Uncertain Territories

GENUS:
Gender in Modern Culture

7

Russell West-Pavlov (Berlin)
Jennifer Yee (Oxford)
Frank Lay (Cologne)
Sabine Schülting (Berlin)

Uncertain Territories
Boundaries in Cultural Analysis

Inge E. Boer

Edited by
Mieke Bal, Bregje van Eekelen, Patricia Spyer

Amsterdam - New York, NY 2006

Cover image: Soussi Albums, from the project *Mapping Sitting: On Portraiture and Photography* by Walid Raad, Akram Zaatari, and The Arab Image Foundation. © Arab Image Foundation, Beirut, Lebanon.

Cover design: Zen Marie

Lay-out: Michael Katzberg

The paper on which this book is printed meets the requirements of "ISO 9706:1994, Information and documentation - Paper for documents - Requirements for permanence".

ISBN-10: 90-420-2120-9
ISBN-13: 978-90-420-2120-4
©Editions Rodopi B.V., Amsterdam - New York, NY 2006
Printed in the Netherlands

Table of Contents

List of Figures

Editors' Preface

This book can be thought of as a trace. Or rather, as a series of traces, perhaps a palimpsest. The word trace is used here in the Derridean sense of a projection forward as much as a material memory of the past. It represents the intellectual legacy of a scholar so generous and stimulating that what she left behind can be said to have inaugurated the future of her work. This book exemplifies and celebrates this open, forward-looking quality of her work by means of the responses written by her close friends and students.

When Inge Boer died on May 19, 2004, her computer files were brimming with life – as she had always been. Her edited volume *After Orientalism* appeared a few days before her passing. Her monograph *Disorienting Vision* appeared posthumously. When we went through her archive to prepare the latter book for publication, we discovered numerous articles, and a book project. The book was to be devoted to boundaries. The papers she wished to rework and include were there. The editing had been cut short by her illness and untimely death. But the vitality of the papers was there, eager to be released into the open.

Critical of current trends to dismiss local cultures in favour of a multicultural globalized view, Inge chose in her final years to study the borders and boundaries that divide the world. She argued against the reification of boundaries as fixed and empty non-spaces whose sole purpose would be to install and uphold divisions. Instead, she contended that boundaries are spaces within, through, and in the name of which negotiations can take place. Understood this way, boundaries need not be the focus of hostility they often are but, instead, may serve the indispensable function of helping people engage and manage an otherwise chaotic world. They are not lines but spaces; neither fixed nor empty but flexible and inhabited.

The first part of the book, *The Function of Boundaries,* comprises chapters in which the notion of boundary is thoroughly explored. In the close readings that constitute this part, either the home, or the lack of it, figures centrally. Thereafter, the writing moves out into a world riddled with boundaries erected for reasons good or bad, but that, in the end, are only productive if taken as loosening, opening up, and yielding to interaction and negotiation.

The second part, *Matter In and Out of Space,* sets up an equally stark initial opposition – between fashion and the desert – only to be undermined once again. In both parts of the book, the author proceeds by following a kind of intellectual sketch that, in its shape, outlines the contours of the argument of the study as a whole. Similarly, between the beginning of the first part and the end of the second, a symmetrical outline of the argument takes shape. This structure has led to an enfolded form; the final paragraphs of the last chapter take up, a bit like a palimpsest, what the end of the introduction suggested. After this summoning of the spirit of earlier chapters, the book refuses to offer closure. This open end, due not simply to Inge's untimely passing but more to her open mind, inspired us to continue this iconic writing and give the book the critical openness that the author herself pursued time and again.

It is in this same dialogic spirit of Inge's person and intellect that we asked some colleagues and students to write responses, presented in the third part. These were to be genuine contributions to what, in our view, Inge's legacy most importantly is: a body of thought that lives on and grows not withstanding her passing. The authors were asked not to pay homage except in the sense of continuing their own work while conversing with Inge, so to speak. In Inge's own spirit, we wished to avoid a solemn tribute in favour of a lively engagement. This led to the third section.

The contributions engage a multitude of artefacts and media, ranging from literature to photography, to art installation and presentation, to film and song. They share an acute concern with the way in which these artefacts challenge the rigidity of boundaries. Fanning out from Inge's central focus – the Middle East – to other parts of the world, they remain committed to the artefact as cultural stimulant, as the embodiment of thought. Thus, this afterlife of Inge's work demonstrates intellectual process at its best: not as following a leader but as engaging with what most deeply moved her. She was never moved by firm positions but, rather, by ways of interacting, thinking through, and learning from the beautiful objects that surround us and provide cultural life with all its sheen, warmth, and fun. And, in an ultimate enfolding, these qualifiers describe quite nicely how we most remember Inge.

As two of Inge's close friends and intellectual mates, we, Patricia and Mieke took it upon us to curate these remainders of her mind. We started out with some trepidation – trying hard to do justice to the subtleties of her thought – yet we grew confident that we knew her lively mind well enough to present her passions, her views, and her commitment to her subjects of study in this book. Between the two of us, we represent the two sides of Inge's interests and knowledge: anthropology and the arts; the more social and the more cultural side of the divides she sought to unmoor.

We also both talked a great deal with her during the months leading up to her death. Thus, we feel we are more loyal to her thought by intervening in her earlier writing, tragically curtailed, than we would by leaving it unsoiled out of ill-guided respect. Unlike *Disorienting Vision*, these papers needed more interventions, some updating, editing out of overlap, and extension of arguments shortened for the sake of earlier publications. The complexity of this work called for the additional expertise of a professional editor, and we took Bregje van Eekelen on board. As it happens, Bregje rapidly developed a close and productive relationship to Inge's work, and became a dedicated and engaged editor of this book.

Finally, Inge loved to discuss, dispute, argue, as much as she loved to travel, experiment, and write. Her favourite verb, we can guess, must have been "encounter". Of encounters, at any rate, this book is full, and as an encounter among the many who continue to benefit from Inge's work, we offer this volume. There are a few people we would like to thank especially. We would like to thank the Lebanese artist, Walid Ra'ad, another of Inge's friends and intellectual companions, for generously contributing the illustration on *Uncertain Territories*' cover. Zen Marie carefully crafted the cover composition. We thank Michael Katzberg for formatting this book. We thank the colleagues at ASCA, the research institute to which Inge was wholeheartedly devoted, for their ongoing support. Most of all we thank Inge's husband, Carel Smith. From the start, he encouraged and supported our efforts, helping us to retrieve old files from Inge's computer, locating drafts and hard copies of different papers, and recalling where we might find the many illustrations that Inge draws upon in her work. Most importantly, he made us feel that it was appropriate to edit and revise "in her spirit" what Inge left behind. For all of this, and much more, we thank him deeply.

Introduction

Boundaries in the Age of Globalization

Boundaries and globalization appear at odds with each other. Hence, to write a book about boundaries in the age of globalization might seem a bit quaint. Even so, I propose to enter this study of boundaries through the problem of globalization – and through globalization as a problem. For in debates about globalization, the presence or absence of boundaries is invariably at stake. Protagonists of globalization tend to frame the discussion in terms of the economy and mobility. Hence, globalization and its effects involves movement, free flow – the overcoming of boundaries – and mobility as a way of life. In this line of reasoning, globalization promises a better life with higher standards of living – and by extension "democracy" – for all citizens of the world.

According to its critics – who march the streets as well as the information highway – globalization and its alternatives are also to be understood primarily in terms of the economy and boundaries. The local, in the view of these critics, is the exact opposite (and victim) of the global. Globalization is a disturbance of local stability, a stability that is often captured in economic and nostalgic terms. The International Forum on Globalization (an anti-globalist organization) suggests for example that the viability of local communities and culture can only be secured through the local control of local markets for local consumption. Ideally, one moves up the regional or national levels of power only if the local level is ineffective. What globalization entails, according to this agenda, is a "de-localization and disempowerment of communities and local economies".[1] Interestingly, then, whereas the prime culprits in the eyes of the anti-globalization movements are international organizations such as the World Bank or the International Monetary fund, banks and corporate finance, and transnational corporations operating on a worldwide scale, the local, while lacking this expansive scale, is also captured in terms of the economy.

I use the word "captured" here on purpose. For the discourse on the economy remains prevalent even in the proposed alternatives to

---

[1] <http://www.ifg.org/beyondwto.html>.

globalization. Just like the discourse it opposes, the Forum's alternative is a master-discourse on economy transplanted from "the global" to another arena, called the local (for powerful feminist critiques of such economic representations, see Gibson-Graham 1996 and Tsing 2000). Moreover, in this evocation the local is infused with forms of nostalgia, of a golden age when all was well and centred around the village commons. But as Audre Lorde and many other feminists after her have declared: the master's tools will never dismantle the master's house (1984).

What concerns me in these narratives (whether pro or con), is that a gap seems to appear between the term "globalization" and two other terms that continue to be at the forefront of cultural analysis, "gender" and "ethnicity", or, if you like, sex and race. As so often happens when gender and ethnicity are ignored, the debate on globalization and its effects remains caught in binary oppositions, a structure of thought that is invariably reductive, hierarchical and simplistic. The reductive debate about globalization centres on the binary opposition between the global and the local, and it portrays each pole of this opposition in exclusively economic terms (see also Massey 1994 and Gupta and Ferguson 1997b). As a structure of thought, binary oppositions are problematic because of three successive logical moves: 1) the reduction of an infinitely rich and chaotic field into two centres; 2) the articulation of those centres into polar opposites and 3) the hierarchization of these two poles in which a (usually preferred) positive term is opposed to a (usually disdained) negative term (Bal 1997: 128). This is exactly what happens in the globalization debates. In the context of my approach in this book, it is important to notice that a binary opposition is itself a boundary, though not one that I would like to sustain. Rather, I seek to develop another meaning of boundaries.

What interests me most for the purpose of this book is the question as to how one gets from one extreme to the other, or rather, how one reorders such sharply drawn borders so that we perceive and can inhabit a wider space "in between". What, indeed, happens in between? Isn't there something of a relay in between, a boundary space, a contact zone, where different beliefs about life and what it consists of meet or clash (for an elaboration of the concept of contact-zone, see Pratt 1992). By posing this question I seek to move from an economy-only standpoint about globalization to a cultural perspective, and from a reductive opposition to the creation of a space – rhetorical as well as cultural – where opposition yields to negotiation. In such a space, the multifaceted reality of intercultural relations takes on more prominence than the mere demarcation of a binary opposition would allow. The globalization debate stands, here, as an allegory for the moves I will be proposing in the book concerning the notion of boundaries.

Boundaries as Confrontations, Lines and Obstacles

> A few decades ago, it was still possible to leave home and go somewhere else where the architecture was different, the landscape was different, the language, lifestyle, dress and values were different. Today, farmers and filmmakers in France and India, and millions of people elsewhere, are protesting to maintain that diversity.

What strikes me in this evocation of a much longed for, nostalgically evoked past by the Forum is that boundaries had to be crossed in order to undergo the beneficiary effects of diversity. A sense of diversity in existence *at home* is not available. The here and now is contrasted with the then and there. In both evocations, the presence and absence of boundaries has major significance.

To be honest, both the nostalgic memorization of boundaries and the apparently liberating effect of their absence resonate with my own sentiments. When, as a child I went on vacation, one of the attractions was the crossing of boundaries between countries. The mystery of being far away was reinforced by the illusion that one or several boundaries dividing and defining Europe were to be transgressed. Beyond that boundary, life, in all its aspects, was different. The childlike fantasy of that other space provides a good image of how boundaries are often perceived: as geometrical lines in a landscape (a landscape which to my disillusion did not really differ), marked by stones, customs officers and the showing of passports. Geographical boundaries do not differ much from those dividing ethnicities, religions, sexes, cultures and so on. They share the characteristic of simply being there, of an immutable presence no one has the power to question, or so it seems.

As Michel Foucher (1991) has argued, boundaries have a tendency to be perceived as anonymous, and to supersede the individual. Dividing spaces and groups of peoples, yet no one's possession, the anonymity of boundaries is guaranteed by naturalizing impulses that strengthen their stable and immobile qualities. I wish to foreground in this book the ways in which such naturalizing impulses erase the human activity entailed in *constructing* boundaries. This naturalization occurs even in the most savvy of intellectual pursuits, such as cultural analysis (see Kaplan 1996). As a result, the question of boundaries has been directed toward the definition of *what* a boundary is and *where* it is located, rather than towards querying the construction of such views of boundaries. In this book, I seek to explore the consequences of these two questions.

To introduce this inquiry I will use some examples from that monument of rational, enlightened Western thought, the *Encyclopédie*, to illustrate this point. The question of what a boundary is and where it is located narrows the possible range of considerations down to an artificial exactness. In a lemma on bounds, limits and ends, the *Encyclopédie*'s primary editor Denis Diderot gave the following descriptions:

> BOUNDS, ENDS, LIMITS. Terms that are all related to a finite expanse; the *end* marks up to where one can go: the *limits*, that which it not permitted to cross: the *bounds*, that which it prevents from going forward. The *end* is a point: the *limits* form a *line*; the *bounds* an *obstacle*.

> BORNES, TERMES, LIMITES, termes qui sont tous relatifs à l'étendue finie; le *terme* marque jusqu'où l'on peut aller: les *limites*, ce qu'il n'est pas parmis de passer; les *bornes*, ce qui empêche d'aller en-avant. Le *terme* est un *point*; les *limites* sont une *ligne*; les *bornes* un *obstacle* (Diderot 1751, II: 236; italics in original).[2]

Two conspicuous features drew my attention in this passage. On the one hand, I was struck by the use of geometrical notions such as points or lines. On the other hand, note how the point of view of the observer is formulated. This perspective is phrased in terms of inside and outside, so that bounds, ends and limits prevent or hinder someone from what would otherwise be transgressed. Each in their own way, bounds, limits and ends seem to impose restrictions on the freedom and mobility of human beings. All three terms have a forbidding quality to them, closing off expanses within from those beyond.

---

[2] All translations into English are mine, unless otherwise stated.

One might object that terms such as bounds, limits and ends are only related terms when speaking about boundaries. In the lemma on "frontière" however, we encounter a similar usage of terminology and perspective. "Frontier is used for limits, confines or extremities of a kingdom or a province". The text continues:

> The word can also be used as an adjective: we say frontier town, frontier province . . . According to several authors this word is derived from the latin noun *frons*; the frontiers being, they say, like a kind of front opposed to the enemy. Others have this word come from *frons* for a different reason. They say that the frontier is the most exterior & most advanced part of a state, like the front is of the human face.

> FRONTIERE se dit des limites, confins, ou extrémités d'un royaume ou d'une province. Le mot se prend aussie adjectivement: nous disons *ville frontiere*, *province frontiere* . . . Ce mot est dérivé selon plusieurs auteurs, du latin *frons*; les *frontieres* étant, disent-ils, comme une espece de front opposé à l'ennemi. D'autres sont venir ce mot de *frons*, pour une autre raison; la *frontiere*, disent-ils, est la partie la plus extérieure & la plus avancée d'un état, come le front l'est du visage de l'homme (Diderot 1751, VII: 341; italics in original).

A frontier is thus relative to a finite expanse, but specified here to administrative or governmental forms. Where bounds, ends and limits seemed to impose restrictions on human beings, no mention was made of *who* applies the restrictions. Generously, various interpretations of the derivations of *frons* are handed to us. Here, we encounter possible reasons for the restrictions and perhaps even a justification: on the other side of the frontier we look the enemy in the eye. The transgression of a frontier is seen as a risky business. The second explanation takes the human forehead in its quality as extremity or limit. Both explanations share, again, a perspective where a frontier or boundary is perceived from within, from a notion in which "we" all participate and acquiesce.

One more example will further clarify the point I am trying to make. In the *Encyclopédie*, the act of setting boundaries (*action de bornage*) is primarily interpreted in the legal sense of separating inheritances, i.e. carving up land:

> One comes to mark out the boundaries of two inheritances by three means: by the landmarks which are placed on the confines to serve as limits, by title-deeds & by witnesses. The way to pursue the last two proofs is the same as in every

other act. With respect to the first, one recognizes that a stone has been placed to serve as landmark & as limit, when one finds guarantors or witnesses underneath, that is, two or three pieces of a flat stone, which the measurers & land-surveyors are accustomed to place aside the landmark when they plant it. Those little stones are called *guarantors* or *witnesses* because they are mute witnesses that certify the truth.

On parvient à borner deux héritages par trois moyens: par les bornes qui ont été mises sur les confins pour servir de limites, par titres & par témoins. La manière de pratiquer ces deux dernieres preuves est la même qu'en toute autre action. Par rapport au premier, on reconnoît qu'une pierre a été mise pour servir de borne & de limite, quand on trouve dessous des garants ou témoins, c'est-a-dire deux ou trois morceaux d'une pierre plate, que les mesureurs & arpenteurs sont accoûtumés de mettre aux côtés de la borne quand ils la plantent. On appelle ces petites pierres *garants* ou *témoins*, parce qu'elles sont des témoins muets qui certifient la vérité (Diderot 1751, II: 236; italics in original).

In its foregrounding of what the boundary is and where it is located, the encyclopaedia calls attention to the act of *setting up* boundaries. Initiated by measurers and land-surveyors, this boundary-work is followed up by witnesses in stone, anthropomorphous forms to which the task of certifying the truth is relegated. The very existence of stones in a particular place provides a recursive answer to what the boundary is – it is right there where the stones are.

In response to this discourse I wish to argue is that even when human activity is involved, such as in the act of setting boundaries, the role of particular people, of their interactions, is subsequently erased. The question as to *what* a boundary is and *where* it is located therefore limits our possibilities for interpretation. Boundaries assume an anonymous form, to which truth value is assigned – a value that seems imposed on us as a God-given and which uses an inside perspective opposing us to whomever we find on the other side. This is the discourse of boundaries that even anti-globalization movements have inherited from our Enlightenment predecessors. It is the discourse I wish to suspend in this study, in order to elaborate an alternative vision of boundaries.

Travelling Theory

Let me return to my own memories. Boundaries not only figure in the debates on globalization or in actual travel, they matter in intellectual work as well.

As an adult, I continued to travel, both practically and intellectually. Crossing boundaries became a more and more frequent practice, and the joy in doing so doubtlessly linked up with my childhood memories. But since my aim has always been to contribute to theories about cross-cultural representations, foregrounding the notion of boundaries and the ways in which boundaries function continues to be a theme on my intellectual agenda. This led me to ask, in the wake of Edward Said's notion of travelling theories (1983), how feminism as a travelling theory operates in shaping the relationship between feminists in the so-called First and Third worlds, and more specifically, between feminism in Western Europe and the Middle East.

Said indicates a discernible and recurrent pattern in the way in which any theory or idea travels:

> First, there is a point of origin, or what seems like one, a set of initial circumstances in which the idea came to birth or entered discourse. Second, there is a distance transversed, a passage through the pressure of various contexts as the idea moves from an earlier point to another time and place where it will come into a new prominence. Third, there is a set of conditions – call them conditions of acceptance or, as an inevitable part of acceptance, resistances – which then confronts the transplanted theory or idea, making possible its introduction or toleration, however alien it might appear to be. Fourth, the now full (or partly) accommodated (or incorporated) idea is to some extent transformed by its new uses, its new position in a new time and place (Said 1983: 226-27).

In what seems a rather banal itinerary of theories that travel – point of origin, a distance in location and time traversed, conditions of acceptance or resistance, and finally the transformed concept – I am struck by the fairly linear development in time and direction from point A to point B. Said seems to imply a one-way ticket, so that "emigrating theories" might be a suitable term. However, if we want to hold on to the word *travelling* theory, I suggest taking into account its everyday sense, which implies not just a departure from one place to another, but also a return. If a theory, after its travels, returns to the same location, is it still the same?

James Clifford offers a wonderful contribution to the combined notions of theory and travel:

The Greek term *theorein*: a practice of travel and observation, a man sent by the polis to another city to witness a religious ceremony. "Theory" is a product of displacement, comparison, a certain distance. To theorize, one leaves home. But like any act of travel, theory begins and ends somewhere. In the case of the Greek theorist the beginning and ending were one, the home polis. This is not so simply true of travelling theorists in the late twentieth century (Clifford 1989: 177).

Said took the example of György Luckács' theory of critical consciousness as the point of departure, a theory that in turn was taken up and modified by Lucien Goldman and finally found its temporary port of call with Raymond Williams (Luckács 1971 [1917-1918]; Goldman 1964; Williams 1980). Said perceives *theories* that travel, things arriving on a one-way ticket in Great Britain via Paris from Hungary. Clifford, by contrast, adds the figure who undertakes the travelling, the theorist her or himself. Most important, however, is his critique of the linearity of Said's argument with respect to travelling theories in a postcolonial context. Clifford formulates his critique in terms of "feedback loops", and the ambivalent positions of theorists occupying a site of "betweenness", addressing audiences in different situations and contexts (1989: 184-85).

However we turn these arguments, the question of boundaries is present in them, whether with respect to theories, theorists, or other people who travel. But the question is not analysed for its own sake. The travelling theories and theorists conjured up by Said and Clifford, might easily be taken to enjoy a freedom of movement, a situation of limitless possibilities, maybe even a utopian free exchange of ideas, much like the freedom attributed – but wrongly in my view – to the people who enjoy the masquerade discussed in Chapter Five of this book. I question the idealized view implicit in this assumedly limitless circulation of ideas, thoughts and reflections, which has appeared in a host of publications in which nomadism, migration, and the exiled or diasporic individual are used as jubilant metaphors. How can theories travel if not across boundaries? And why dismiss boundaries so quickly if they might turn out to be central to the process of travel? As I argue in Chapter One, we must take seriously the conceptual metaphors we use, and take into consideration what their implications are, perhaps especially in discussions on travelling theories.

In my insistence on boundaries the material referent in the shape of national boundaries is the first to come to mind. But one could also think of the ways in which boundaries function in our way of perceiving the world and informing our meaning-making processes. Following feminist art historian Lynda Nead, I would argue that "meaning is organized and regulated at the edges or boundaries of categories" (1992: 33) or as Edward Said in *Culture and Imperialism* states: "no identity can ever exist by itself and without an array of opposites, negatives, oppositions" (1993: 52). My aim in this book is not a redefinition of boundaries as such, but to achieve another way of theorizing dynamic processes of cross-cultural representation in which boundaries are explicitly included.

Spaces for Negotiation

In order to overcome this limitation in our thinking about boundaries I propose to consider boundaries not in their definition of *what* they are and *where* they are, but instead to theorize them as a *function*. The possible range of questions this allows for is infinitely more interesting and revealing, because they do away with the anonymity of boundaries and ask questions of an altogether different kind. For example: Who draws up the boundaries? Who takes those boundaries for granted? Who is afraid the boundaries will get crossed? Who do cross boundaries? Whose boundaries are transgressed? These questions thus address the how and why of boundary construction, as well as what happens "at" the boundary when people from both sides meet. By way of introducing the analyses in the chapters of this book, in what follows I give some examples of the kind of questions that can result from this refocusing of the concept of boundaries.

In an article that is highly relevant for this inquiry, François Béguin analyzes how army engineers in the late eighteenth century by order of the French and Spanish kings set out to decide on the boundary between the two countries (1991). The whole process was not initiated because the territory lacked boundaries. In fact, there was a boundary that had been recorded in so-called "*faceries*", agreements made between the farmers of the region. The agreements settled the movement of herds on territories belonging to a person, allowing them to make use of the pastures across the "border". As soon as the engineers started their work of fixing the boundary, the inhabitants of the Pyrenean valleys, supported by the parliament of Pau, mounted a host of protests:

> In each of their protests, they invoked the antiquity and the conclusiveness of the old limits, as well as the arbitrary and harmful character of the frontier of the military engineers. The commissionaires [two government officials to oversee the engineering operation, IB] retorted by having local notaries carried off and imprisoned to then oblige them to come to recognize the new boundaries (Béguin 1991: 50).

This dispute about boundaries shows us some very interesting processes in which the struggle takes on different forms. The inhabitants of the Pyrenean valleys try to resolve the conflict by invoking the past, in other words, their history, and the "well-foundedness" of the old boundaries. The new frontier is experienced as a structure without grounds, arbitrarily and haphazardly imposed, and oppressive.[3]

Violence and the sense of violation come together in the imprisonment of the local notaries, who are forced to recognize the new boundaries. As a *pars pro toto* or synecdoche of the communities involved, their recognition stands for general acceptance. Both parties claim exactness for their boundaries, the engineers and commissionaires based on the latest scientific methods of triangulation, and the communities on the basis of negotiated agreements from the past (Béguin 1991: 51). Notwithstanding the justification on both sides of the conflict of their respective understanding of the boundary, what is important for my purposes is to note how the boundary functions.

I allege Béguin's example because in his case, the boundary is not stable, but rather mobile or, more precisely, a "space" of negotiation. It is a space in which different and contrasting visions, more often than not unequal in terms of power, come into play. The inhabitants of the Pyrenees contest, through legal means, the state intrusion upon their own negotiated agreements; an intrusion personified by the army engineers. Ultimately, the state emerges victorious. However, boundaries, one could argue, are negotiated in a process that does not end with the provisional designation of a boundary. The boundary is arbitrary in character, temporary and changeable.

---

[3] For a longer-ranging study on the invention of the national boundary line in the Pyrenees and the making of Frenchmen and Spaniards, see Peter Sahlins 1989.

So far, the boundaries discussed are taken to have a material referent; i.e. a boundary one could point out between two nations. This supposedly physical existence of boundaries has often been used to justify the division of peoples according to religions, ethnicities, cultures, sexes and so on. Needless to say that the mapping of "real" boundaries onto different religions, ethnicities, cultures or sexes, leads to the search for justifiable and visible referents as well. It leads to divisions – and then, easily exclusions – according to colour or dress and the naturalization of norms of the dominant discourse and culture. These norms are consequently imposed upon those subjected to a strict application of racist and sexist boundary principles. As I argue in different ways throughout this book, analyzing how boundaries function provides a critical tool for undermining a continuous recourse to visible referents (see also Madan Sarup 1994).

Probing the function, not the definition of boundaries, then, I will approach boundaries in two distinct but related ways. In the first part of this book, *The Function of Boundaries*, I will explore different aspects of this function. In the first chapter, highlighting the function of imprisonment, a deeply troubling, depressed view of boundaries emerges from a contemporary novel by Algerian-French writer Nina Bouraoui (1991). This novel depicts boundaries in keenly visual terms, a partiality to the sense of vision that extends as far as the novel's title. I will use this text to question an all-too-cheerful endorsement of the allegedly generally available "nomadic" condition that, in the wake of the popularity of Gilles Deleuze, has been rampant in some recent feminist theory.

Equally depressing, however, is the state of constant transgression of boundaries, especially when these are protective of individuals and enabling humane existence. I am referring to the systematic destruction of the boundaries of the private sphere, a destruction that comes about with the state of civil war. In Chapter Two, I analyse a novel by the Lebanese author Hanan al-Shaykh (1995). Strikingly, both Bouraoui's testimony and al-Shaykh's novel are both written in the first person. But whereas Bouraoui's character has no one to speak to, al-Shaykh's heroine is exuberantly expressive. This felicitous access to language cannot fool us, however, once we realize that the personal letters the novel consists of are all addressed to non-existing or non-accessible addressees. This fictitious epistolarity provides the entrance to a further exploration of the function of boundaries as a site of negotiation. The linguistic nature of this negotiation in this instance will be further explored with the support of another writer who wrote in the situation of civil war, the Algerian writer and essayist Assia Djebar (1999). Djebar's view of language – in her case, her use of French – proposes language itself as both a boundary and an area of negotiation. Here, *translation* becomes an example of the production of boundaries as functional spaces.

This function becomes even more evident, while being, also, compounded with visual equivalents, in Chapter Four. Here, I return temporarily to an earlier time, one I studied before embarking on this book, namely the late eighteenth century. The writings of two travelling French women who practiced their own version of globalization in relation, not opposition, to locality, serve to propose the *encounter* as an enabling concept in the analysis of boundaries. Through a focus on encounters, boundaries can be approached as a space in which events can happen, shedding the guise of boundaries as demarcating lines. The writings in question, more than mere travel documents, are ethnographies of sorts. I argue in the chapter that some of the most fundamental features of these writings are proto-ethnographic, betraying the pros and cons of what is now called "fieldwork".

Once the principal elements of boundaries in their function of negotiable spaces have been outlined, the second part of this study, *Matter In and Out of Space*, is devoted to more material aspects of boundaries. A primary example of this materiality is the desert – an allegedly natural phenomenon that produces a kind of landscape easily mistaken for emptiness. Deserts are inhabited, traversed, and negotiated, and can stand for those spaces, considered boundaries, that turn the allegedly globalized space into a criss-crossing of localities, and their perceived eternal, a-historical naturalness into a busy palimpsest. In Chapter Four I traverse five different accounts of deserts in order to tease out those aspects of the desert that are contingent upon their "fullness".

As in the first part, gender insinuates itself regularly as a decisive aspect in my analysis of boundaries. In Chapter Five, therefore, I take on the phenomenon of fashion, so easily considered frivolous and feminine – perhaps frivolous because feminine. Nothing is farther from the truth, on both counts, as the chapter demonstrates. I consider contemporary phenomena of cultural cross-dressing to be profound statements on the negotiation of boundaries, negotiations beyond the global-local opposition. In order to anchor contemporary fashion habits – if that phrase is not an oxymoron – I look at an historical antecedent in the same era as the travellers who anticipated our ethnographers, namely the late eighteenth century, through the example of Madame de Pompadour.

When we try to understand boundaries as spaces of negotiation, there is one question that can hardly be avoided, because it so tenaciously challenges an all-too-cheerful view of these matters. This is the question of authenticity – fetish of contemporary "high culture" and specifically of art history and practice. Again, it is the artist who guides us, here, the artists united in a particularly strange art museum on the one hand, and the French novelist Georges Perec on the other. A museum that refuses to frame art with text labels, betrays in that very reluctance a fetishistic investment in an authenticity that re-affirms all the boundaries between the categories of cultural value: culture versus nature, high art versus artefact, modern versus ancient. It is the fiction of the French novelist that makes these investments visible, through an allegorical tale of utter, dizzying deception as the highest form of authenticity.

In the end, then, I will argue that boundaries cannot be wished away but will serve their ordering purposes better – that is, without the lack of understanding and the ensuing hostilities that usually accompany them – if we accept their existence but take them as uncertain; not lines, but spaces, not rigid but open to negotiation. The resulting uncertain territories are the ground we stand on, together.

PART I

THE FUNCTION OF BOUNDARIES

The World Beyond My Window: Nomads, Travelling Theories and the Function of Boundaries

As a first case of the shift in the meaning of boundaries I am exploring in this study, I resort to a literary genre that itself transgresses boundaries: autobiographical fiction. The function rather than the nature of boundaries is explored in Fatima Mernissi's book of that hybrid genre, *The Forbidden Roof-Terrace*, in which the author describes the life in a harem of a Moroccan upper-class family.[1] As a mythical place construed as a site of confinement and inequality between the sexes, the harem is a good place to start. It is, incidentally, also the figure that binds this study to my previous book, in which I offer detailed analyses of the fantasies of the harem produced in the Western imagination (Boer 2004b).

In Mernissi's book, the harem is presented from the inside perspective, so to speak. A young girl worries about the rules of the harem and how to negotiate the boundaries involved. She seems to have found inspiration and a splendid "role-model" in Mrs. Bennis, a woman regarded with suspicion by the young girl's father and uncle, because she was of Tunisian or Turkish descent, meaning that she put the revolutionary ideas of Kemal Atatürk,

---

[1] In the Netherlands, where the book was first presented in translation in 1994, the title is *Het verboden dakterras* (The Forbidden Roof-Terrace). I will quote from this Dutch edition. In a public interview (Amsterdam, De Balie, April 27 1994) Mernissi spoke of the title she proposed for the English edition. She suggested *The Harem Within*, but the publisher decided on *Dreams of Trespass: Tales of a Harem Girlhood* (1994a). Note the different implications of the latter title.

concerning the full social participation of women, into practice. She drove around, unveiled, in her husband's black Oldsmobile and her platinum dyed hair was trimmed à la Greta Garbo.

But Mrs. Bennis would wear a traditional djebella and a veil when going to the medina, the old city. Her expert handling of the boundary mesmerizes the young girl:

> You might well say that Mrs. Bennis led two lives: one in the Ville Nouvelle, the European part of the city, where she went about unveiled, and one in the traditional medina. Everybody thought this idea of a double life attractive and it made Mrs. Bennis famous. It was much more attractive to live in two worlds instead of one. Everybody was taken by the idea of commuting between two cultures, two personalities, two codes and two languages! Mother wanted that I would be like princess Aisha, the teenage daughter of our king Mohammed V, who made public speeches in Arabic and French, and who wore both long kaftans and short French dresses. Indeed, the thought of switching codes and languages was as spellbinding for children as the opening of fairy-tale doors. The women enjoyed it too, but the men did not. They deemed it dangerous and my father especially did not like Mrs. Bennis, because, according to him, she made transgressions into something normal. She transferred too easily from one culture to the other without respecting the sacred boundary, *hodud* (Mernissi 1994b: 175-76).

Hodud, the holy boundary the father speaks of – and wants respected – is what protects the cultural identity of Arabs. Mrs. Bennis' continuous travel back and forth across this boundary evokes his fear of dissolution of identities. This form of cultural cross-dressing, at the same time, evokes the elation of women (see also Chapter Five). I would not go so far as to argue that crossing the boundary is a women's thing systematically opposed by men. The I in *The Forbidden Roof-Terrace* does see, like many others with her, that Mrs. Bennis loses nothing in the process. Negotiating boundaries, she gains independence, knowledge about both cultures, both codes and both languages. Mrs. Bennis also shows that the boundary should not be taken as a given, but as something that can be critically approached. In the process the boundary might change.

One objection against my example of Mrs. Bennis might be that it has very little to do with cross-cultural representations and pertains to the negotiation of internal boundaries within Moroccan society of the mid-twentieth century. However, my point here is that this reflection on human agency in the construction and transgression of boundaries does not leave the position of the interpreter of that process unaffected. Therefore, the analysis of cross-cultural representations needs to take yet another boundary into account, in view of which cross-cultural representations are part of an interactive process that problematizes deeply entrenched ideas about one's own identity with respect to that of others.

As I have suggested in the *Introduction*, James Clifford's notion of feedback loops, expanding Said's initial four stages in a theory's travels, sheds light on the dynamics of that process. Therefore, I wish to return to the question of travelling theories and the relationship between feminism in Western Europe and in the Middle East, and point out why feedback loops in relation to boundaries are necessary elements to be considered. In this regard, let me first acknowledge that Western feminism can hardly be seen as a unified theory, but rather as a disparate set of critical aims and theoretical approaches, varied in forms and situated in different socio-political and cultural contexts. It did not arrive in the Middle East as one package, nor was it received as such.

To substantiate my claims, I will discuss the work of two influential feminists, Fatima Mernissi and Nawal el-Saadawi. While they work on very different projects, they both elaborate parts of a local, specific theorization of feminism. I will briefly sketch out some of their ideas, since they have, each in their own respect, become important and exemplary advocates of female intellectual production in the Middle East. Then, I will turn to a novel by a young Algerian writer, Nina Bouraoui's *La Voyeuse interdite* (1991). This novel is constructed around the classical topos of the window as a boundary. Physically separating the inhabitants from the world, the window's transparency nicely sums up the contradictions on boundaries.

Feminism's Travels

In her most well known book, *The Hidden Face of Eve* (1980), Nawal el-Saadawi displays an almost programmatic approach with respect to women's issues. The book starts with an account of a personal experience, el-Saadawi's cliterodectomy as a six-year old girl. El-Saadawi sets up the basic framework of her argument by extending this experience into reflections of a more general and generalizing nature on the condition of women in the Arab world. Focusing on the need for comprehensive social and economic changes in the Middle East, she argues for liberation from neo-colonial forces, which will also entail changes in the position of women.

Importantly in light of the contemporary over-emphasis on religion, Islam is not the major force in the alleged backwardness el-Saadawi observes in the Middle East, nor in the inferior position to which women are relegated. Imperialism and reactionary forces in the Middle East collaborate in maintaining ignorance and norms targeted specifically at women, such as virginity, veiling and cliterodectomy. Her indictment of the patriarchal class system reigning in the Middle East does not lead to a further analysis of the ideological grounding of this system. Instead, el-Saadawi directs her attention to the violation of the rights of women and the pressures society exerts upon them. Her approach is action-oriented and practical, calling for women to unite their forces.

What el-Saadawi has taken from Western feminism is the insistence on equality between the sexes and a critique of commonplaces about female sexuality. She has transformed and adapted feminist theories for usage in the specific context of the Middle East and thereby focused on practices like cliterodectomy. By contrast, Fatima Mernissi focuses on Islam, but not in an essentialist sense either. In *The Forbidden Roof-Terrace* (1990), Mernissi, like el-Saadawi, starts with a personal question. "Can a woman actively participate in politics and/or rule over others?" The search for an answer leads Mernissi to an analysis of Islam and its ideological roots in patriarchy. Her project is to find access to the *mémoire-histoire* (remembered history) that nobody can control to its full extent. Mernissi analyses the various interpretations of the *Hadith* (the Prophet's recitations) and concludes that the sacred text has always been manipulated in order to exert and maintain male power. This manipulation, not the text itself resulted in the exclusion of women and their relegation to a position of powerlessness. To recall the roles of women in Islam and to insert them back into the sacred text implies pulling at the texture of a socio-political and religious construct. As a result, women re-enter the arena of manipulation.

Mernissi's question obtained further relevance when Benazir Bhutto was elected prime minister of Pakistan in 1988. Despite the outcry from Islamist parties and their assurance that Bhutto's election was unprecedented,

Mernissi advances, in her book *Sultanes oubliées* (1990), the hypothesis that women did rule in the Islamic world, but have become the victims of "historical assassination". She subsequently uncovers the names of a host of female rulers. Hence, Mernissi elects to work within the framework of Islamic culture and to retrieve, from within, the neglected role of women. The process of reintroducing women into the tradition through a careful rereading of its textual sources results in important modifications and transformations, which, in turn, lead to claims for women's rights. Her strategy is to seek a foundation for such claims. Thus, she uses the boundary between religious and social life as a space for negotiation:

> Progressive persons of both sexes in the Muslim world know that the only weapon they can use to fight for human rights, in general, and women's rights in particular in those countries where religion is not separate from the state is to base political claims on religious history (Mernissi 1988: 338).

In response to Mernissi's and el-Saadawi's positions, a vigorous and fruitful debate has developed among feminists both from the West and the Middle East. After one of the various conferences held on the occasion of the UN Decade of Women, both Mernissi and el-Saadawi voiced their discontent with the organization's tendency to situate Third World participants as passive audiences. Their arguments broke the ground for a fundamental rethinking of the relationship between Western feminists and those from the Third World. And here I see what James Clifford described as a feedback loop (1989: 184-85). I consider feedback loops as a return home, albeit a home changed along the way. Feminism in the West, in other words, cannot exist unscathed from the trip to the Middle East.

One seminal outcome of the debate on the relations between different feminisms was Chandra Mohanty's "Under Western Eyes" (1991). In this article, she argued that Third World women are still too often perceived as victims, dependent, encroached in underdevelopment or as sisters in a global struggle without their own strategies and policies being taken into account.[2] In a similar vein, Marnia Lazreg critically analyzed the all-pervasive presence

---

[2] First World and Third World are terms hesitantly used because of their totalizing implications, but following Chandra Mohanty I insist on the potential for common political struggle and not on a division along lines of race or sex.

of religion in studies of women in the Muslim world (1990; 1994). She does not hesitate to raise charges against Mernissi and el-Saadawi as well as against Western feminists, indicting their use of a compact set of categories which stereotype women in the Muslim world over and over again. Marie-Aimée Hélie-Lucas, by contrast, argues that the dichotomy between Western feminism and Third World feminism is false and "prevents women from benefiting from each other's experiences" (1993: 218). She interprets the resistance to Western feminism as a fear for contamination. What works most effectively in her eyes is to bring women across the Islamic world in contact with each other so that differences among them are exposed and the myth of a homogeneous Muslim world is exploded.

I see in all these examples the mechanism of feedback loops, because these female intellectuals, wherever they work or reside, take the transformed and adapted notions of Western feminism developed in the Middle East as their point of departure (or should I say point of return?) and contribute from their specific positions to important reconsiderations of the relationship between Western and Middle Eastern feminism. Consequently, feminisms, both in the West and the Middle East, take on aspects such as the practice of veiling, the reconsideration of religion as a major ideological force, the issue of cliterodectomy, and strategies for the feminist movement in a global context. As a result of these feedback loops, Western feminism is transformed and modified. Anyone working on cross-cultural representations, and especially feminists working within cultural studies, will have to take these transformed notions of feminism into account.

In this book, I attempt to offer yet another example of a feedback loop. An important aspect of such loops is self-reflection, because in following the itinerary of a travelling theory one needs to re-evaluate one's own position and location. It changes one's theorizing and practice, leading to, as Donna Haraway has phrased it, a "feminist accountability", which requires a "knowledge tuned to resonance, not to dichotomy" (1991: 194-95). In the process of a theorizing that includes such self-reflection, one indeed leaves home, to return to the same location, but not quite as the same person.

More Metaphors of Travel

Let me now focus on ways in which boundaries operate in cross-cultural representations as flexible spaces of negotiation and sites of contestation. More specifically, I will investigate writings by women from the Arab-Islamic world and the relationship between First World women and Third World women in light of cross-cultural interpretational practices. While investigating boundaries in relation to cross-cultural representations, I was struck by a very angry, claustrophobic text that belies the rhapsodic, open and joyous tone of some Western feminists who endorse mobility as a guideline. This novel, written by a twenty-four year old woman born in Rennes, France, of French-Algerian descent is entitled *La Voyeuse interdite* (1991).

Nina Bouraoui won critical acclaim for her first work, a disconcerting and disturbing account of a young woman's life in Algiers. In a street in Algiers a young girl behind a windowpane watches life pass by and anguishes about her existence. Enclosed in her room she will slowly become definitively encapsulated within the situation if she does not resist it with all her might. She pities her mother and her sisters who bear the signs of an unbearable life made liveable through resignation, their bodies and minds tired for lack of impulses from outside. This seems to be the frightening future for Algerian girls waiting for marriage, an evocation of a slow suffocation, of energy wasted, of a life lost . . . for what?

The title raises many interesting questions about gender and sexuality. The masculine French word *voyeur*, a Peeping Tom, has no feminine equivalent. Just like the *flâneuse*, the *voyeuse* thus departs from the connotations attached to *voyeur* and *flâneur*, while simultaneously maintaining crucial links with them (see also Janet Wolff 1990). The qualifier *interdite* qualifies the voyeuse in important ways, as its meanings can be prohibited, forbidden, to be amazed or bewildered, and to be under restraint. Bouraoui's novel plays on all these meanings.

The novel manages to suck up its readers, into the forbidden space of imprisonment. In so doing, it is anchored firmly in the "willing suspension of disbelief" that characterizes literature's power to persuade. Reading Bouraoui's *La Voyeuse interdite*, I felt as trapped as the young girl, as desperate to find a way out of a nightmarish labyrinth of rules and obligations. And therefore, I started to read it again. Let me begin with a short analysis of an excerpt from the very beginning of the book. The novel opens as follows:

> This morning the sun is higher. Haughty I would say. Perched on an invisible throne, it pours out its energy into my street that turns proudly away from the rest of the city. Epicentre of adventure, it is here that everything is happening for that woman hidden behind her window, for that red-faced grocer seated on his stool, for that man spying on a closed curtain, for those small boys and girls who are running in a rectangle well-limited by gloomy, rigid buildings.
>
> One yells, idles about, looks, cheats and steals. And they rape. The rest exists no longer.

> Ce matin, le soleil est plus haut. Hautain je dirais. Juché sur un trône invisible, il déverse son énergie dans ma rue qui se détache orgueilleusement du reste de la ville. Epicentre de l'aventure, c'est ici que tout se passe pour cette femme cachée derrière sa fenêtre, pour cet épicier rougeaud assis sur son tabouret, pour cet homme guettant un rideau clos, pour ces petits et petites qui courent dans un rectangle bien délimité par des bâtisses sombres et anguleuses.
>
> On hurle, on flâne, on regarde, on triche, on vole. Et ils violent. Le reste n'existe plus (Bouraoui 1991: 9).

In the translation, some of the rich word play is lost. Nevertheless, I would like to draw attention to some striking elements in Bouraoui's text that persist in translation. Even in such a short, opening paragraph, and even within Western literary concepts, it is easy to see why this book was such a literary success. This opening is the narrator's negotiation of the invisible boundary that separates her from the outside world.

The narrator is located in an I who – through the use of "my street" – attaches herself firmly to her lived environment. Indeed, the very first word – the little deictic element "this" – positions the narrator in a diegetic timeframe as well as space. The sun is "higher", this morning; higher, presumably, than the day before. Thus, the narration bleeds into an ante-story we have no access to, binding the reader to a life longer than the duration of the diegesis. The narratorial voice is foregrounded by the first of an innumerable amount of puns, when "haut" (high) becomes "hautain" (arrogant, haughty), "je dirais" (I would say). Through this small sentence, the narrator's power over the diegesis is supplemented by an explicit arrogation of the power over language.

This combined power of language and diegetic timespace doubles itself when the sun and the narrator appear to become one, the power and energy of the former transferred to the latter. The sun is invested with royalty by means of the metonymic throne on which it sits (trône invisible), a royal status immediately translated into actual power when its energy "proudly" pours out over the street. The boredom of the everyday, embodied in the grocer sitting on a stool we see a fraction later, is lifted when the sun's arrogance transmits itself to the street.

As a result of this transference of creative power from sun to narrator this deictic narrator suddenly appears to turn into a distanced, perhaps "omniscient" speaker when the view on the outside – illuminated by the haughty sun – becomes the object of description. The reader "sees" street life. This is the third power the narrator takes: the world beyond the window is hers to represent – hence, in a tale of fiction, to create. The street itself is separated from the city at large only to become a synecdoche of it, its epicentre. One could even suggest that seen from behind the window, the street *becomes* the world. Invested with the sun's arrogance, it seems a powerful place.

Until, that is, language's metaphoricity alerts us to disasters to come. When the street is called "epicentre" of adventure, the metaphor recalls images of earthquakes, of violent action leaving people powerless against the natural forces unleashed. Its power to shake up the world, however, only works to a certain extent, since everyone has his or her own place in the street life. The grocer is sitting idly, there is an invisible man spying on an invisible woman, and the children, still allowed to mingle, are locked up in a rectangle firmly delimited by buildings that appear none too cheerful. At the end of the paragraph, the synecdoche of the entire world seen from the window – from the sun overlooking it from its haughty position – is turned inside out. The world, unlimited for a split second, shrinks before our eyes to become a claustrophobic tiny square. In the wake of that shrinking, the narrator resumes her proper, tiny place behind the window.

From behind a window, then, a woman, the I, looks at the street where men do their business and act as Peeping Toms, and where children play. The division between the sexes is played out ruthlessly, although with the children who still have a future, the street has the promise of boundless adventure. The sequence of activities described comes to a forced stop when

the neutral *on* in French (one in English) is replaced with the masculine
pronoun indicating the act of rape. *Violer* is used in the absolute sense here,
reminding us that the verb is ambiguous because *violer* can also mean to
transgress a law or to violate rules. Who is able to transgress in this street, a
space of freedom and movement and yet seemingly rigid in its gender
organization? On what terms would the I herself have the possibility to
transgress rules, to act out her desire? The double sense of violer, rape and
transgression, brings up questions of boundaries, of gender, of inside and
outside, of movement and stasis, of transition and change.

In its thematization of the street as epicentre of adventure and of the gaze
as the only means of existence, *La Voyeuse interdite* calls forth the
perspective of looking from the inside out, a perspective that resonates with
my analysis of the figuration of the nomadic subject, on which more in
Chapter Four. At the same time, Bouraoui's narrator, attempting to borrow
the sun's power, represents the opposite of the idealized figure of the
nomadic subject circulating in contemporary feminism. Inspired by Gilles
Deleuze's concept of the nomad, Braidotti, for example, endorses the
intellectual nomad's point of being, which concerns "crossing boundaries
. . . the act of going, regardless of the destination . . . The nomad enacts
transitions without a teleological purpose" (1994: 22-23).[3]

Braidotti proposes to speak about the nomad as a figuration, i.e. as "a style
of thought that evokes or expresses ways out of the phallocentric vision of
the subject. A figuration is a politically informed account of an alternative
subjectivity" (1994: 1). In some cases the figural mode functions according to
what Braidotti has called, "the philosophy of 'as if' . . . It is as if some
experiences were reminiscent or evocative of others; this ability to flow from
one set of experiences to another is a quality of interconnectedness that I
value highly. Drawing on a flow of connections need not be an act of
appropriation. On the contrary; it marks transitions between communicating
states or experiences" (1994: 5).

This easy travel between metaphor and the conditions of life of groups of
people gives me pause. What does the figuration of the nomad imply?
According to Braidotti, it entails both a style and a mode of being. The

---

[3] Janet Wolff has also drawn attention to "vocabularies of travel [that] seem to have been proliferating
in cultural criticism", and that are gendered in nature (1993: 224).

nomadic style foregrounds transdisciplinarity (or deterritorialization as Deleuze called it) and the mixing of various ways of speaking. One of the explicitly stated goals of the nomadic style is a continuous critique of the concept of the unified subject, while proposing instead a situated but heterogeneous subjectivity. The nomadic style "is about transformations and transitions without predetermined destinations or lost homelands" (1994: 25). However, through the creation of trajectories – trekking from oasis to oasis – the nomad returns with regularity.

The figuration of the nomad also implies a mode of being, an existential circumstance, a polyglot who lives in between languages. As such the nomad has a sceptical attitude concerning identities that are thought of, or presented as stable. Time and again the mobility of the nomad is emphasized: "The nomad's identity is a map of where s/he has already been . . . The nomad represents moveable diversity, the nomad's identity is an inventory of traces" (1994: 14). In a questionable effort to separate the "real" nomad from the intellectual nomad, Braidotti claims to use the latter as "a myth, that is to say a political fiction, that allows me to think through and move across established categories and levels of experience: blurring boundaries without burning bridges" (1994: 4).

At first sight, the figuration of the nomad seems to open up possibilities. Women, women's voices and their experiences can be situated differently, it seems to imply, which would be a welcome counterweight to the universalizing discourses about women. It functions, as Braidotti states, in similar ways as Foucault's notion of countermemory, as "a form of resisting assimilation or homologation into dominant ways of representing the self" (1994: 25). As I understand it, the nomad is a rebel with a cause. She resists, and is not always particularly peaceful in so doing.[4]

This begs one pressing question: who can be or become a nomad? Citing Dale Spender, Braidotti takes the nomad as the prototype of the "man or woman of ideas" and she summons feminists and other critical intellectuals to cultivate a nomadic consciousness. Hence, no more than a woman, one is not born a nomad; instead, a nomadic consciousness or subjectivity is

---

[4] In fact, Braidotti overemphasizes this privileged link between the nomad and violence, depicting him/her as raiding, looting and sacking cities, and killing the sedentary population. In so doing, she draws upon, but greatly simplifies, Deleuze's notion of "war machines" (1994: 25).

cultivated. Akin to becoming a *femme de lettres* one needs to work to become a nomad. Describing her own intellectual nomadic activity, Braidotti refers to her frequent use of the image of the map and her writing as cartographies: "The nomad and the cartographer proceed hand in hand because they share a situational need – except that the nomad knows how to read invisible maps" (1994: 17). As a prelude to the discussion in Chapter Four I now return to Bouraoui's novel, where we also encounter a figuration of the nomad. I wish to explore some of the questions related to this figuration, and consider Bouraoui's text as an entry point to a critical reflection on the function of boundaries.

In the apparently static world of Bouraoui's text some figures from outside break the silence of the house. The most significant of these is Ourdhia, a woman from the south of Algeria. This somewhat mysterious and, indeed, nomadic woman knocks on the door one day. She needs food, a drop of water and a roof over her head. She becomes the cleaning woman of the household. As often happens in situations of social inequality within the home, Ourdhia comes to function as a source of comfort for the young girl as well. Moreover, Ourdhia's experience as a woman of the desert is transformed into an image of alleged, doubtlessly projected freedom: "My nomad, look, I say my nomad, belonged to a large Touareg tribe dispersed over a land without apparent boundaries where beauty was the worst danger" (Ma nomade, voyez, je dis ma nomade, appartenait à une grande tribu targuie dispersée dans un pays sans frontières apparentes où la beauté était le pire des dangers [Bouraoui 1991: 53-54]). As I have already indicated, the narrator of *La Voyeuse* uses the personal pronoun to suture her own voice to the diegetic space and its inhabitants. The use of personal pronouns is often indicative of deeply felt ties. Such ties are self-evident between the narrator and Ourdhia, and they are just as self-evidently severed. Ourdhia has something to offer just like the street, "my street", had something to offer: she offers a narrative, the story of her travels through the desert. The narrator describes the nomadic voyage she cannot have witnessed in a language that deploys fictionality to create strong identificatory sensations:

> Ourdhia had refused every company on her march through nature . . . Guided by the stars she had reached the barest region, the beauty without display, the essence itself of the sublime: le Ténéré. Emptiness of emptiness, absolute of the

absolute, centre of the earth, epicentre of nothingness, this place finally
crowned the disciplined walk of the nomad, there, she was in intimate
conversation with the truth. Le Ténéré, vast empire of sand, is represented on
my map by a large yellow spot. But I did not know. Ourdhia taught it to me.

Ourdhia avait refusé tout accompagnement dans sa marche à travers la nature
. . . Guidée par les étoiles, elle avait atteint la région la plus nue, la beauté sans
apparat, l'essence même du sublime: le Ténéré. Vide du vide, absolu de
l'absolu, centre de la terre, épicentre du néant, ce lieu couronnait enfin la
marche disciplinée de la nomade, là, elle communiait avec la vérité. Le Ténéré,
vaste empire de sable, est représenté sur ma carte par une large tache jaune.
Mais je ne savais pas. Ourdhia me l'apprit (Bouraoui 1991: 54-55).

Several metaphors from the opening paragraph recur here. The sun's majesty,
the epicentre, are again invested with immense power (e.g. "crowned", the
absoluteness recalling the absolute power attributed to monarchs) and at the
same time, undermined by the emptiness that characterizes the place. Beauty
and emptiness go hand in hand.

The narrator also uses the metaphor of the map to suggest the bond
between knowledge and power – or powerlessness. The spot on the girl's
map, at first indicating an emptiness of knowledge, now, through Ourdhia's
narrative, becomes an almost over-determined space. From the white of
ignorance it is now coloured with the yellow of sterility and emptiness.
Although described as the ultimate emptiness, it stands in sharp contrast to
the emptiness of the girl's life or the gap in her knowledge. Ourdhia's march
leads her to the epicentre of nothingness, where truth resides, a truth the
young girl badly wants to know about but lacks the ways or means to attain.

The girl's perception of Ourdhia differs sharply from that of her mother
who considers the nomad as no more than a maid. Significantly, this
subservient position also allows some measure of freedom – a freedom,
however, that turns out to be a highly dubious asset. The maid is the only one
permitted to leave the house to do some shopping. In this function she
embodies the negotiable boundary as such. The girl jealously watches
Ourdhia since she has access to that other epicentre: the street. Thus, the
street becomes the counterpart of the empty, awesome beauty of the desert.

Urban Desert

The confrontation of the nomad with the street reveals an additional truth, the ugly truth of the epicentre of what was called "adventure" at the beginning. One day Ourdhia leaves the house, closely followed by the young girl's gaze from her window:

> In the beginning, everything went well, her teeth held the traditional veil, Ourdhia never covered her head, only her shoulders: first signs of a perfect body able to stir up the desire of those men always in heat. Her pace was dignified . . . The men of my street then began to regroup, the illusion of freedom was soon going to disappear. The city seemed to be a vacuum-sealed bell jar that closed itself little by little over her shoulders.

> Au début, tout allait bien, ses dents retenaient le voile traditionnel, Ourdhia ne couvrait jamais sa tête, uniquement ses épaules: premières marques d'un corps parfait pouvant attiser le désir de ces hommes toujours en rut. La démarche était fière . . . Les hommes de ma rue commençaient alors à se regrouper, l'illusion de liberté allait bientôt disparaître. La ville semblait être une cloche sous vide qui se refermait peu à peu sur ses épaules (Bouraoui 1991: 56).

From the young girl's vantage point behind the window, a tragedy is about to unfold. Assuring us that "in the beginning" everything went well, the narrator makes the reader aware from the start of impending danger. Like the silence before the storm, the actors of the play position themselves for what is to come. Not only do the men in the street take up their positions, the city itself is ready for confrontation, as if a classical drama is soon to come to its inevitable conclusion.

As expected, the situation explodes into violence. Like the earthquake promised in the novel's first paragraph, the personified space senses the man-made catastrophe about to erupt. The city holds its breath, the men become a wall, and the children turn rigid. His majesty the sun turns away:

> The children had stopped their playing. The little girls knew and, just like me, had not foreseen the danger. She [Ourdhia] walked faster . . . Suddenly, she halted. A brat threw a stone at her, another, more courageous, hit her full in the face, two young men let their repugnant hands run over her beautiful body, I screamed. She alone knew. The increasing noise of the city smothered her cries, yes, Ourdhia defended herself. She wasn't afraid, but what to do confronted with those unleashed hordes? Ourdhia was a woman and moreover, oh

desolation, she was black! Kahloûcha! Kahloûcha! [Kahloûcha: a denigrating term for a black woman].

Les enfants s'étaient arrêtés de jouer, les fillettes savaient et, comme moi, elles ne prévinrent pas du danger. Elle marchait plus vite . . . Soudain, elle s'arrêta net. Un morveux lui lança une pierre, un autre, plus courageux, lui cracha en pleine figure, deux jeunes hommes faisaient courir leurs mains répugnantes sur son beau corps, je hurlais. Elle seule savait. La rumeur grandissante de la ville couvrait ses cris, oui, Ourdhia se défendait, elle n'avait pas peur, mais que faire devant ces hordes déchaînées? Ourdhia était une femme et en plus, ô désolation, elle était noire! "Kahloûcha"! (Bouraoui 1991: 57).

This figure of the nomad is a far cry from Western feminism's joyful figure of liberty and boundary-crossing. On the contrary, against her sheer appearance, the personified city erects the most solid boundary of all: that of patriarchal appropriation and racism. Indeed, this confrontation with the abusive hordes of hyper-testosteronic men solicits the first mention of her racial identity.

The nomad's fate in this episode, then, made me profoundly uneasy about the idealization of this figure in recent feminist theory. Just because she was a woman and black, she was punished for being present in the street. The aggression expressed in the behaviour of the boys who attacked Ourdhia is experienced as a grave transgression, by the young girl as well as, the latter imagines, by Ourdhia. The girl cries out, but the window, that invisible boundary that precludes effective solidarity, silences her voice. The rape does not have to take place in all its sordid details, because the sense of violation is already multiple as well as total: physically and mentally Ourdhia is made to undergo the law of the dominant patriarchal order where gender, race and class all work against her.

This scene at the heart of the novel questions any sense of idealization of the nomad. Not coincidentally, this figure is a woman – like the Western feminist, minus the protection the latter enjoys. Being a nomad is not only an exposure to hunger and thirst, it is also potentially an exposure to total violation. For the young girl, Ourdhia represented freedom and royalty. In the eyes of the girl hungry for adventure, the nomad was a princess. This proud woman walking through the desert taught her about choice, knowledge of truth, and movement for women. Nomadism became connected to these concepts in the girl's eyes.

Ourdhia seemed to be able to transgress the boundaries that were strictly applied to the girl. In this sense the two epicentres are related: just as the street represents adventure and limitlessness, the desert does the same. But as in the baroque beginning of the novel where extremes touch and royalty becomes imprisonment in the blink of an eye, the world widens and shrinks in a single breath. After Ourdhia is attacked in the street, the girl must reach the shocking conclusion that she had constructed a fantasmatic image of the nomad. In the most extreme way possible Ourdhia is subjected to the restrictions of a society that applies rules to everybody, but more stringently to women, and even more stringently to women of colour. From her window looking out, in the young girl's perception the street and the desert seemed without boundaries and Ourdhia seemed able to move around in this apparently heavenly state. But altered by the language of the opening paragraph, as readers we know better. The girl was only able to contemplate the world beyond her window as adventurous and borderless if she turned a blind eye to a major boundary, to her perspective from the inside. Therefore, what renders the outside into a beyond without boundaries is exactly the boundary operating between "our window" and the outside, or rather, "our window" is, metaphorically, a boundary itself. Hence, in my reading, the girl acquires knowledge about the boundaries one lives with – and which one tries, and ultimately needs, to negotiate. And, as we will see, the negotiation is not confined only to restrictions and limitations.

In Braidotti's and other feminist analyses of the nomad, the nomad functions in a field of references: evocations of the desert, freedom, limitlessness and violence. The distinction between the figuration of the nomad and actual nomads is hard to maintain given the strong and vivid notions that come with the use of the term. Within this framework, I immediately made associations with representations of the Orient, and with Orientalist imaginings of the Orient, which I studied in a previous book (2004b). I refer to this field as the Orient so as to emphasize that I am not trying to get at a notion of Middle-Eastern reality, but to a representation that has fantasmatic overtones. In this context, it is sad to see how the figure of the nomad in feminist theory becomes the noble savage functioning as the identificatory knot, as the mirror image, of what one wishes to critique in the West. This trajectory based on projection remains locked in a fiction that dates back at least two centuries. The stereotypical representations of the Middle East in Orientalism, connected to imaginations of violence and free-roaming hordes of nomads in the desert, are deeply embedded in Western notions of the Orient. Threat and admiration go hand in hand, as it were, and belong to an ideology of dividing the world into what is horrifying but attractive and what is common to oneself and one's self. To my mind, it is necessary for theory to distance itself from this imagination, and instead of unreflectively reiterating these figurations, to make it the critical mission of theory to undermine their power.

In this context, I share Caren Kaplan's concern that the figuration of the nomad is in danger of becoming romanticized; nomadic life should not become a desired state (1996). What I see operating here is a similar problem to the one the young girl encountered in *La Voyeuse interdite*: only from the perspective of the inside would it be possible to postulate the freedom of the nomad, intellectual or otherwise. Moreover, the privileged links between nomadism and violence, and between nomadism and movement, imply the existence of a boundary. However, rather than recognizing this boundary so as to facilitate its negotiation, these theories are predicated on their presumed absence. This invisibility of boundaries keeps us from apprehending the very conditions in which nomads live.

Bouraoui's novel sets the girl behind the window up against the reality of street violence. Thus, while remaining within the focalization of the powerless young girl, the structure of fiction enables us to understand a reality that is more real, perhaps, than the reality suggested in feminist theory. The novel suggests that the violence and movement of nomads are inspired by outside conditions that impose restrictions upon them. For example, running up against a boundary can motivate violence. And even though nomads share their situational needs with cartographers like Braidotti, nomads know not only how to read invisible maps, but also know that mapping invisible maps into visible ones went hand in hand with colonialism and struggles over the uncertain territories around which boundaries were drawn. Therefore, the relevant question is *not* how to achieve a state of freedom without boundaries. Thoughtlessly crossing these boundaries on an endless travel makes them disappear as an area of contention and contestation. Rather, I propose to take precisely these boundaries – and their function – as a point of departure.

The analysis of change and transition can take place in vastly different ways. One end of the continuum we find fenced-in notions and rigid divisions between categories. On the other end we can find the limitlessness of the figuration of the nomad in feminist theory. In my insistence on the importance of boundaries, I find myself at neither end of this continuum. Instead, for me boundaries function even where one postulates their absence. Ultimately, the movement is *in* the boundaries, not just in the spaces it separates or in a borderless harmony.

My insistence on the study of the function of boundaries is confirmed in Fatima Mernissi's later work, an autobiographical fictional text describing life as a member of a harem in an upper-class Moroccan family (1994b). *The Forbidden Roof-Terrace* describes the life of a young girl – the I in the narrative – amidst an extended family in which women, especially elder women, function as sources of all kinds of information. One of the notions capturing the attention of the young girl, the I, is the harem. Her grandmother Jasmina gives some clarification. Jasmina explains that a harem was the space where a man would safely accommodate his family, his wife or wives, his children and

> other men could not enter without permission of the owner and if they did, they had to obey his rules. A harem had to do with private space and rules that applied there. Essentially, walls were not needed, Jasmina said. As soon as you knew what was forbidden, you carried the harem within yourself. The harem resided in your head, "inscribed under your forehead and under your skin". That idea of an invisible harem, a law tattooed in your head, upset me profoundly (Mernissi 1994b: 65).

The young girl is thrown off balance by a frightening image: a law tattooed in your head. Invisible yet known by all, the harem functions as a space where boundaries operate to separate what was forbidden from what was allowed. How was the young girl to know about the boundary? How was she able to know when she transgressed the boundary or followed its requirements?

Jasmina continues only to complicate the girl's understanding of the function of boundaries:

> This going about with a harem in your head confused me, and inconspicuously I would lay my hand on my forehead to feel whether it was still smooth, to see whether I might be harem free. But after that Jasmina's explanation turned even more alarming, because then she said that every space that you entered had its own invisible rules and that you had to try to find out about them . . . "Wherever there are people, a *qaida*, an invisible rule, exists. If you keep to the *qaida*, nothing can happen to you" (Mernissi 1994b: 66).

The notion of the harem, and its internalization, is not enough to keep one from transgressing, because potentially every space can lead to a breaking of the invisible rule. If the *qaida* governs every space, it is an absolute, vital necessity to know how it works, how the boundary functions and who wants or accepts its functioning. That urgent need is what makes Jasmina's explanation so alarming: negotiating a boundary without knowing what it is.

Resonating with the cultural desire for visible boundaries, discussed in the introduction, the young girl's first impulse is to desire a visible boundary:

> Were there signs or something tangible to watch for? No, she said, unfortunately there were no indications except for the consequences of your transgression . . . In fact, the *qaida*, that invisible rule, was often much worse than walls and gates. At least with walls and gates you knew what to reckon with. At these words I almost wished that all the rules would suddenly materialize in the form of boundaries and visible walls (Mernissi 1994b: 66-67).

Of course, visible walls would at least provide a certainty of sorts. But in fact the advice of Jasmina to the I is to go and find out by herself, because no one would be able to fully teach her how the *qaida* works. Thus, such second-hand knowledge could lead to unintended transgressions of the *qaida*, whereas becoming knowledgeable about its functioning through experience would help avoid such conflicts. What the grandmother is suggesting, then, is that boundaries are uncertain territories in need of negotiation. The young girl needs to insert herself in the process of negotiating the boundary, even when it is as frightful an activity as Jasmina recounts. As we will see in Chapter Four, she undertakes to treat her own situation in her culture as an urban desert: an uncertain space that, like a true boundary, is open to negotiation.

Feminism as Tourism

If feminism doesn't follow a nomadic itinerary, how does it travel? In the most general of terms, the common perceptions about the relation of Western feminism and Third World women have been characteristically shaped from a Western perspective specifically in the sixties and seventies of the last century. It is this Western perspective that I take as my own point of departure in order to critically approach its implicit presuppositions about the relation between Third World women and First World women. The implicit point of departure for Western feminism was the idea that Third World women had something to learn from Western feminism, which in the eyes of the latter was well advanced and fighting for causes that concerned women wherever they were situated and whatever their position. Western feminism set the agenda, presupposing from what might be called a (neo)colonialist perspective that the Third World was a tabula rasa as far as feminist issues were concerned (for a classic critique of this agenda, see Hull et al, eds. 1982).

The imposition of a Western feminist program upon Third World women bears striking similarities to the colonialist's illusion of the Middle East as the mythic white page onto which one could inscribe oneself. For instance, Flaubert, visiting Egypt as a tourist, maintained this fantasy of the white page and was bothered by the evidence of previous tourists' presence:

> One is irritated by the number of imbeciles' names written everywhere: on the steps of the Great Pyramid there is a certain Buffard, 79 Rue Saint-Martin, wallpaper-manufacturer, in black letters; an English fan of jenny Lind's has written her name; there is also a pear, representing Louis-Philippe (Flaubert and Steegmuller 1987: 54).

It is this disturbance of expectations – a growing sense that others have or might have been there before you – which leads to the perception that the point of origin is not you in quiet contemplation of the white page.

A fruitful result of this frustration is the reconsideration of one's own position. When we take a closer look at the point of origin of Western feminism, it is hard to locate. Do we situate it with the famous names of the second feminist wave, Betty Friedan, Germaine Greer? Do we consider the so-called UN Decade of Women, which ran from 1975 until 1985, as the moment that feminism established itself in the discourse as a force to be reckoned with? Or do we go back in history to find the roots of feminism in the struggle for voting rights around the turn of the century, utopian feminism in the 1840s, the Enlightenment ideas on equality between the sexes, Christine de Pisan? The point of origin escapes us, in a truly Derridean movement of continuous deferral (Derrida 1967).

The situation becomes even more complicated when I add the notion of arrival to my considerations. The issue of a theory arriving, for instance in the Middle East, is not as clear-cut as may be expected. Firstly, the arrival of Western feminist theories in the Middle East is intimately tied up with the late nineteenth and early twentieth-century discussions in Egypt and Turkey of nationalism and the advancement of society through economic, social and cultural reforms, as Leila Ahmed has argued convincingly in her work *Women and Gender in Islam* (1992). Secondly, ideas about ameliorations in the position of women in the Middle East came in a mediated form, i.e. through contacts with, for instance, male Egyptian intellectuals travelling to Europe and bringing back information about women's positions in Europe. And finally, Western feminist theories did not arrive as one package; rather, they arrived in bits and pieces. I am thinking of European women who influenced Arab women such as Eugénie Le Brun who instructed Huda Shaarawi, an Egyptian feminist who became well known for publicly unveiling herself on the train station of Cairo in the early 1920s, or Shaarawi herself visiting an International Feminist Meeting in Rome in 1923 in the company of Nabawiyya Musa and Saiza Nabarawi (see Ahmed 1992).

What emerges from this brief contextualization of ideas is that Said's categories of travelling theories, mentioned in the introduction, follow a much more complicated texture of criss-crossing movements, where influences and adaptations are not unidirectional. Nor can they be localized solidly within one or another place. Theories travel and one of the results that come with travel is that interpretational practices have to change as well. Thus, boundary negotiation takes place at various levels, which brings me back to Bouraoui's novel, especially its repeated trope of the epicentre.

The mention of epicentres throughout the novel creates the image of an area of volcanic activity. As all tropes, the epicentres mentioned above – as well as those yet to be analyzed – function as signs, that is, they stand for something else. This something else, I contend, is the negotiation of boundaries. As is well known, epicentres are the points located on a map, and they are just above the true centre of disturbance, from where the shock waves of an earthquake apparently radiate. At first, Bouraoui's epicentres, the street and the desert, are located outside, sending their shock waves in, pointing at what they actually are: spaces of negotiation. In the following three other instances where epicentres are mentioned, however, the direction is reversed: the epicentres move inside, and they are accompanied by references to the earlier epicentres along with their connotations. Again, the sun is present, but not as the source of a contagious majesty. Instead:

> Like the earth turns around the sun, I circle around myself, similar to a fly famished for adventures. Useless round that renders the mind into the epicentre of the body, and the body the epicentre of the mind. And the encaged mouse bites its own tail! I happen to think of Ourdhia.

> Comme la terre autour du soleil, je tourne autour de moi, semblable à une mouche affamée d'aventures. Ronde inutile qui fait de l'esprit l'épicentre du corps, du corps l'épicentre de l'esprit. Et la souris enfermée dans la cage se mord la queue! Il m'arrive de penser à Ourdhia (Bouraoui 1991: 62).

In the circling movement of mind and body, the two are locked together, maybe desiring to break loose but unable to do so at the moment. Avid for adventure, the impasse is merely imaginatively resolved with reference to Ourdhia:

> mythical heroine, dead and buried, but more available than the living. Without emotion, I embrace her body and the landscape to which it belongs.

> héroïne mythique, morte et enterrée mais plus disponible que les vivants. Sans émotion, j'étreins son corps et le paysage auquel il appartient (Bouraoui 1991: 62).

Ourdhia's example has its limits, to use a phrase. I see in this passage both a desire for, and the impossibility of identification. The desire to negotiate boundaries cannot be fuelled by outsiders alone. Yet, the ongoing imagery of cosmic relationships associates Ourdhia with the landscape of the desert from which she came, to which she belonged, and to which the aggression in the city relegated her anew.

In the last part of the novel, the tight interaction of epicentres unfolds. However, this does not lead to complete separation. The section begins with the act that turns the rigid boundary into a negotiable one: "I take the risk of opening my window" (Je me risque à ouvrir ma fenêtre [Bouraoui 1991: 99]). Opening her window, the young girl confronts the sunlight, which both dazzles and strengthens her. Giddy with her newfound power, she sees herself briefly as "the Cassandra of the new age", the "ruler over the Mores" to whom "the street, the city, and the world belong" (la Cassandre du nouveau siècle! . . . dominatrice des Mauresques . . . la rue, la ville, le monde m'appartient! [Bouraoui 1991: 99]).

But this dream of power is short-lived. In the middle of her musings on appropriation and mastery over the world, a car approaches and stops in front of the house: "an insufferably long car pulled me out of my day-dreaming" (une voiture insupportablement longue me tire de ma rêverie [Bouraoui 1991: 99]). The car, described in the terms appropriate for its frightening charge, carries her future husband, who observes her. For the first time, she is named: Fikria. With her name however, she both loses and gains something. Named, endowed with an identity, constituted as a subject, Fikria in the same move becomes an object, subjected to a patriarchal gaze and plot.

During her childhood, she had cultivated the flower of observation in her garden and then, by an odd osmosis, ratified through a pact sealed with blood, she has become object, thing, matter herself. Fikria, the Moorish intellectual, amused herself by spying without being seen and yet, for months, she was unaware of a frightful plot that was being hatched beneath her room: she was going to become a woman. A woman under a man's body. She knows now that the process of entering adulthood does not stop with the first flow of menstrual blood, but will result in an arranged marriage, a pact sealed with blood in which she is supposed to be submissive to her future husband.

In a hallucinatory and horrific encounter with death, she dreams of self-mutilation and rape, prefiguring the rupture of her hymen by enacting the deflowering herself, with the hook of a coat-hanger. Surprised, she wakes up to find her sex intact, but fraught with a new brightness, an unexpected irony. Innocent, yet with its future role known, now Fikria's vagina is itself an epicentre:

Centre of the silhouette, epicentre of pleasure, today it displays its malice, blazing with its entire glow like a sewn emblem that I cannot tear from its target.

Centre de la silhouette, épicentre du plaisir, il étale aujourd'hui sa malice en brillant de tous ses feux comme un emblème cousu que je ne peux arracher de son plastron (Bouraoui 1991: 116).

The vagina as epicentre points at the true centre of disturbance – the boundary to be negotiated, her hymen.

The negotiation is, of course, conducted on multiple levels and within varying relations of power. For instance, her parents value the hymen, carefully preserved as means of exchange in the arrangements for a suitable marriage, thus rendering the young girl into an object for authorized transgression. Fikria, by contrast, perceives the boundary as a place of intersection, where pleasure, anger, pain and convention all coincide. She was ready to forego the strict observation of the boundary.

The hymen is also a boundary to be negotiated by the Western cultural critic. Disconcerting as the examples are, it is too easy to dismiss arranged marriages and the concomitant guarding of virginity exclusively as practices that victimize women. If sexual oppression is perceived as the general ruling condition for women in the Middle East, we might indeed be looking at the world beyond our window, but we might be overlooking how the window influences our perception. Rather than generalizing Fikria's situation, reading her observations as an "outsider within" complicates our analysis.

Immediately following the previous passage, Fikria looks outside. The street has emptied itself; there is nobody to be seen:

Stretched by an enigmatic light, the street is extended as far as the harbour . . . Last protrusion of land, no man's land of nowhere, timeless transit, last instant, unreal sea wall, pause between nothingness and nothing, border of nought, horrible emptiness, the harbour is the last rampart of the prison.

Etirée par une lumière énigmatique, la rue se prolonge jusqu'au port . . . Dernière avancée de terre, no man's land de nulle part, transit intemporel, ultime instant, digue irréelle, temps d'arrêt entre le rien et le rien, bordure du néant, épouvantable vide, le port est le dernier rempart de la prison (Bouraoui 1991: 117).

The street leads to the harbour and, in an ironic reversal of characteristics, at the moment her gaze reaches the water the desert is evoked again, only to meet the harbour as an obstacle.

This interplay between inside and outside, between the contesting forces of convention and a resistant young girl, leads to the last epicentre in the novel. On the day of Fikria's marriage, the bride continues with her angry and ironic observations. Among the cries of admiration for her dress, she is acutely aware of the itching between her legs due to the shaving of her pubic hair. She knows that tradition repeats itself, at least to a certain extent:

> Change of scene, return to the same old monotonous chant. It's your turn, Fikria! Today it is me. Me, me, me! My whole being bears and sustains the adventure, I am its foster-mother, the epicentre, the tourist flyer which prying and interrogative hands fondle in every direction. Wrinkle.

> Changement de décor, retour au semblable sur chant monocorde. A ton tour Fikria! Aujourd'hui c'est moi. Moi, moi, moi! Tout mon être porte et supporte l'aventure, je suis sa mère nourricière, l'épicentre, le dépliant touristique que des mains curieuses et interrogatives tripotent dans tous les sens. Froissent (Bouraoui 1991: 126).

Both subject and object, foster-mother and tourist flyer, Fikria asserts her subjectivity with respect to the women present and is fondled as a powerless object. From this fondling, she does not emerge undamaged, but the damage done (wrinkled) is reparable. Negotiating subjectivity implies taking object-positions as well, as the alternate chanting of "It's your turn, Fikria! Today it is me" indicates. Of the imagery deployed in this passage, it is the tourist flyer that most disturbs me. While the recurring metaphor of the epicentre continues its function of invoking danger as well as adventure, the tourist flyer brings in, at least in the corner of our eyes, the Western feminist.

After the festivities at her home, a car comes to bring Fikria to her new husband: "A start shakes the motor and, surrounded by flowers, I headed for a new story" (Une secousse ébranla le moteur, et, encerclée de fleurs, je me dirigeai vers une nouvelle histoire [Bouraoui 1991: 143]). The phrase "a new story", une nouvelle histoire, bears the irony that is present throughout the novel. There is no certain outcome, no closure to the negotiations that the girl will engage in, now that she is married. *Histoire*, however, also has the meaning of trouble attached to it, as in the phrase "faire des histoires", to make scenes. Negotiation, in her case, will take the form of trouble. Trouble Fikria might experience in her married life, but also trouble she evokes because of her anger and her capacities for critical observation. Ominously, this sentence is followed by the last one of the novel: "Behind the truck, a band of dogs followed" (Derrière la camionnette, une cohorte de chiens suivait [Bouraoui 1991: 143]).

While at this point, closure might actually be desired, the new story with which the novel ends opens up new spaces of negotiation. It is a closure we seek for ourselves in our interpretational discomfort: a solution for the unease of analyzing cross-cultural representations. Yet the very trouble of going through the negotiation of boundaries also offers insights. It offers us glimpses on how the definition of differences and shared goals can and needs to be a multisided process in which hierarchies and inequalities of power relations continue to be problematized. It is this trouble that will rattle our window onto the world.

TWO

Public Violence Hits Home: Civil War and the Destruction of Privacy

What's new? The question couldn't be more mundane, frivolous almost. It seems a superfluous query, ignoring the tragic, utterly painful fate of civilians affected by internal strife. To be sure, it is a question not lightly posed on the subject of literary production in and on civil war. You don't ask "what's up?" or "tell me about it" to people whose lives are threatened on a daily basis. And yet, the question matters. It helps us understand and assess the inventive potential of literature in a political climate where all possibilities have been destroyed. With my analysis of the work of boundaries in the writing of Lebanese Arabophone writer Hanan al-Shaykh, and with help of the Algerian Francophone writer Assia Djebar, I attempt to specify where a focus on newness might take us when boundaries are terrains of encounter rather than division. For this search I will take my cue from Homi Bhabha, who, perhaps unexpectedly, put *newness* in the centre of his imaginings of intercultural worlds (1994).

In his introduction to *The Location of Culture*, Bhabha argued, that "the borderline work of culture demands an encounter with 'newness' that is not part of the continuum of past and present" (1994: 7). Rather than reinscribing such a fatalistic continuum, this encounter creates "a sense of the new as an insurgent act of cultural translation" (1994: 7). Bhabha is speaking of the *rasquachismo* of Mexican and Chicano art, a style attuned to mixture and convergence, with irony as a primary tool (Ybarra-Frausto 1991: 133-34). In the novel under discussion here, the newness is neither ironic nor shaped in the appropriation technique of *rasquachismo*, but rather an insistence on the literal consequences of the in-betweenness in time and space. This in-betweenness, I will argue, is embodied in the impossible epistolary form of the novel.

For Bhabha, the newness of cultural translation resides in its "foreignness". The combination of his two statements seems to put forward newness as a politically productive encounter, where the insurgence (here, against ongoing violence) is in need of cultural translation. That need itself is foregrounded, and the object of almost obsessive reflection. Thus, foregrounding newness implies questions such as: Where does the foreignness of cultural translation take us? What acts of translation occur in civil war literature? And what is my task as a translator? These questions will guide me through the two novels that are central in this chapter. Both are novels of the sad but important genre of "civil-war novels". In such novels, the central effect of civil war is manifest: the destruction of the private domain, or more precisely, the transgression of the boundary that separates, however precariously, the private from the public domain.

In Hanan al-Shaykh's novel *Poste restante Beyrouth* the main character Asma, short for Asmahan, a young Lebanese woman trained as an architect, writes letters in a country torn by civil war.[1] As the book title indicates, the letters are sent "poste restante", to the post office where the addressees supposedly come to collect them. But the poste restante address in Beirut is hardly the safe place where mail can be left until the addressees come to collect it. Most likely, the letters will never reach their addressees. Hence, their writer must know she is in for an interminable wait for replies. Answers, moreover, which are unattainable when the addressees include abstract entities such as "my dear country", "Madame War", or "beloved Beirut", or dead ones, such as "Billie Holiday". Similarly, answers are unlikely to arrive when letters, via poste restante Beirut, go to a good old friend who left

---

[1] Hanan al-Shaykh's novel was first published in Arabic in 1992. I have used the French translation, *Poste restante Beyrouth*, as the basis for my analysis. All translations from the French are mine. The different spelling of al-Shaykh's name (el-Cheikh in French) is a result of varying systems of ortho-graphy in English and French. Unless I cite the French title of the book, I will keep with the British spelling of Beirut.

Lebanon for Paris; to an ex-boyfriend, a Palestinian, forced to leave the country; and to another ex-boyfriend in exile. If the letters have such difficulty reaching their addressees, why write them at all? To write, or not to write: that is the question. In a country plagued by civil war, this novel demonstrates, the question is every bit as fundamental as that Shakespearean one about being.

As we will see, the question "Why write?" receives more depth and poignancy than ever in the case of civil war, and can, thus, come to stand for the poetics of civil war in general. This is why I pursue a different line of inquiry than Miriam Cooke, who interprets *Poste restante Beyrouth* as a narrative about emigration (2001: 24-25). Indeed, emigration forms a theme in the novel, especially in the letters to Asma's girlfriend in Paris, to Palestinian refugee Nasser, and to émigré Jaouad in Chapters One, Three and Seven respectively. However, since emigration is not addressed in many of the other letters – especially those directed at inanimate, abstract, or collective addressees – the novel's thematic and formal centre must lie elsewhere. Indeed, I contend, *address* – the futile and desperate writing of undeliverable letters – constitutes both the thematic and the poetic centre of the novel.[2]

Hanan al-Shaykh takes up this question in her pseudo-epistolary novel. Her earlier novel, *The Story of Zahra* (1986), also had the civil war as its focus but is not epistolary in form, nor does it have the question "Why write?" at its heart. I would like to speculate that the later novel offers a poetological reflection on the point of writing, a point her earlier book may have brought up in the author's mind as well as her readers. If we consider a writer her own first critical reader, the question "Why write?" may well have emerged from a novel that *describes* the state of civil war but does not *perform* it. It is in relation to this question of a performative poetics that I invoke, later in the chapter, the writings of Assia Djebar who reflects on her own writing. Where, for al-Shaykh, the question of writing is elaborated around the impossible addressee, for Djebar it is the impossibility of a single language that haunts her. For Djebar, the question is "why write in French?" Both authors, through different means, "introduce invention into existence" where they had been left depleted.

---

[2] See also Cooke's information on the so-called Beirut decentrists of which al-Shaykh is a member (1992: 454-56).

Assia Djebar has dealt with this issue a few years ago in her collection of essays and personal memoirs *Ces Voix qui m'assiègent* (Those Voices That Haunt Me [1999]). I will examine al-Shaykh's work in light of Djebar's, with the common framework set against the background of the violence of civil war in Lebanon and Algeria in the 1990s. These two books foreground the question of why one should bother to write under civil war in two distinct ways. Whereas al-Shaykh doubles the question by compounding the thematic with the poetic issue in the way I have outlined, through epistolary form and undeliverable address, Djebar simply and continuously raises the question explicitly in a form – a collection of essays about her writing – that stands for the inquiry itself. In line with these two texts' central focus, then, my investigation centres around the issue of writing: how one writes and what one writes about when one is faced with this violent and cruel environment that presses against the relevance of writing. What influence, ultimately, does the violence of and in civil war exercise on writing – and how can writing offer a different environment? Invoking Frantz Fanon, Bhabha said it thus: "I should constantly remind myself that the real *leap* consists in introducing invention into existence" (1994: 8; emphasis in text).

When Home and the World Melt Together

In a country torn apart by an internal war, a war that ravages the privacy of its people, and that divides the capital city into two halves, the notion of borders changes. In *Poste restante Beyrouth*, the motive of the border runs through the entire novel. But it is only towards the end that Asma is able to describe the border itself. This boundary is cast, not as an imaginary line with soldiers on the different sides, checking passes and harassing people who wish to visit a sick relative in a hospital or to go out on the town for an evening, but as a concrete, physical space. Here is what Asma sees:

> to end up in a wasteland. There he told me to get out and traverse on foot:
> – When you see the Pepsi-Cola sign, you will have arrived on their ground. Right there, you will find taxis to take you wherever you wish to go.

> pour déboucher enfin sur un terrain vague. Là il m'avait fait descendre et dit de traverser à pied:

> – Quand vous verrez l'enseigne Pepsi-Cola, vous êtes arrivée chez eux. Tout
> près, vous trouverez des taxis pour vous amener où vous voudrez (Al-Shaykh
> 1995: 274).

The wasteland, which Asma describes a few lines further as "that deserted
space" (cet espace désert), is vast. A bit later, this vast scale, literally a waste
of land, is explained in terms that foreground the tragic pointlessness of
internal warfare:

> The gap between the two zones became wider, not even because of the small
> hills and the barbed wire that obstructed the passage points, but because each
> zone had chosen a road that widened the distance from the other.
>
> Le fossé entre les deux zones s'élargissait, non pas à cause des monticules et
> des barbelés qui obstruaient les points de passage, mais parce que chaque zone
> avait choisi une voie qui l'éloignait de l'autre (Al-Shaykh 1995: 277).

As we will see, the constant hesitation between metaphoric and literal use of
language is characteristic for this novel. It mobilizes the imagination in order
to understand and render understandable the absurdity of what cannot be
understood. In the previous quote, for example, we don't know where
metaphor begins and ends. A zone, a piece of land, makes the *choice* – that
human agency par excellence – to widen the boundary. It is not the fatality of
the naturalized obstructions, erected by humans but henceforth inevitable, but
the choice of the zones that matters. Agency is both questioned and
attributed, in the same way that the city itself has become an addressee of the
letters.

A bit later still, this address is, precisely, based on the destruction waged
by the boundary itself:

> They took us back to your reality, Beirut, which was no longer anything but a
> hyphen; your beauty was only a product of import-export.
>
> Ils nous ramenaient à ta réalité, Beyrouth, qui n'était plus qu'un trait d'union; ta
> beauté n'était plus qu'un produit d'import-export (Al-Shaykh 1995: 286).

A hyphen that separates and binds at the same time, while – importantly for
the poetics of this novel – it occupies no space.

Both Algeria and Lebanon have known periods of civil strife and ethnic warfare in the mid-twentieth century, due to the dissolution of the French colonial empire that exercised its influence over both countries from the nineteenth century onward. Algeria suffered a prolonged war of independence (1954-1962), pitting a large European community living in Algeria against an indigenous population avid for independence. The country faced the formidable task of breaking away from France, not as a colony, but as an integral part of metropolitan France. Lebanon became independent in 1946, striking a delicate balance in a country inhabited by Shi'ite and Sunni Muslims, Christian Maronites, Greek Orthodox, Druzes and Palestinian refugees after 1948, a balance which broke down in a civil war that lasted a few months in 1958 (Hourani 1992: 429-30).

Tragically enough, the history of both countries includes yet more civil war in the 1990s. Lebanon's civil war started in 1975 and lasted until 1992. In Algeria, civil war broke out when the army took over the government in 1992, because polls for the upcoming elections showed the Islamist party, the FIS, to be on the winning side. This sad summary is not meant, of course, to suggest, as many tend to do, that Arab countries are continuously involved in civil war, but rather that *the memory of civil war* is part and parcel of the recent history and hence, continues to act up in the culture of both countries. Civil war, to a large extent, constitutes that culture.

Although the civil war in both countries has a definite international angle to it, something the world community and its politicians should not forget, I want to foreground the effects of civil war violence perpetrated against the civilians of Lebanon and Algeria. And the first and foremost effect is a perversion of boundaries. As political scientist Luis Martinez argues, the violence of civil war leads to the collapse of a political community which, in turn, results in the emergence of interior frontiers or autonomous territories within the state (1998: 12).[3] The collapse of the political community sends its devastating shockwaves through every level and aspect of people's lives. No statistics or even journalistic accounts can make us understand this

---

[3] In addition to Martinez' thorough analysis, see Hannoyer (1999) and Benrabah et.al. (1998) for specific investigations on the Lebanese and Algerian civil wars of the 1990s. Fisk's classic (1990) continues to be reprinted. For a personal account, see Ghoussoub (1998); also, earlier, Makdisi (1990). I have elected to elaborate the effects of civil war through fiction rather than autobiography.

devastation, but literature "from within" can. This literature tells us how the fighting of and in civil war is also a violence against oneself, one's country, one's village or city, and one's street, with the effect of alienating family members from each other, rendering neighbours into strangers, making everyday life hardly bearable and household chores a day-filling job (Hannoyer 1999: 9-30).

In the writing of Hanan al-Shaykh, civil war reverberates in ways even more profound than Martinez describes. Not only do new and previously non-existent boundaries appear within the country, but existing boundaries are affected as well. Borders such as familiar markers of gender, class, ethnicity and religion undergo significant changes. Most deeply felt, however, are the alterations, if not outright destruction, of the boundaries between the private and the public. The use of this pair of terms runs the risk of reinforcing an unwarranted dichotomy, which I wish to disavow. To be sure, no such binary opposition can be absolute, since holding on to such an opposition would facilitate ongoing abuse and violence within the private domain under the protection of privacy.

In the introduction to a collective volume on privacy, Beate Rössler maps the different ways in which privacy is conceptualized. She lists three historical domains whose transformations have yielded concepts of privacy. The first is derivative, a supplement (in the Derridean sense, I would add) to the changes in the public sphere, changes effected by cultural redefinitions of individuality and authenticity. The second is the impact of feminist thought that led to a redefinition of the relations between the sexes, and, in its wake, a reconfiguration of privacy. The third is the development of information technology and its intrusive potential (Rössler 2004: 5).

Rössler then proceeds to list five different ways in which privacy has been defined. The first is place-based: privacy lies in the domestic sphere of the household; a naturalized locality. A second, negative definition holds that privacy is the right to be left alone. Thirdly, privacy has been defined in terms of access: to enjoy privacy is to be inaccessible. A fourth definition focuses on control over means of access to one's person, including information. Finally, a broad definition conceives of privacy as the protection from interference. Inexplicably, Rössler never mentions violence as an element, both in the definition of privacy as a normative category and in the opposition between private and public. If the philosophical debate about privacy is blind to violence, then the "newness" al-Shaykh's novel creates must first of all be seen in the removal of those blinders.

The first consequence of the situation of civil war is in fact the melting down of the private-public distinction, not only in the rigidity of the boundary but also as the sustaining possibility to be protected from invasion. This invasion from the outside in, where the public violence destroys the right to be left alone, accrues to the second problem of the definition of privacy as the opposite of public. The most private of institutions, the family, epitomizes the untenable nature of the opposition, since family is at the same time the stronghold of the nation-state, hence, the emblem of the public domain, as well as the locus for the private sphere. In addition, even though I am using the terms private and public I do not intend to situate those terms within a Habermassian discourse on the formation of a bourgeois liberal public sphere and its counterpart, private sphere. Many of Habermas' critics have pointed out that his exclusion of gender has profound implications for his understanding of public and private spheres (see various contributions in Calhoun 1992). Likewise, Claire Wills has shown – with respect to Northern Ireland and its modern poetry – that Habermas' theory creates difficulties in terms of its relevance to colonial and postcolonial situations (1993: 64-66). In light of all these objections, the deployment of the privacy-public dichotomy must be conducted with caution – as under erasure so to speak. Yet, in the face of civil war, it cannot be avoided.[4]

Homi Bhabha takes the argument contesting the divide between the public and the private one step further when he proposes that the two become confounded in an unhomeliness that is paradigmatic for colonial and post-colonial conditions. But even if the borders between home and the world become confused as an inherent product of (post)colonial movements and cross-cultural encounters, as Bhabha argues (1994: 9), it remains a task for the cultural critic as a translator to contextualize the repeated instances of such unhomeliness. The first gesture must be to suspend not the terms but their status as dividing line. Indeed, in the context of my project the boundary

---

[4] I want to thank John Goodby for pointing out to me the relations between Claire Wills' work and mine. Jean Hannoyer discusses a different perception of public and private spheres in the Middle East in terms of custom and law (1999: 14-15).

between private and public is not a divide but a space. It is a contested space whose function it is to question – rather than endorse – both the divide between private and public and the invasion of the private in the name of the public. In other words, instead of being an ontological domain that naturalizes the respective power and powerlessness of its inhabitants according to public divisions that impose particular interpretations, the distinction between private and public becomes a boundary on which and for which the rightful occupation of space can be contested.

To make this case, I want to translate Bhabha's contention that "(t)he unhomely moment relates the traumatic ambivalences of a personal, psychic history to the wider disjunctions of political existence" to my examples of women's writing on that situation of such contestation par excellence, the state of civil war (1994: 11). What I wish to demonstrate here is the profound impact civil war violence exerts on people's lives.

In her influential *Sexuality and War: Literary Masks of the Middle East* (1990) literary scholar and writer Evelyn Accad diagnoses (civil) war as a masculine, sexualized power trip. What is needed, she argues, is a sexual revolution, a boost in love, a boost that spreads from sexual partners, to families and society in general. Linking women to love, Accad contends that if women's issues would be dealt with from the beginning, wars might be avoided (1990: 27). Accad's analyses of literary work on civil war by women focuses on a gendered dichotomy between war and love in which women's writing foregrounds love, as against the male public space of war. Investigating Assia Djebar's literary work, Danielle Marx-Scouras (1993) echoes Accad in the binary differentials that define men's and women's writing on war, emphasizing how Djebar counters war with love, passion and poetry as a means to heal the wounds. In a more generalized sense, she asserts that women writers from the Maghreb "depict the devastation of revolutionary and civil war on their writing bodies, the 'body in pain' becomes, so to speak, the textual signifier" (1993: 176).[5]

As with all forceful dichotomies, I have trouble underwriting Accad's and Marx-Scouras' setup of male public space and war versus female private space and love. The problem is the figure of dichotomy itself and the

---

[5] The phrase "bodies in pain" refers to Elaine Scarry's important book, of which the chapter "The Structure of War" is particularly relevant for the present chapter (1985: 60-157).

conception of boundaries in which it is anchored. Establishing a dividing line between the two domains, no space is left for contestation. Boundaries in the present study, by contrast, are to be imagined as spaces, not lines. Spaces that, in the sense of Derrida's parergon, can belong to either of the two domains they are supposed to separate, but in which encounters between the two are possible as well.[6] Not, that such encounters should be idealized; they are not likely to be peaceful. The point of this focus on the space of boundaries is to shake up their sheer immovable rigidity. Where contestation is possible, newness may occur. Without idealizing conflict, nor sinking into cynical despair, my analysis of al-Shaykh's work, as well as my comments on Djebar's reflections focus on those elements in their writing that are split and schizophrenic. This writing responds to, and attempts to translate, a condition, namely a condition of dissociation, passivity, withdrawal, depression and autistic fantasies, which results from and is an expression of civil war. If anywhere, it is in the precarious boundary space, however, that the weeds of newness can grow against all odds; the literalized cracks in the concrete of the destroyed streets of Beirut, in the one case; the figurative, allegorical "French" as the only available language of writing in the other.

    To bring this view of boundaries as contested spaces to bear on al-Shaykh's letter-writing protagonist, my tentative answer to the question as to how she deals with the intrusion of the public into the private, would be that Asma writes letters to silence the voices that haunt her, so as to reinstate a boundary between herself and an outside world that intruded her private sphere at will. But the struggle to attain that goal is prolonged and difficult, leading through extensive efforts to name the losses suffered. At the same time, her efforts to rebuild a destroyed boundary also demonstrate the need for a kind of boundary that forms a space, not a simple and tight divide.

---

[6] In *Truth in Painting*, Derrida takes up Nietzsche's concept of the parergon to further theorize how the frame not only separates (inside from outside) but also connects the two, so that they can no longer be considered opposites (1987). Instead, inside and outside are entangled supplements of each other. For a clear and concise explanation, see Culler's "Author's Preface" to his book *Framing the Sign* (1988).

Writing for Life

Writing to an unreachable addressee is, for Asma, also a way to reach herself. In a letter to Jill Morell – fiancée of McCarthy, a man taken hostage in Beirut – Asma starts out with nervous banter about the confusion of names. When the news of the kidnapping first broke, Asma thought Paul McCartney of The Beatles was taken hostage, and in the letter she rambles on about her admiration for the pop star, to end with a confession: writing to Jill Morell is a means to turn the attention to herself. She likens her situation to that of being held hostage.

> I have the impression that I own nothing, except this body and mattress, because my mind does no longer belong to me. When I force myself to think and pull myself together I know that I am in possession of my body, but not at all, not even provisionally, of a place to put my steps. In short, I am a hostage just like your friend or fiancé.

> J'ai l'impression de ne rien posséder, sauf ce corps et ce matelas, car mon esprit ne m'appartient plus. Quand je me force à réfléchir et à me reprendre, je sais que je possède mon corps, mais non pas, même provisoirement, une terre où poser mes pas. Bref je suis un otage, tout à fait comme votre ami ou votre fiancé (Al-Shaykh 1995: 41).

When we as readers imagine the situation of hostages, this image might emerge: a body (naked, or scarcely clad) on a bare mattress. It is a small step from this image to the next, that is, to identify with the loss of mind, the taboo on thinking that comes with fear for life. Hostages, as has been apparent so often, are prone to identify with their captor. This is a theft of mind, not only of body. As much as this idea goes against the ingrained Western idea of the body-mind split and the free spirit that can endure life in captivity, Asma describes herself in terms of the hostage, and as incapable of holding onto her free mind.

Indeed, thinking causes profound difficulty, a great effort that only confronts Asma with a deep feeling of dread. When it kidnaps its victims, civil war does more than corroding the mind. It also takes the pleasures and reassurances out of everyday life. Life becomes a tedious chain of small routines inside, at home, a home whose status as a safe haven is threatened, yet which is the only place left where the people can at least attempt to find refuge. Home, the space that, in the words of Gaston Bachelard, "allows one

to dream in peace", is no longer the shelter against a civil war raging outside
(1994: 26).

This is poignantly felt when we read in the same letter to Jill Morel how
Asma's own bedroom is badly damaged, and how the outside enters her
private sphere in a frightening way:

> And the idea of death does not leave me alone; it is there, every so often really
> close. I keep my eyes open or shut, depending on whether I feel like seeing,
> eating, living, or whether I feel indifferent to everything, overtaken by despair.
> In this kind of games that I imagine myself, I can see, or not, the walls of my
> room crumbling, the new windowpane in the window (in reality it is an
> ordinary plastic bag), the debris of the mirror hurled on the ground in the latest
> battles. I haven't picked up the pieces, nor repainted the rectangular mark it left
> on the wall. The houses are no longer kept up. I let everything go to the dogs.
> Like the hostages, I no longer have any plan.

> Et l'idée de la mort ne me quitte pas; elle est là, parfois toute proche. Je garde
> les yeux ouverts ou fermés, selon que j'ai envie de voir, de manger, de vivre, ou
> que tout m'indiffère, prise par le désespoir. Dans cette sorte de jeux que je me
> représente à moi-même, je peux voir, ou non, les murs de ma chambre qui
> s'écroulent, la nouvelle vitre de la fenêtre (en réalité, c'est un vulgaire sac en
> plastique), les débris du miroir que les derniers combats ont projetés à terre. Je
> ne les ai pas encore ramassés, et n'ai pas repeint la trace rectangulaire qu'il a
> laissée sur le mur. Les maisons ne sont plus entretenues. Je laisse tout aller à
> vau-l'eau. Comme les otages, je n'ai plus aucun projet (Al-Shaykh 1995: 45-
> 46).

In the face of the continued threat of death, all Asma is left with is the child's
world of games. The game Asma plays when she hides or seeks, when she
elects to see or not to see the destruction surrounding her – crumbling walls,
a plastic bag for a window-pane, a mirror in pieces – is a game of negation
alternating with recognition. She seems aware that if only she were to be able
to recognize the mess in her room, Asma might clean up and recognize her
situation – a recognition that might be generative of plans for restoration.
Instead, the lack of a timeframe within which restoration would be a
meaningful thing to do paralyzes her and she lets everything go to the dogs.

The lack of ordinariness, of which a timeframe is an integral part, is a
symptom of trauma in its effect of discursive incapacitation. As Ernst van
Alphen has argued, the lack of a frame of ordinary life expectation – such as,
here, the expectation that repairs would be worth the effort – makes events

traumatogenic. He lists four symptoms, all of which are present in al-Shaykh's novel. Two pertain to the subject, who is either ambiguously suspended between action and inaction, or cancelled out altogether by the incompatibility of complicity and powerlessness. The other two symptoms concern action: either the event is too overwhelming to be integrated into an experience, or it cannot fit into a frame of life expectations (Van Alphen 1999; see also 1997).

The description of physical space offers insight into the mode of symbolization in place in this novel. In Asma's room, the walls and windows represent thresholds between inside and outside (see also Chapter One on windows as thresholds). Instead of offering protection, these elements are crumbling and provisionally patched up with the flimsiest of means, a plastic bag. The boundary between inside and outside has become an uncertain one as Asma will never be sure when the next bomb might crumble the walls even further or rip the plastic bag to pieces. The outside invades or threatens to invade the inside at all times. What is valued as private, one's bedroom, is not the safe haven it should and used to be, and even less a space that permits Asma to dream. Instead, the room imprisons Asma, keeping her locked in, precisely, like a hostage, without offering the protection from invasion that privacy is said to provide. The third element that has shattered is the mirror, the instrument of self-awareness. Routinely placed in the privacy of bed or bathroom, the broken mirror deprives the isolated figure of even herself. Hence, without her mind, without herself, and without her walls and windows, this trained architect lacks all the means to rebuild her life.

In a letter directed to *Ma Terre chérie* (My beloved land), Asma sings the praise of the village of her grandparents. She has moved to this village because fighting in Beirut became too intense, putting her life on the line. Her family name is well known in Lebanon – it is related to the land through varieties of apples and pears that carry the name of the family. In the ancestral village, Asma's family was influential, but the civil war has changed their position. Fields, bringing forth vegetables and other produce for the family in former times, are now covered with poppies, the raw material for the production of heroin. Drugs were much in demand; used by militias of the various parties, intoxication offered an escape from the full control over mental capacities when committing atrocities. The fields that used to feed the village, are now nourishing the madness of civil war.

Suddenly, as if in protest against the definition of privacy in opposition to the public domain – of which the state is the clearest instance – Asma makes the following connection between the history of her family and the history of the country:

> my gaze rested on the poppies that were swaying in the gentle breeze and were shining, white and red, under the sun, while bringing out hues of yellow and green that belong to you [i.e. the land] properly. For the first time, perhaps, the drama of my grandfather and grandmother, my tragedy and yours, became clearly visible for me: all this no longer belongs to us.

> mon regard s'est posé sur les plants de pavots qui se balancent à la brise légère et brillent, blancs et rouges, sous le soleil, faisant ressortir les tons de jaune et de vert qui t'appartiennent en propre. Pour la première fois peut-être, le drame de mon grand-père et de ma grand-mère, mon drame et le tien, m'apparaissent clairement: tout ceci ne nous appartient plus (Al-Shaykh 1995: 130-31).

Here we begin to see the point of impossible epistolarity as a privileged form for civil-war writing. The apostrophe to the land knots the tight bond between land and inhabitants when the land that feeds is abused to become the land that destroys. The deceptive beauty of the poppies shimmering in the sun in their changing coloration only enhances the trauma of their violent use. Addressing the land as if in a letter, Asma appears to desire to write the land back to life, to the life of before the war when it was allowed to be predominantly green and yellow. It is as if she is writing the land into privacy, that is, into a relationship where privacy begins.

But the land has already been violated from within, its function abducted and its beauty repainted. The colours of wheat and grass still shimmer through, but the predominant colours are now white and red. As if talking to a comatose patient, she ascribes to the land its former colours and functions. What used to belong no longer does – neither to Asma's family, nor to the land that merged with the former as each other's metaphor. But this is a metaphor that cannot be disentangled. It forms a rupture that is also exposed in the writer's use of the word "en propre" when land and people are described together in the moment that "proper" has ceased to be a meaningful term.

The rhetorical figure that addresses the inanimate has been theorized by a great number of scholars, among whom I would like to draw attention to Barbara Johnson and Jonathan Culler. In a beautiful essay Johnson wrote about poems written from the vantage point of a woman addressing her aborted foetus, the potential child, and derived from those poems a theory of apostrophe as essential for lyrical poetry (1987). Culler also considers apostrophe essential to the lyric, and argues for apostrophe's power to provide a place for the reader from where to overhear what can otherwise not be accessed. A propos of a poem by Wordsworth he sees the apostrophes in that poem as "nodes or concretizations of stages in a drama of the mind" (1981: 148).

If we consider drama as the modality that offers a model of trauma in that it happens apparently outside of the will of the subject suffering or rather, assaulted by it, we can no longer consider the lyric as the privileged domain of apostrophe. The specific epistolarity that shapes this novel – where the impossibility of address raises the question "Why write?" – turns civil-war writing into a new domain of apostrophe. Asma's image of herself as hostage, deprived of her mind, returns here.

The losses catalogued by Asma are numerous and those that are immaterial are felt most deeply: loss of language, loss of mind, loss of safety, loss of ground under her feet. Asma is affected by the civil war in every relationship of her life: in her family life in Beirut and her ancestral village, in her friends who have left the country, a country itself invaded by foreign troops, and divided by different factions at war with each other. Roadblocks are erected everywhere, thus creating boundaries where they do not belong, whereas other boundaries are dissolving where they are most needed.

Asma is right, then, to equal her position with that of a hostage, a position that signifies a situation of involuntariness; she is locked in, her safety disrupted, her mind on halt, her bodily integrity violated. Likening herself to a hostage is Asma's way of identifying the unsettling of her sense of inside and outside, and of a foreignness expressed with extreme difficulty. Because, as Victor Burgin, quoting Melanie Klein (1987), argues,

In psychosis, the internal and external world are poorly differentiated, or not differentiated at all; for example, whereas, in "normal" life we may encounter a person A who "reminds us of" another person B, the schizophrenic patient may simply substitute the latter for the former; or, again, he or she may experience the internal representations of "fantasy" as actual representations of external reality (Burgin 1996: 100).

It is because of this pervasive sign of disruption that I call the writing here split and schizophrenic. If we read *Poste restante Beyrouth* along these lines, some of the havoc wreaked on the lives of civilians in the midst of civil war becomes visible. To put Burgin's words in touch with the terms I have been using throughout, Asma's sense of boundaries is profoundly disturbed. The violent outside intrudes the private at any particular moment, always unwanted and unexpected. We might see a certain likeness between Asma's situation and that of a hostage, but then the image of the hostage functions as a metaphor of involuntary seclusion. Asma however, *identifies* with the hostage, *becomes* the hostage in an act of substitution that is repeated throughout the letters.

Writing from the position of a hostage is the alternative to writing from the position of exile. The "newness" at stake here is, precisely, the creation of a form of writing that is deeply entrenched in a place from which one cannot escape or even be exiled. Whereas an exile, as has been maintained, connotes a position of in-betweenness from which one needs to construct an "architecture of exile" – a life space where "home" is no longer the unreachable other of "not-home" – the hostage is unable to construct anything. For the hostage, at least in al-Shaykh's metaphorical evocation of this figure, is locked into a "home" that is depleted of its defining features.[7]

But Asma does manage to forge a newness that will allow her to stay in the impossible place. In the last letter – addressed to her émigré friend Hayat whom was addressee of the first letter as well – Asma appears to have found a sense of stability. While waiting for a delayed plane at Beirut airport with her lover Jaouad, the plane that is supposed to carry her to Paris, Asma replays her life during civil war:

> Why deny that I was feeling like a stranger, even at home? Didn't I start these letters writing that I had the impression of being abducted and of finding myself

---

[7] Noble (2002: 186; 190), writing about the art of Mona Hatoum. Hatoum is a Palestinian artist who grew up in exile in Beirut, lives and works in London as a double exilic.

in a place where I did not even understand the language? Why did the other passengers seem like a flock of stupid sheep?

Pourquoi nier que je me sentais comme une étrangère, même chez moi? N'avais-je pas commencé ces lettres en écrivant que j'avais l'impression d'avoir été enlevée et de me retrouver dans un lieu dont je ne comprenais même plus la langue ? Pourquoi les autres passagers m'apparaissaient-ils comme un troupeau de moutons stupides? (Al-Shaykh 1995: 344).

The moment of possible displacement is the moment of insight and healing. This validates Cooke's interpretation in terms of emigration, albeit in limited ways (2001). At this point, Asma can put into words what until then she had *enacted* in her disturbed state of mind. She is no longer bound to the opposition between exile and hostage; she is able to reject exile because she is no longer a hostage.

What she is able to articulate, here, is the diagnosis of civil war. Civil war literally makes people strangers at home, alienating them from themselves. This alienation takes a very precise form in this programmatic passage. The description of Asma's bedroom quoted earlier offers the concrete images of what it means to be a stranger at home. The state of being held hostage conflates the sense of displacement with the foreignness that remains untranslatable, because the hostage doesn't even understand the language. Djebar will come up with a different answer, concretely performing a kind of linguistic appropriation comparable to *rasquachismo*. Thus, she achieves the ability to translate even in the face of the loss of language. Finally, if all others seemed like stupid sheep, Asma's fellow passengers cannot connect to her because they are not traumatized the way Asma is. Yet, at this moment of understanding Asma can separate between what is hers and what belongs elsewhere, between inside and outside. And, since she projects her insight onto the letters she has been writing, it is possible to speculate that it is by and through her letter writing that she has rebuilt a provisionally safe haven.

It was, Asma concludes,

As if the city was imprinted in my spirit, with the war. Beirut had acquired a dimension and a form I could grasp, whereas in times of peace, life was but a garage full of dead cars and loose parts I didn't know what to do with. Now, Beirut appeared to me as a big hole covered with ditches, narrow cavities and minuscule openings, without the least vegetation *except for some small tufts of herbs clinging to the edges.*

Comme si la ville s'était imprimée dans mon esprit, avec la guerre. Beyrouth avait acquis alors une dimension et une forme que je pouvais saisir, tandis qu'en temps de paix, la vie n'était qu'un garage plein d'épaves et de pièces détachées dont je ne savais que faire. Beyrouth m'apparaissait maintenant comme un grand trou avec des fossés, d'étroites cavités et des ouvertures minuscules, sans la moindre végétation *hormis quelques petites touffes d'herbes accrochées aux bords* (Al-Shaykh 1995: 353; emphasis added).

Those tufts of herbs clinging to the edges, do very precisely and concretely the work of reconfiguring boundaries. Against the non-space of ditches and crevices – a negative space consisting of holes and cavities – the beginning of life manages to escape from the dire emptiness. This emergent life morphs boundaries from dividing lines into space – but only by virtue of Asma's desiring gaze. The passage continues:

At the beginning of these letters, I wrote that I was a hostage; now I was trying to perceive those small herbs, the only thing that is growing on my soil. Here was my life.

Au début de ces lettres, j'avais écrit que j'étais otage; maintenant j'essayais d'apercevoir ces petites herbes, la seule chose qui pousse sur ma terre. Ici se trouvait ma vie (Al-Shaykh 1995: 353).

While Paris, image of freedom for other Lebanese fleeing the war, beckons continuously, Asma decides at the very last moment to stay in Beirut. She begins to see through the smoke that blinded her, and she latches onto the beginnings of life and the spaces they create.

In a sustained effort, Asma wrote her letters from Beirut to her various addressees, all of them at a remove from the city torn by fighting. Whether she writes to her best friend Hayat, who lives in exile; to Jaouad, her lover, dead; to Nasser, her Palestinian ex-boyfriend; to Billie Holiday, conjured up in connection to the misuse of land for drug production; or to a place at a distance in time, as the description of her ancestral village demonstrates, the addressees signify different aspects of being "there", not here with Asma. Even the country, even the beloved city itself, addressed poste restante, is "not here".

What the letters allow her to do in the end is to make a two-fold move. On the one hand, the letters mediate between her, a hostage, locked up inside but not in safety, and the outside. The letters thus create the possibility, through a detour, to *stay* in Beirut. Through writing, Asma provisionally creates a sense of place; a safe haven precariously perched on the edges of destruction. On the other hand, and in the meantime, Beirut also transformed into a different city. Asma describes Beirut in her last letter as a third space, to use Edward Soja's words (1996; 1999: 276; see also Lefebvre 1991). A space that goes beyond the mappable, observable space, third space is the one that is practiced and lived. What she has created, then, in the precise sense I am theorizing it in this study, is a boundary that remains open to contestation.

The Newness that Remains

In order to see how the "newness" proposed by Bhabha emerges from *Poste restante Beyrouth* I now turn briefly to a second text written under civil war. A recent collection of essays and memoirs by Assia Djebar, titled *Ces Voix qui m'assiègent* (Those Voices that Besiege Me [1999]), sheds another light on a disturbed sense of boundaries. Preceding a section on autobiography, an epigraph taken from Samuel Beckett's *L'Innommable* (The Unnameable [1953]), serves as inspiration for Djebar's book title. The passage stages, again, a subject assaulted by a voice that is not hers; a subject subjected to the assault of traumatic repetition:

> This voice that speaks . . .
> It comes out of me, it fills me, it clamours against my walls, it is not mine, I cannot stop it, I can't prevent it from lacerating me, from besieging me.
> It [this voice] is not mine, I do not possess it, I have no voice and yet I must speak, it is all I know, it is this one must think about, it is this one must speak about, with this voice that is not mine, but that can only be mine since there is nobody but me.

> Cette voix qui parle . . .
> Elle sort de moi, elle me remplit, elle clame contre mes murs, elle n'est pas la mienne, je ne peux pas l'arrêter, je ne peux pas l'empêcher de me déchirer, de m'assiéger.
> Elle n'est pas la mienne, je n'en ai pas, je n'ai pas de voix et je dois parler, c'est tout ce que je sais, c'est autour de cela qu'il faut tourner, c'est à propos de cela qu'il faut parler, avec cette voix qui n'est pas la mienne, mais qui ne peut être que la mienne puisqu'il n'y a que moi (Beckett quoted in Djebar 1999: 95).

In Beckett's novel an unnamed being sits in a jar, unable to move. Like Asma in *Poste restante Beyrouth*, Beckett's unnameable is a hostage. A single voice appears to exist, separated from the narrator, acting according to its own wishes, yet belonging to this narrator. In Djebar's book title, this voice has become multiple.

But, whether singular or multiple, a voice that assaults the subject, a voice that is separated from her but not leaving her alone, is first and foremost to be interpreted as the voice of trauma that fails to protect the subject from invasion, a protection evoked earlier as a definition of privacy. The context for Beckett's alienation is of course quite different from that of Assia Djebar. The Irish migrant writer struggling for recognition in the 1950s in Paris obviously differs from the Francophone Algerian migrant residing in the same city since 1980. His novel about "the obsessive-compulsive need for words" (Bair 1990: 423), verging on a complete break-down, is at first sight incomparable with Djebar's literary or essayistic production; in that sense, the epigraph would be more suitable for al-Shaykh's apostrophic novel. But what matters for my argument here is the intertextual relation Djebar forges through the use of the epigraph. This relation circles around the notion of the unnameable, the title of Beckett's book and the signifier of the pain, horror and silence in Djebar, evoked by the Algerian civil war. The *unnameable* is the element of foreignness that needs to be brought to expression. This call for translation is what intertextually links Djebar's essays with Beckett's novel.

By inserting a quote from Beckett's bleak narrative – a narrative seemingly devoid of humanity – into a section on autobiography, Djebar translates the narrator's alienation and lack of control over his own voice in *L'Innommable* into another situation signifying lack of control, that is, civil war. The situation of civil war forces Djebar to confront the voices, multiple and varied, that haunt her. She experiences difficulties, just like the narrator in *L'Innommable* does, to recognize where the voices come from and where they are located. The boundaries between what is "mine" and "other" become blurred. This situation describes, at the level of the individual subject, the situation of the hostage, that figure of the trauma of losing the negotiable boundary space where privacy begins, or is suspended.

Djebar takes up one of those voices that haunt her in the introduction;

voices that ask her why she writes, and more explicitly, why she writes in French. Djebar tentatively answers that her writing in French is

> Carried by those "voices that haunt me", my own voice, registered here, has attempted, above all in the course of those tumultuous and often tragic years for my country, to simply defend the Algerian culture, which appeared to me in danger.

> Portée par des *"voix qui m'assiègent"*, ma propre voix, ici transcrite, a tenté, surtout au cours de ces années tumultueuses, et souvent tragiques, de mon pays, simplement de défendre la culture algérienne, qui me paraissait en danger (Djebar 1999: 7-8).

Amidst the voices that haunt Djebar, she manages to keep her own voice, a voice in defence of an endangered Algerian culture, albeit at the cost of speaking the language of the very culture that has endangered hers. But in defending Algerian culture, her voice is a paradoxical one. Djebar struggles to create and maintain her own voice, while writing in French, the language Djebar learned in school, and the language of the former colonizer.

Ever since her debut *La Soif* (1957), Djebar's writing in French has been a source of contention. In the midst of the war of independence-cum-civil war, waged against the French colonizers and a large *pied noir* community, Djebar started publishing in French and continued to do so. Critics have been puzzled by this choice, which at first sight appeared to be a sell-out to the enemy. Writing in French connected her voice willy-nilly to a particularly charged political position, a position that became once again contested in the Algerian civil war that erupted in 1992. Yet, her essays contend, both the plurality of voices and the alien voice in which she writes are inevitably part of her. It is from that position of "hostage" that she must, like al-Shaykh's Asma, introduce newness into existence.

In an essay "Etre une voix francophone" (To Be a Francophone Voice), Djebar fleshes out the book's title when she explains how she perceives her writing:

> The multiple voices that besiege me – those of my characters in my fictional texts – I hear them for the most part in Arabic, a dialectal Arabic, or even in a Berber tongue that I understand badly, but whose raucous respiration and whisper inhabit me in an immemorial manner.

> Les multiples voix qui m'assiègent – celles de mes personnages dans mes textes de fiction –, je les entends, pour la plupart, en arabe, un arabe dialectal, ou même un berbère que je comprends mal, mais dont la respiration rauque et le souffle m'habitent d'une façon immémoriale (Djebar 1999: 29).

The voices her written French must negotiate are those of fiction, as well as those of her most intimate memories, the acoustic mirror of her childhood. The sequence from Arabic, via dialectal Arabic, to an ill-understood Berber also forms a series of increasing physicality. The less she understands of a voice, the more the sounds are cosmic accomplices to her linguistic schizophrenia. The alliteration of *respiration rauque* turns the phrase into a sonic image accompanied by *souffle*: whisper or wind, human or cosmic. All those sounds inhabit as well as envelop her.

A French written from within that acoustic tent cannot be a case of selling out in any simple sense. Djebar acts as an intermediary between voices haunting her in Arabic or Berber, and the French into which these voices will be transformed and subsequently heard in a public space. In this, Djebar can be usefully contrasted to Jaouad, the lover with whom Asma almost leaves Beirut at the end of al-Shaykh's novel. Djebar doesn't leave her acoustic tent; rather, she mediates from within, speaking to a world where whispers/winds are muffled.

Significantly, after leaving Lebanon for France, Jaouad has become a writer, and like Djebar, he writes in French. In her last letter, to her exiled friend Hayat, when she is pondering the possible decision to leave, Asma writes about language in the following terms:

> there where you reside reigns such calm, such security, that the voices seem to raise no echo at all.

> là où tu résidais régnait un tel calme, une telle sécurité, que les voix paraissaient ne soulever aucun écho (Al-Shaykh 1995: 310).

The multiplication of voices in which Djebar grounds her French is not possible in a safe, calm, and, it is implied, homogeneous environment. Jaouad struggles with this linguistic erasure of the war. He says so to Asma, who remarks that his success depends on the suffering of others:

I know I pluck the bitter fruits of the war, I write in a European language the emotions hidden behind the letters of my own language, in the back of my conscience. The more I am successful, the more I feel remorse, because within myself [intérieurement] I have been praying for a long time for the annihilation of this country.

Je sais, je cueille les fruits amers de la guerre, j'écris dans une langue européenne les émotions qui se cachent entre les lettres de ma propre langue, au fond de ma conscience. Plus j'ai du succès, plus j'ai de remords, car intérieurement je fais depuis longtemps des prières pour l'anéantissement de ce pays (Al-Shaykh 1995: 345).

Although the last sentence of this passage retains an ambiguity that saves the statement from total cynicism, Jaouad's use of French cannot be compared to Djebar's, for whom that language allows the resonances of the other, multiple languages.

Hence, Djebar is able to hear various voices, connecting her to Algeria and its languages and providing her with a language in which to express herself. But as Benrabah has argued, the language policies of the successive Algerian governments do not allow one such freedom. In its choice for classical Arabic as its official language and thus against the dialectal Arabic and Berber languages spoken by Algeria's population, the government has turned itself against the language of the former colonizer, but also against the indigenous languages of the country (Benrabah 1998).

Djebar's decision to write in French is an attempt, not to lose but to hold onto the languages threatened by the civil war. Al-Shaykh's Asma highlights another relation between civil war, words, and language, when she writes that Jaouad has lost everything for having missed the war. His departure, his escape from the war's violence and destruction, has deprived him of his own language. When he considers staying in Beirut, Asma doesn't believe this is an option:

To stay here and live like me? He had even lost his power over the words! That's the effect Beirut exerts on those who had not known the war.

Rester ici et vivre comme moi? Il avait même perdu son pouvoir sur les mots! Voilà l'effet de Beyrouth sur ceux qui n'avaient pas connu la guerre (Al-Shaykh 1995: 351).

The loss of his language makes it impossible to return, especially for a writer. But more poignantly, this loss is due to the fact that the subject he is writing about, the civil war, has escaped him as much as he has escaped it. It is this loss that Djebar's ponderings about the use of French try to negotiate.

However, Djebar's choice to use French as a creative language (and her choice to live in France as many others do with her), renders her suspect under the current circumstances of civil war.[8] As a result, she doesn't even have the option to live like a hostage. Under the pressure of civil war, choices for a creative language or an intellectual language in general can come at great cost. It can be perceived as maintaining relationships with the former colonizer and result in death, as Algeria witnessed over the years during the nineties when many intellectuals, writers, and journalists were killed.[9]

Djebar's choice for a Francophone voice does not solve the most basic problem: her lack of *control* of her literary voices. Rather, these voices haunt her, exceed her, binding her in incontrollable ways to a larger, complex political context. This haunting evokes both trauma, as the assault of voices no longer under the subject's control, as well as privacy as defined in terms of control over access to oneself. The voices that haunt Djebar are voices from Algeria, speaking – whispering – to her in dialectal Arabic or Berber, and like Beckett's narrator, Djebar has difficulty deciding whether those voices belong to her or not. Do they come from outside or from inside? They control her and tell her to do things, but how to stop them? In fact, they can't be stopped, the voices will keep on haunting whenever and wherever. The voices violate the boundary between you and the outside world, whether you live as an Algerian writer in France or not. And because they defeat every attempt to control them, they are non-negotiable. Hence, there is no "good", creative or safe boundary left to speak from.

In her writing, Djebar, like al-Shaykh, diagnoses civil war as a condition with the symptoms of schizophrenia. Following the logic of the intertextual relations between the title of the book, the motto taken from Beckett and the references to this motto throughout the book, voices that besiege me are an

---

[8] In a contribution to a special issue of *World Literature Today*, devoted to Assia Djebar, Katherine Gracki has argued that Djebar's use of French is a poaching of sorts, and a taking of war booty (1996).
[9] See also Djebar's *Le Blanc de l'Algérie* (1995), a narrative mourning, in a long funeral procession, all those who died in both civil wars.

expression of a disturbed sense of boundaries. Voices haunting her in Arabic or Berber are rendered into French, a transgression of boundaries where Djebar would not want boundaries to exist. Yet, among the voices haunting her from Algeria are also those that want to force her to comply with their anti-French aims and goals. In a political manifesto of sorts on writing and language, Djebar asserts:

> The Maghrebian writer . . . can no longer play his/her role as a spokesperson or even as a ferryman . . . But [what about] the writer, poet, novelist, storyteller who, chased away from home, finds refuge in the North, or at least in the language shelter, the language of yesterday's colonizer, the language that has proven an instrument of creation for him, that seemed the forge for his work, and henceforth his safest haven? One more time, how to bear witness by writing? The ground has slipped under your feet. You have got to understand . . . that your one and only territory was indeed the language and not the soil.

> L'écrivain maghrébin . . . ne peut plus jouer son rôle de porte-parole, ou même de passeur . . . Mais l'écrivain, poète, romancier, fabulateur qui, chassé de chez lui, trouve refuge au Nord, ou tout au moins dans la langue-refuge, la langue du colonisateur d'hier, elle qui s'est avérée pour lui outil de création, qui lui a paru sa forge pour son travail, et désormais son plus sûr havre? Encore une fois, faut-il témoigner en écrivant? Le terrain a glissé sous vos pas. Vous avez à comprendre . . . que votre seul véritable territoire était bien la langue, et non la terre (Djebar 1999: 215).

Ardently defending the use of language as her one and only territory, Djebar unties the strict bonds between physical territory and the language(s) belonging to it. But the safe haven of language, this "finding back an 'in the word' that, alone, remains our fruitful fatherland", as Djebar asserts twice in almost the same wording, does not guarantee her that the voices besieging her will leave (retrouver un "dedans de la parole" qui, seul, demeure notre patrie féconde [Djebar 1995: 276; 1999: 249]). Because of her position as intermediary, a translator of foreignness in multiple ways and directions, Djebar will be a sounding board for the various haunting voices between which she mediates and whose demands she will need to negotiate time and again.

I suggested at the beginning of this chapter that in newness the issues of translation and foreignness figure prominently. In an analysis of translations of Wittgenstein into English, Lawrence Venuti, a prominent theorist of translation, has argued strongly for the importance of the enduring presence, in the target text, of what he calls the remainder of the source text (1998). Resisting naturalization into the domestic language of the target text, the remainder preserves the foreignness that Walter Benjamin also cherished as the "untranslatable" (1968a). The remainder is, precisely, that foreignness that emerges when Djebar's haunting voices make themselves heard, in the middle of the most literary, almost classical French. It may sound paradoxical, but no less important to emphasize, that what introduces newness is exactly the enduring remainder of the old acoustic environment taken along into exile.

Clearly, al-Shaykh and Djebar both address civil war as a situation in which boundaries are confused: undermined where they should be protecting and popping up where they don't belong. Nevertheless, one might argue, what's *new* about that? Are these boundaries, as Bhabha contended, not part and parcel of the (post)colonial condition? Of course, we may recognize the transgression of boundaries in postcolonial literatures in general and assume that a similar thing happens in Lebanese or Algerian literature. But my analysis has focused on something more specific: how can the unhomely moment be lived – how, in other words, can literature create a home for the unhomely?

In order to frame the unhomely in Djebar and al-Shaykh, I have foregrounded boundary confusion and its relation to foreignness. Both authors appear to proclaim – albeit in different ways – that civil war renders the analysis of foreignness an urgent matter. Al-Shaykh's protagonist likens herself to a hostage, identifies to a frightening degree with that position and nevertheless wrests something new in the midst of it. This key metaphor of the subject under civil war as a hostage him- or herself constitutes a contested boundary: in view of Asma's descriptions of her living spaces, it is not immediately clear that the identification of herself with a hostage is "just" a metaphor. I propose to consider the image as a translation-with-remainder, a tool to transform a culture of devastation into a liveable space, however minimally and minimal.

The same can be said of the use of epistolarity in this specific mode of apostrophe. Conjuring up interlocutors who are not really available, Asma manages to translate what is unbearable otherwise. From the narrativity of a discourse of representation, as in her earlier novel, she has transformed her writing into a form of writing that has incorporated as well as answered the question "why write?" in a discourse that is performative. By imagining a "there", a space geographically distant and historically remote, she can stay "here". The trauma of the dissolution of boundaries finds a precarious but relatively safe cure in the home of writing. This safety finds a footing in physical sense as well: over the course of the book, Beirut is transforming into a different place, a potentially liveable space, where tiny weeds pop up among the ruins.

Djebar speaks of translation in a different way, literally multiplying languages and voices. In Djebar's essays, translation appears in different forms and at different levels. She compares her position as a writer with a ferryman, someone crossing boundaries, shuttling between North and South. She also evokes translation in the voices that haunt her in languages native to her fatherland. Djebar transcribes those voices into French. But the voices that haunt her are also voices asking her the difficult questions that link up private and public, politics and home. They ask her why she doesn't speak up about the violence and the killing in Algeria; they ask her why she writes in the language of the colonizer; and they demand sharp-edged boundaries from her where she refuses to draw or even recognize them. Djebar's response is to investigate the foreignness not of the French of her place of exile but of civil war in her unhomely home, the unnameable that she attempts to address through intertextual links with Beckett's novel. And even though she diagnoses civil war as a schizophrenic condition, she knows how to brave the ensuing sense of disturbed boundaries by insisting on her own role as a third: not territory but language is her true home. Her acts of translation are the tools with which she, too, brings newness to light. To speak once more with Bhabha: both al-Shaykh and Djebar write in order to *touch the future on its hither side* (1994: 7).

THREE

Uncertain Territories: Travel as Exchange

Thinking through the connections between imperialism, culture and gender, I realized that recent publications seem to have taken a "geographical turn". Two related issues have come to the fore in these geographical interests. On the one hand, they call for a redrawing of the "cartographies of struggle" on the basis of changing conceptions of how histories of colonialism, capitalism, race and gender are interrelated (Mohanty 1991: 3). On the other hand, geography is perceived as constitutive of the ways in which imperialism functions. Whereas the former view departs from an idea of geography as open-ended and hence, open to negotiation, the latter sees geography as always-already implicated in a conquest that closes it down.

In his influential book *Culture and Imperialism*, Said addresses this tension when he argues "just as none of us is outside or beyond geography, none of us is completely free from the struggle over geography". The struggle over geography is not just a history of conquest, but also, in Said's words, "a struggle about ideas, about forms, about images and imaginings" (1993: 7). This struggle is performed not only in real space but also in acts of mapping, charting, and producing cartographies. These activities, formerly among the means of conquest and domination, are now offered as a critical practice of cultural analysis. These practices have parallels with those writings that, for all intents and purposes, we can call "ethnographic".

I use the term ethnographic writings deliberately in a somewhat loose sense, not bound to the profession of ethnography, because in this chapter I will deal with travelogues, accounts of experiences of travel and the intercultural encounters travel inevitably entails. If we consider that travel, and especially the kind of travel that inspires the desire to write, is propelled by a curiosity about other cultures similar to the professional interest that inspires ethnographers, travelogues can be considered forms of writing akin to ethnography. Both practices share a keen attention to the everyday practices of Europe's "others", and employ techniques that are both descriptive and "writerly". I will analyse in this chapter how these techniques characterize the writings of women who travelled to the Orient in the late eighteenth and the nineteenth century. In many ways the descriptions of their experiences and perceptions prefigure the ethnographies of a later moment. One might see travelogues, especially in the nineteenth-century variety I analyze here, as a hybrid genre that mixes personal experiences with descriptions of a more general nature. Indeed, they attempt to generalize from inside the intimacy of personal encounters. This mixture turns such writings into representations of a particular kind of border, namely that between the personal and the exterior, as well as between the singular and the general, which is typical of ethnography as well.

Ethnography, in light of these remarks, can itself be seen as a practice of and on the border. While ethnography has been – and still frequently is – an account by a Westerner who charts the strange and not-so-strange habits of another culture, most ethnographers invest enormous efforts in bridging the gap between themselves and their "subjects" or local informants, establishing contact that goes well beyond the informational exploitation of "natives". What is dubiously called "the field" is a ground where ethnographer or traveller and local inhabitants meet, whatever the terms of that meeting, so that any "field" is always already an intermediate zone of the kind I call here a boundary space, comparable to the window, in Chapter One, and the open home or the urban space, as in Chapter Two (for a genealogy of the "field" in ethnographic practices see Gupta and Ferguson 1997a).

In order to understand how the endeavours of travel – as well as ethnography – have been marked by this ambiguity from the very beginning of these practices, I will pursue the question of how ethnographic devices or topoi function in travel writing and how we can historicize these ethnographic devices. By ethnographic device I mean ways of describing and inscribing a particular kind of knowledge – that is, the kind of knowledge that is always and inevitably focused on "others", and that tends to generalize on the basis of singular moments of knowledge production through personal experience. I use the term "techniques" because I am interested in practices that construct and produce knowledge.

Two travelogues by nineteenth-century French women, never intended as a contribution to the anthropological discipline, form the basis of my analysis. The mapping of unknown territories in the Middle East – or the Orient in nineteenth-century terms – by Madame de Gasparin in *À Constantinople* (1867) and by Jane Dieulafoy in *La Perse, la Chaldée et la Susiane* (1887) is of particular interest for my purpose here, because both record their various encounters with women.[1] Being women themselves, and finding themselves in the unusual position, at the time, of gaining access to local women's intimate sphere, they were in a position allowing them to produce precisely the kind of boundary space I am seeking to bring into view. Moreover, Dieulafoy and de Gasparin use modes of constituting knowledge in relation to subjectivity that draw on what I here call ethnographic devices, including – besides writing – photography. Jane Dieulafoy accompanied her husband on an archaeological expedition and published the travel journals afterward. Her *La Perse, la Chaldée et la Susiane* is significant here because it contains a host of photographs, many of which feature women. De Gasparin travelled in the company of five women and her husband.[2]

Imagining Boundaries

Valérie Boissier, comtesse de Gasparin, travelled with her husband and some lady friends to Constantinople in the mid-1860s. Their itinerary by boat along

---

[1] Dieulafoy's travelogue was reprinted in a three-volume edition by Phébus: *Une Amazone en Orient: Du Caucase à Persépolis* (1989); *En Mission chez les immortels: Journal de fouilles de Suse* (1990a) and *L'Orient sous le voile: De Chiraz à Bagdad* (1990b). In the Phébus edition the engravings are assembled in sections after the photographs so that unfortunately the relation between text and image in the original edition is lost. I will give references to both editions.

[2] See for the role of husbands in the travelogues and the division of labor in publishing travelogues, my book *Disorienting Vision* (2004b). See also Birkett (1989) and Pratt (1992: 155-71) for further discussion on the gendered content of travelogues by female authors.

the Danube took them from Vienna across the Balkans to the Black Sea and
ultimately to Constantinople. Let me start with a quote from De Gasparin's
travelogue *À Constantinople* describing the travellers just on their way from
Vienna heading south:

> And it is a funny thing, you can believe me in this, to find yourself suddenly the
> neighbours of the Turks, like with us, on the other side of the Jura, we are the
> neighbours of the Bourguignons.
> Here we have the hills of Presburg . . . The castle places forward its four pieces
> of wall, the castle of which the Turks (our neighbours the Turks) have broken
> open the interior . . .
> On the square stretching along the river . . . the Austrian Emperors came to
> have themselves crowned as King of Hungary. The Monarch arrives on
> horseback, receives the diadem and brandishes the sword of the Holy Stephen
> to the four corners of the horizon. Isn't he the leader of that nation that guards
> the boundaries of the civilized world?
>
> Et c'est une drôle de chose, vous pouvez m'en croire, que de se trouver tout à
> coup les voisins des Turcs, comme chez nous, de l'autre côté du Jura, nous
> sommes les voisins des Bourguignons.
> Voici les collines de Presburg . . . Le château assied en avant ses quatre pans de
> murs dont les Turcs (nos voisins les Turcs) ont effondré l'intérieur . . .
> Sur la place qui s'étend le long du fleuve . . . les empereurs d'Autriche viennent
> se faire couronner rois de Hongrie. Le monarque arrive à cheval, reçoit le
> diadème et brandit aux quatre coins de l'horizon l'épée d'Etienne le Saint.
> N'est-il pas le chef de cette nation qui garde les frontières du monde civilisé?
> (De Gasparin 1867: 34).

This fragment shows a peculiar mix of past and present, of neighbourly
relations and tensions along boundaries, of comparison and difference. To be
sure, Hungary was part and parcel of the Habsburg Empire at the time of de
Gasparin's writing. Hence, the reference to the Austrian Emperors is
understandable, but how about the neighbouring Turks? And where do we
find the boundary between the neighbouring Turks and the civilized world?

No one's possession yet dividing spaces and groups of peoples, the
anonymity of boundaries is solidified by naturalizing impulses that
strengthen their stable and immobile qualities. The very question of what the
boundary is and where it is located, participates in their naturalization by
narrowing the possible range of considerations to an artificial exactness. In
Chapter One I argued that the human activity of setting boundaries, the role
of individuals and their interactions is subsequently written out of existence.

In my analysis of the travelogue by Mme de Gasparin, I will investigate the how and why of her boundary constructions in her cross-cultural encounters in the Balkans. The Balkans – partially under the influence of the Habsburg Empire, partially under Ottoman reign – was a region in transition during the nineteenth century. Processes of nationalism, the influence of powers such as France, Russia and Germany, the introduction of steamboats and the oppositional powers of the Habsburg and Ottoman Empires deeply changed the make-up of the region.

Edward Said argued that the line separating Occident from Orient is "less a fact of nature than it is a fact of human production, which I have called imaginative geography" (2001: 199). In the Balkans, this imaginative geography does not result in fixed boundaries distinguishing Occident from Orient; nor does it result in an answer to the where and what of boundaries. Rather, it consists of a set of flexible border zones of contact and interaction, or "contact zones", as Mary Louise Pratt has called them (1992). If I speak of boundaries, then, I analyse the how and why of their construction – whether material or immaterial. The possible range of questions related to the how and why of boundary construction comprises precisely questions that attempt to come to grips with interaction in a contact zone, to come to grips with the imaginative geography of encounters between East and West.

Mme de Gasparin's imaginative geography is elaborated and clarified in the following fragment:

> In front of the Gönyä monastery, some Slovaks come aboard . . . These people, with their tallness, square shoulders and thick limbs pass in everything the bust of their masters, the Madgyars . . . their small, round head . . . completes these monumental figures who call to mind the profile of the Dacians such as antique bas-reliefs return to us. I find their slow gait and quiet movements alike to Orientals. Grave, astonished but not looking around them, they go and squat in a corner. Seated races, squatting races, thus in one trait the separation between Orient and Occident is marked . . .
> Well, I'll tell you, these four immobile, pensive giants, half hidden in the draperies of their wool cover, this attitude of Bedouins in the desert, of the Arabs of Palestine, of all the pastoral peoples who are also warlike . . . let pass before me pretty visions of the great primitive life in wide-open free spaces.

> Devant les tours du monastère de Gönyä, des Slovaques montent à bord . . . Ceux-ci, qui ont la taille haute, les épaules carrées, les membres épais, passent de tout le buste leurs seigneurs les Madgyars . . . leur tête petite, ronde . . .

complète ces figures monumentales qui rappellent le profil des Daces, tel que
nous le restituent les bas-reliefs antiques. Je leur trouve la démarche lente et les
mouvements tranquilles des Orientaux. Graves, étonnés, mais ne regardant
point autour d'eux, ils vont dans un coin s'accroupir sur leurs talons. Races
assises, races accroupies, ainsi d'un trait la séparation se marque entre l'Orient
et l'Occident . . .
Eh bien, je vous le déclare, ces quatre géants immobiles, pensifs, ensevelis à
moitié dans les draperies de leur couverture de laine, cette attitude des Bédouins
au désert, des Arabes de Palestine, de tous les peuples pasteurs qui sont aussi
des peuples guerriers . . . font passer devant moi les belles visions de la grande
vie primitive dans les grands espaces libres (De Gasparin 1867: 36-37).

Whereas in the previous fragment the past was evoked as part of an ongoing
tradition in a repetitious scene of monarchic mastery over the world – by
brandishing the sword – here the past has different connotations. The Slovaks
are likened to the Dacians (Dacia was an unruly province of the Roman
Empire located in what is now Romania), monumental in their size and as
such reminding Mme de Gasparin of Dacians on antique bas-reliefs.

This simile comparing Slovaks to Dacians serves various purposes. First,
Mme de Gasparin shows her knowledge of Antiquity by "recognizing", as it
were, the Dacians. This is a strategy often practiced in ethnographic writing,
and it serves to make the strange familiar enough to understand it. More
specifically, the author repeats a well-known trope by naming the Slovaks
Dacians, to wit, relegating unknown others to a distant past. In so doing, the
little distance in space – the Slovaks share the same room on the boat – is
changed into a temporal distance of centuries. The anthropologist Johannes
Fabian has called this phenomenon the "denial of coevalness", a "persistent
and systematic tendency to place the referent [i.e. the Slovaks, IB] . . . in a
Time other than the present of the producer [i.e. Mme de Gasparin, IB] of . . .
discourse" (1983: 31). By relegating the Slovaks into a distant past, Mme de
Gasparin indicates that they do not share the same time with her. In fact, by
using a classificatory term (Dacians) that serves as a time-distancing device,
she not only denies the Slovaks the same time, but also the same level of
civilization. The Slovaks lag behind, forever unable to catch up with Mme de
Gasparin and her company.

With this denial of coevalness, Mme de Gasparin certainly inserted herself
in a tradition of Western travel writing. A famous predecessor of hers, the
Comte de Ségur, wrote in a similar vein about the people he observed in St.

Petersburg:

> This clothing, and the thick bands of wool around their feet and legs that form a
> kind of coarse buskin, bring to life before your eyes these Scythians, Dacians,
> Roxolans, Goths once the terror of the Roman world. All these demi-savage
> figures that one has seen in Rome on the bas-reliefs of Trojan's column seem to
> be reborn and become animated before your gaze (1859: 329-30 quoted in
> Wolff 1994: 22).

But the Slovaks are not only placed at a temporal distance from the French
travellers, they are spatially removed as well. Their slow gait and quiet
movements render them Oriental, a trait that is elaborated in the remainder of
the fragment. And in the difference between squatting and sitting, Mme de
Gasparin discovers the boundary between Orient and Occident.

I am interested in the various boundaries and their construction in the
quotations so far. First, Mme de Gasparin thinks it is funny to "suddenly"
find oneself the neighbours of the Turks. In order to illustrate her point, she
invokes the example of her region of birth, the Vaud, the French-speaking
part of Switzerland located across the Jura Mountains. Just like the
inhabitants of the Vaud happen to live next to the neighbouring region of the
Bourgogne, the Turks happen to live "next to" the Habsburg Empire. Here,
we might still be inclined to perceive the relations as natural, as defined by
geographical coincidence, since mountains have traditionally been seen as
"natural" borders. But there are signs that relations are perceived as less than
neighbourly.

Leaving Vienna, capital and stronghold of the Habsburg Empire, and
heading toward the Black Sea, the conciliatory tone of neighbourly relations
is replaced with a more contentious one. The idea that a mere thin line, the
boundary of the civilized world, divides Mme de Gasparin from the – by
implication uncivilized – Turks, scares her to death. The Austrian Emperor is
the one who needs to guard that contested boundary of the civilized world –
Mme de Gasparin's civilized world – against the Turks, even though the last
time the Turks had threatened Vienna was in 1683, almost 200 years prior to
Mme de Gasparin's writing. When her travelogue describes how she
perceives the boundary between civilized and non-civilized, the narrative is
based upon her focalization, that is, upon the "relation between the vision and
that which is 'seen'" (Bal 1997: 142). Hence, the narrative is located firmly

within the civilized world she is now leaving. Still within the Habsburg
Empire, near the Gönyä monastery, her encounter with the Slovaks incites
Mme de Gasparin to further elaborate on boundaries ("in one trait the
separation between Orient and Occident is marked" and "the great primitive
life in wide-open free spaces").

These two examples of boundary construction show how boundaries in the
imaginative geography of Mme de Gasparin are made, and yet, they are not
fixed. Time and again, Mme de Gasparin needs to establish the boundary
between her and the regions where she travels or the people she meets.
Hence, we can already formulate some rules according to which the process
of boundary construction works. People focalize from the inside; they divide
between a "we" that blocks or runs up against a "they"; they invoke history
as justification for the boundary; they construct differences or similes to
make sense of boundaries; they create (and reinforce existing) differences;
they never question their own position.

In light of these techniques, let me turn to another fragment of Mme de
Gasparin's travelogue. The moment the company approaches Belgrade
clearly demonstrates the impact of this "grammar" of travel writing that, as I
will argue below, is congenial to ethnography. Belgrade was, at the time, a
frontier town that had been Ottoman until 1717 when the Habsburg Empire
decided on a policy "to throw them [the Turks, IB] completely out of
Europe" (such was the policy of Vienna throughout the eighteenth century as
Karl Roider argues [1982, quoted in Wolff 1994: 165]). In 1739 the
Habsburgs had to give up Belgrade. If you wish to speak of a geographical
boundary, Belgrade constituted the passage point from travelling among the
civilized to entering the world of squatting uncivilized races, as Mme de
Gasparin would have it. She sketches a bleak picture:

> Yes, but change direction and you'll see, Belgrade! All the Oriental lights come
> up against the Turkish city. It sure is here. The white houses, the mosques and
> the minarets thrown upwards as if in a single fountain. Green gardens strew
> their acacias at random, the flag of the Islam unfolds its starred crescent in the
> morning breeze, the fort heavily set on the hill protects the palace of the pasha
> that presents its radiant front; have you seen the turban? Have you seen the
> scimitar? And as our steamer speeds over the water, Semendria, another citadel
> of the Ottomans, appears in the distance.

Imagine, in a treeless country, without grass, burnt, an age-old wall, high, grey and grim . . . that whole sight of the times of Suleiman I bristles up on the banks of the river, in an austere country under a blue sky that does not please. No inhabitants, not a sentinel, not even Mohamed's banner. It remains standing for no reason, it watches time pass, flotsam of another world. It looks as though through that enormous gate the half-savage hordes would leave, the great Asian armies, those peoples that the conquering Sultan kept on reins to launch onto a trembling Europe.
Nothing is leaving, nothing moves, all is dead.

Oui, mais tournez le cap, et vous verrez. Belgrade! Toutes les lumières de l'Orient ont rencontré la ville turque. C'est bien elle. Les maisons blanches, les mosquées, les minarets lancés d'un seul jet se montrent à la fois. Des jardins verdoyants sèment au hasard leurs acacias, le drapeau de l'islam déroule son croissant étoilé sous les brises du matin, le fort lourdement assis sur la colline protège le palais du pacha qui présente son front radieux; avez-vous vu le turban? Avez-vous vu le cimeterre? Et comme notre vapeur vole sur les eaux, Semendria, une autre citadelle des Osmanlis, paraît au loin.
Figurez-vous, dans un pays sans arbres, sans herbe, brûlé, une muraille séculaire, haute, grise et farouche . . . toute cette vision du temps de Soliman Ier se hérisse au bord du fleuve, dans un pays austère, sous un ciel bleu qui ne réjouit pas. Point d'habitants, pas une sentinelle, pas même l'étendard de Mohamet. Cela reste debout on ne sait pourquoi, cela regarde passer les années, épave d'un autre monde. Il semble que par cette porte colossale doivent sortir les hordes à demi sauvages, les grandes armées asiatiques, ces peuplades que les sultans de la conquête tenaient en laisse pour les lancer sur l'Europe frémissante.
Rien ne sort, rien ne bouge, tout est mort (De Gasparin 1867: 62).

All is dead: this, it seems, is the result of viewing the world beyond "our" boundary from hither.

The Difficulty of "Writing About"

Although the links between anthropology, ethnography and travel may seem obvious, none of these terms can be simply mapped onto the others. Many practices akin to ethnography exist which are not incorporated within or are marginal to the discipline of anthropology proper, in much the same way that travel might lead to an ethnographic style of writing without being exclusively oriented toward the production of ethnographic knowledge. I would argue nonetheless that travel, whatever else its aims might be, does involve an "ethno-graphic impulse". This impulse is to perceive, and subsequently describe and order what one encounters. This mechanism implies a selection based on pre-established as well as "found" categories expected to help understand strangeness. Although selection is thus deployed from the beginning, this is not inconsistent with what earlier manuals on the art of travel advocated as an encyclopaedic, inclusive genre of writing. In epistemological terms, the ordering principle serves in the first place to integrate new phenomena within the existing epistemological framework and, in the second place, to allow the traveller to transmit the newly acquired knowledge to others. One way in which we might analyze travel writings as producers of boundary space is, therefore, by attending to their use of ethnographic devices. Specifically, such an analysis would attempt to examine how the travellers negotiate the problem of "writing about" in a situation where they are also "inside".

Of the categories that structure selection and perception, the educational one has a strong presence, whether the traveller is aware of it or not. Education was a strong force in eighteenth and nineteenth-century thinking. Stagl (1990) argues that in the tradition of the "Ars Apodemica" which extended its influence well into the eighteenth century, travel was defined in terms of education and the acquisition of useful knowledge. The selection entailed in the description of the travel concentrated therefore on the noteworthy, "for the usefulness of travel was the experience of what was worth seeing and knowing" (1990: 321). Even though extensive advice accompanied the traveller in what s/he was to describe, the question of what was worth seeing and knowing underscores not only the normative context of travel but also the context of a readership for travel writing.

But what kind of things are worth noting? One of the reasons why travel writing was heavily mortgaged on educational ideals is that it made the object world of "elsewhere" readily available for perception. In her contribution to visual culture studies, Eilean Hooper-Greenhill draws attention to the ambiguity of the word "object" itself, an ambiguity that becomes particularly trenchant when it comes to travel, where the objects of description are not merely things but people and their customs. Hooper-Greenhill writes that according to the *Chambers Dictionary*, an object is a material thing, but also an aim or purpose, a person or thing to which action, feelings, or thoughts are directed: thing, intention, and target (Hooper-Greenhill 2000: 104).

As Bal (2003b) has noted in her discussion of Hooper-Greenhill, the conflation of thing with aim does not imply attributing intentions to objects, although to some extent such a case could be made (Bal is alluding to Kaja Silverman's philosophical study of vision, *World Spectators* [2000]). The conflation, instead, casts the shadow of intention of the subject over the object. In this guise, the ambiguity of the word "object" harks back to the goals of nineteenth-century object-teaching and its roots in pedagogical positivism, which was surely no stranger to the impulse of travel: "the first education should be of the perceptions, then of memory, then of the understanding, then of the judgement" (Calkins 1880: 166; quoted in Hooper-Greenhill 2000: 105). This order is clearly meant as a recipe for progressive education, in which the child is empowered to form its own judgments based on perception, and the travelling adult, similarly, opens her mind to new experiences. At the time, this was a much-needed emancipation of the young subject, as well as of women. However, it is also precisely the reversal of what cultural analysis ought to disentangle and reorder. For, in the then-welcome attempt to counter the newly "invented" ideological brainwashings produced by the primacy of opinion, the sequence established proclaims the supremacy of a rationality that represses subjectivity, emotions, and beliefs. It is an attempt to *object*ify experience.[3] Travel, instead, established a ground for the interaction between subjectivity and the "object" – goal, other, or thing – encountered, not grasped but met halfway.

At this point I wish to rephrase my initial question, "how do these travel writings negotiate the problem of 'writing about'?" in order to extend the analysis to both text and reader. In travel writing a description of something is stated in terms of something else – the new and unknown is stated in terms of the known. Here, a translation of sorts takes place. But since the traveller hardly masters the "foreign language" constituted by the culture encountered, the success or failure of the cultural translation is subject to hesitation, relativization, and provisionality. Hence, such moments of "translation" are all-important, and merit scrutiny.

True to the ambiguity of "object" intimated above, the text does not function as a thing in and of itself that conceals its secrets only to be disclosed by an attentive reader. Instead, I would argue that the meaning of a

---

[3] On the history of the concept of ideology, see Vadée (1973); on textual manifestations and their analysis, Hamon (1984).

text is – always provisionally – established in an interaction between the text and the reader. The latter brings certain readerly conventions to bear on a given reading. Indeed, a semiotically-inspired theoretical focus like the interactive model of meaning production implies that meaning is variable: the reader inevitably employs different conventions of reading dependent upon her/his cultural and historical situatedness. The moment of cultural translation occurs when such conventions are both deployed and, however marginally, subjected to intercultural hesitation.[4]

This brings me also, once again, to the moments of translation. Based on what – and how – do I assume the presence of such moments and what do these consist of? Moments of translation occur not only within the travelogues, but also when my own position as a twenty-first century reader of the nineteenth-century texts unfixes my readerly conventions. I am reading as a feminist and cultural theorist working on (post)colonial discourses, and trying to explore boundary spaces. Therefore, the moments of translation I focus on are those pertaining to situations in the text in which an exchange takes *place* – as event and in space. These are instances where something of the production of a text and the forces at work in this production become visible. At those moments the work of knowledge production in "writing about" can be analyzed in terms of discursive practices, inequalities in power relations, and the specificities according to which gender, race and sexuality are constructed.[5]

For these reasons I now take up and further pursue a combined analysis of the travelogues by de Gasparin and Dieulafoy, a study I began in an earlier book (Boer 2004b). My reading here will focus on the ethnographic devices these women writers use in their representations of the Orient and, more specifically, of local Persian women. In view of cultural translation as well as the production of boundary space through the deployment of the text in the double sense of "object", I consider in particular the moments in which an audience is addressed; those moments, in other words, when a goal-oriented text asks its readers to consider a certain mode of reading; when a detail

---

[4] For a very useful discussion of text-reader relations see Ernst van Alphen (1988: 201-11). For a seminal study on situated knowledge, see Donna Haraway (1991).
[5] For exchange and its implications in intercultural representations see also Boer (1994). My interest in moments of translation, incidentally, also pertains to the practice of historical reading, or in reading, "pre-posterously", from the vantage point of today.

strikes me specifically in my guise of reader or when an exchange takes place that can be said to yield or make available for analysis a "scene of production".

The Traveller's Eye

> Les Échelles du Levant! Do you feel the sea breeze? Views bathed in sun have opened up, a sky more vivid than sapphire has unfolded over our heads, over there beautiful Circassian [female] slaves are passing, and there Osman's scimitar flashes; happy is the one who, with the foot on a caravel, heading to the Orient, is gliding this luminous route that Vernet's paintbrush cast before our eyes!

> Les Échelles du Levant! Sentez-vous le souffle de la mer? Des perspectives baignées de soleil se sont ouvertes, un ciel plus éclatant que le saphir s'est déroulé sur nos têtes, là-bas passent les belles esclaves de Circassie, là-bas le cimeterre d'Osman jette son éclair; heureux qui, le pied sur une caravelle, le cap sur l'orient, glisse dans cette voie lumineuse que jeta devant nos yeux le pinceau de Vernet! (De Gasparin 1867: 1).

The very first sentence of Madame de Gasparin's travelogue immediately deploys the double sense of "object" twice: as the rhetoric of a sentence directly addressing the reader, and as an invocation of a visual representation, an object that itself addresses its viewer directly. After all, the sentence starts with the evocation of a painting, *Les Échelles du Levant* by Joseph Vernet. Vernet was a well-known painter of seascapes in the mid-nineteenth century, and readers of Madame de Gasparin's text could safely be assumed to know his work. Using vision to solicit a tactile experience is a clear statement of a rhetoric that can be called synaesthetic, appealing to a multi-sensorial experience. It uses painting to re-present, to make present, something that is not simply of the order of vision – it extends well into the realm of touch: the touch of the sea breeze on the skin of a reader who, most likely, is sitting in an armchair at home.

What does this introduction tell us as readers today? In the first place it proposes a mode of reading where we are addressed in ways relevant for the ethnographic endeavour of the text. By inviting us to identify with the sensory aspects of the Orient – the sea-breeze, the sunlight and the sapphire-coloured sky – de Gasparin appeals to common experiences to which one could relate, whether one knows the Middle East, or not. The shared knowledge of what a sea breeze feels like and of a clear, bright-blue sky, is enough to make the next step and "travel" to the Orient. But the rhetorical appeal is more complex than this. The address is voiced as a direct question: "Do you feel the sea-breeze?" or as a reference to a shared viewing: "*our* heads . . . *our* eyes". This viewing is invoked, not as the retinal objectifying viewing but as an embodied one, for which the body parts involved are spelled out. Whether through interpellation or the use of the first person plural, the reader becomes quite concretely *incorporated* within the scene evoked. Or, to characterize the viewing in different terms: de Gasparin acts as a focalizer, as the point of view from which a narrative is proposed, privileging a particular mode of reading and/or viewing. The discourse of embodiment specifies not only the focalizing subject – de Gasparin, along with her readers, imagined as standing before Vernet's painting – but also the nature of the act of perception, as multi-sensorial, eager, and forcefully engaged.

Let me expand on some of the implications of de Gasparin's focalization and the way in which it positions me as a reader. Her pointing exclamations direct my readerly gaze. "Over there" (là-bas) for instance, a deictic element that positions the reader in a space and moment, is a strong and insistent means to point out specificities of the scene evoked, such as beautiful female slaves passing by or the flash of Osman's sword. These elements are spatially indicated, in a gesture of pointing that would be an emblematic example of the Peircean *index*. In its indexical function, it suggests the travel to "over there" that the reader is about to embark on, through the mediation of the traveller's text. Much like a camera-eye zooming in on a detail, the field of vision narrows to what I am asked to contemplate – aspects of the Orient that are stereotypical in Western representations: beautiful but subjected women, glittering riches. In this fashion, I am also invited to recognize the gendered, double image of sexuality and violence – the beautiful female slaves and the flashing male weapon of the collective Orientalist imagination – whose fantasmatic nature is foregrounded by means of exotic terminology. These elements are evoked within a setting of spectacular natural scenery that at first – in its bare, generalized version – is known to all, and then becomes deepened by specific Orientalist aggrandizement: from a common sun bath to "a sky more vivid than sapphire".

In the last part of the passage a fantasmatic image is conjured. This image is based on a painting, and forms a way of staging the subsequent narrative. Only here ambivalence is introduced. We see the selection and ordering at work – according to categories we know – in order to rhetorically invite the reader to partake in the travelling. The narrative that tells of a travel that is about to take place, is represented as already having happened, as captured on the surface of a canvas; but it is also as if one has travelled before, so that seeing inevitably means re-cognition, and experience entails absorbing the unknown within the known. Dreaming in front of a painting, one travels to the scene of that painting.[6]

By the same token, among European writers who actually travelled to the Middle East in the mid- to late nineteenth century, the experience of strangeness or disorientation was frequently expressed as the inability to form a picture, as the absence of pictorial order. As Mitchell observes, "it was as though to make sense of it meant to stand back and make a drawing or take a photograph of it; which for many of them actually it did", including, as we will see, de Gasparin and Dieulafoy (Mitchell 1988: 22).

De Gasparin's use of the image of Vernet's *Les Échelles du Levant* addresses an audience and conjures possible readings and viewings of the Orient, but not without insisting at the same time, I suggest, on certain privileged modes of doing so. Of course, I could speculate as to the actual make-up of de Gasparin's intended audience, but it is the work of *creating* and *imagining* an audience that is the focus of critical attention here.

The beginning by way of a painting, as the ready-made image of what we are about to see, conforms to the predominance of vision as a mode of cognition. With this predominance comes a particular conception of visual perception: not the general idea of vision, nor the embodied act of looking that was evoked by means of the Vernet painting, but that of perspective. A second quote from de Gasparin's travelogue shows the insistent pattern in which the eyewitness report is combined with the use of perspective (in the figurative sense) to guarantee that we do not miss a beat in her account. Much in the mode of the realist novel, the reader is taken by the hand and shown a view whose focalisation is motivated by the itinerary of the ship:

---

[6] For an elaboration of travel writings as the already-seen and the already-read, see Boer (2004b).

Thus the *Imperator* advances. It turned its prow to the clear horizon of
Marmara, where one after another the islands of the Princes are rising. Soon its
course is changing, it describes a curve; the Head of the Seraglio comes out of
the waters in the magic spectacle of its airy silhouettes; Constantinople is
appearing as a whole, splendid; a cry escapes from our breast.
– Lower the anchors, yes, captain, and leave us here.

Ainsi l'Imperator s'avance. Il a tourné sa proue vers le clair horizon de
Marmara, où l'une après l'autre se lèvent les îles des Princes. Bientôt sa ligne
fléchit, il décrit une courbe; la Pointe-du-Sérail est sortie des eaux dans la féerie
de ses silhouettes aériennes; Constantinople apparaît tout entière, splendide; une
cri nous sort de la poitrine.
– Jetez les ancres, oui, capitaine, et laissez-nous ici (De Gasparin 1867: 116).

Now that we actually find ourselves on a boat with the ironic name of
Imperator, the luminous path painted by Vernet stretches out in front of us.
The sweeping views of a city, splendid in its scenery, unfold and provide the
spectator with a panorama that holds promises in its fairy-tale like staging.
De Gasparin describes the sense of moving toward the city in terms of
anticipation, an eagerness to see it all. However, the sentence harbours
ambivalence, which characterizes the traveller between gaze and encounter.
The city *appears*, as if Constantinople, not the traveller, moved towards the
encounter; and it appears *as a whole*, to be captured in a single glance, an
appearance made possible by distance – a distance that will not allow
encounters to take place. It is almost as if the reader will cry out with de
Gasparin in surprise, and beg the captain to allow some time for a closer look
at the city.[7]
The supplication has been heard and the description continues:

In the middle of the bustle, the colours, forms, movement and life, some main
features attract the eye. Facing us, this sea-arm that the bridge of the Sultane
Validé cuts across will penetrate into the heart of Stamboul to form there the
Golden Horn. In there swarm steamers, caiqs, caravels, feluccas, and tartans.
Wheels strike the water, wakes interweave; garlands of smoke which mark in
the air the different courses that ships are keeping, soon mingle and float
aimlessly, casting their fawn veils at the old Byzantium. She rises, the city, she
enlarges.

---

[7] The idea that descriptions are narratively motivated has been extensively theorized by Philippe
Hamon (1981).

Au milieu du tumulte, des couleurs, des formes, du mouvement et de la vie, quelques grands traits saisissent les yeux. En face de nous, ce bras de mer que coupe le pont de la Validé-Sultane va s'enfoncer dans le cœur de Stamboul pour y dessiner la Corne-d'Or. Là dedans fourmillent paquebots, caïqs, caravelles, felouques et tartanes. Les roues battent l'eau, les sillages s'entrelacent; les écharpes de fumée qui marquent dans l'éther ces routes diverses que tiennent les navires, bientôt mêlées et flottant a l'aventure, jettent leur voile fauve à la vieille Byzance. Elle monte, la ville, elle s'élargit (De Gasparin 1867: 116-17).

Again, in line with the realist tradition of her time, the description moves from distant overview to detailed entrance. The general overview is substituted by a much more particular description. Where confusion reigns in the first instance in this part of the description – the bustle, colours, and movement, which form such a staple of travel accounts – soon enough an ordering appears, according to the categories that facilitate re-cognition. The depiction of the spatial arrangements of water and city provides not just information about the main features of Constantinople, but offers a focus through which the eye is to enter the city as well. These two elements join information in such a way that it reveals the construction of the text.

The particularity here resides, on the one hand, in the post-facto construction of what was seen, and on the other hand in the present tense form of the narrative. How is de Gasparin able to report so exactly what she sees, or rather, has seen, in the past of her travel and now present for the reader to see in the present? While she is approaching Constantinople for the first time, she nevertheless confidently produces the names of the main waterways and what one can see there; at the same time, she entices us to pretend that we, too, already know what we see. The continuous use of the present tense creates a sense of timelessness and of presence (Pratt 1992: 64; see Fabian [1983] for a discussion of temporal terms in which cultural differences are staged and naturalized). The final close-up of the city forms the provisional finale that personifies it: she rises, she enlarges. It becomes difficult to ignore the many subtle ways in which the city is feminized and presented as (an) opening to the incoming traveller. Here, a relation of mastery is established under the guise of awe.

As Mary Louise Pratt has argued, landscapes in travel writing are frequently aestheticized and obtain the quality of a painting (1992: 201-05).

Such landscapes acquire a semiotic density, which can also be seen in de
Gasparin's representation of Constantinople. In the arrival scene the city is
anthropomorphized while all human beings are absent, save for the gazing
eye of the traveller. I wish to point out, however, that in addition to aesthetic
and anthropomorphic similes, the description of Constantinople and the
activities in its surrounding waters makes use of metaphors alluding to
textures and human clothing. The wakes trailing different watercrafts
interweave with each other, and garlands or scarves of smoke (*écharpes de
fumée*) cast their fawn veils over old Byzantium. A city draped in veils and
garlands, a magical spectacle that catches the eye of the beholder, renders
Constantinople not only a gendered landscape, but almost a bodyscape as
well. A body to be, at the very least, read and interpreted.

The Ambiguous Act of Unveiling

Moving from the feminized bodyscape of Constantinople to the female body
as represented in Jane Dieulafoy's travelogue is to move from a staging of
apparent mastery to a much more ambivalent encounter. Two decades after
de Gasparin's visit to Constantinople, Jane Dieulafoy travelled through Persia
and Iraq, assisting her husband in his archaeological research. Archaeology
might be seen as a form of ethnography, but more than the latter archaeology
is a form of inscription par excellence, insofar as the landscape is mapped
and altered through excavation and measurement. In this sense, archaeology
could be considered the next step, taken after the traveller-ethnographer has
penetrated the landscape. Parallel to the archaeological inscription runs Jane
Dieulafoy's travelogue, describing the work, the places they visit, and the
people they meet along the way. The photographs she took during the
couple's travels make her travelogue even more interesting. Dieulafoy shows
repeated interest and concern with the position of Muslim women, and her
photographs of these women, in relation to her writing, are particularly
compelling. Consequently, my analysis of Dieulafoy's travelogue focuses on
those photographs of Oriental women. I read the photographs as ethnographic
devices and elicit from them scenes of knowledge production pertaining to
issues of gender.

As Walter Benjamin claims, photography

can bring out those aspects of the original that are unattainable to the naked eye yet accessible to the lens, which is adjustable and chooses its angle at will. And photographic reproduction, with the aid of certain processes, such as enlargement or slow motion, can capture images which escape natural vision (Benjamin 1968b: 220).

Although in early photography the technology of slow motion was yet unavailable, the notion that a photograph can capture more than the eye is a useful insight with which to approach Dieulafoy's photographs. In his discussion about the working of a film camera Benjamin reiterates his distinction between the naked eye and the camera, but with a crucial addition: "Evidently a different nature opens itself to the camera than opens to the naked eye – if only because an unconsciously penetrated space is substituted for a space consciously explored by man" (1968b: 236-37). The translation unfortunately blurs the meaning a bit, but the argument Benjamin is trying to make is that the camera adds a level of knowledge of which the naked eye is unaware or even "unconscious" (even though a person might consciously "see" something).

But what he also appears to say is that the space seen through the camera is ontologically different from the one the traveller enters. This ontological difference, here expressed by the use of the verb "to substitute", is, in Benjamin's words, an absolute difference. In the context of my analysis, the opposition between an unconsciously penetrated space and a space consciously explored by man must be turned upside down. Far from being unconscious – Benjamin's term "the optical unconscious" comes to mind here – the difference is of distance, exploration, and surface versus proximity, penetration, and – potentially – an encounter. In terms of Benjamin's distinction, then, Dieulafoy mediates between the two forms of exploration.

Seen in this light, photography as an ethnographic technique employed in a context such as Dieulafoy's travelogue, does more than add to personal observation. If it can be said to become a necessary supplement to the text, the term supplement must be taken in its strong, ambivalent, Derridean sense. The photos do not simply illustrate what was being written anyway. They are part of the account, a form of writing, not with ink but with light. From this perspective it is important to analyze the photographs within their textual context, as they appeared in the first edition of the travelogue published in 1887, as I do here.

Dieulafoy gives an extensive account of the Babi revolt that took place while she was in Zendjan, a North Persian city heavily involved in this revolt. Babi were adherents of Mirza Ali Mohammed, who claimed to be the twelfth imam.[8] Babism offered mixture of Islamic and mystical elements, but bore many characteristics of a social reform movement as well. Women were especially attracted to the new movement and played an important part in its diffusion, as Dieulafoy intimates:

> Since its emergence, the new religion had known to its success how to gain the interest of women, so annihilated by the Koran, by promising them the abolition of polygamy, correctly considered by the Sublime Highness [Mirza Ali Mohammed, IB] as a source of vice and immorality, by inciting them to reject the veil and by attributing them next to their husbands the honoured and respected place that the wife and mother must occupy in the family. All the intelligent Persian women appreciated the indisputable advantages of this social revolution, embraced ardently the beliefs of the reformer, took it upon them to spread Babism in the harems, inaccessible to men.

> Dès son apparition, la nouvelle religion avait su intéresser à son succès les femmes, si annihilées par le Coran, en leur promettant l'abolition de la polygamie, considérée à juste titre par l'Altesse Sublime comme une source de vice et d'immoralité, en les engageant à rejeter le voile, et en leur attribuant auprès de leur mari la place honorée et respectée que l'épouse et la mère doivent occuper dans la famille. Toutes les Persanes intelligentes apprécièrent les incontestables avantages de cette révolution sociale, embrassèrent avec ardeur les croyances du réformateur, se chargèrent de propager le babysme dans les andérouns, inaccessibles aux hommes (Dieulafoy 1887: 78; 1990b: 48).[9]

It is clear that Dieulafoy saw Islam as an oppressive religion for women while she upheld the place assigned to women in the Babi movement – that of honoured and respected mother and wife in the family.

At the same time, however, the gesture of sympathy towards Muslim women contains a duplicity: that of favouring a bourgeois-like existence for

---

[8] The Shi'a variant of Islam in Persia holds the belief that after Ali, founder of the Shi'a, eleven imams succeeded him. The twelfth imam disappeared and is believed to come back one day to establish a regime of righteousness. Claiming to be the twelfth imam, Mirza Ali Mohammed excited large popular support.
[9] In the Phébus edition the whole section about the Babi movement has been displaced from the context in which it appeared in 1887.

Persian women, a position from which Dieulafoy wished to distance herself in her own culture.[10] These passages clearly show that Dieulafoy's frame of reference remains her own background, however much she wanted to escape from it. In turn, she projects this background as a desirable goal for Persian women. This move underscores how much the interpretation of reforms in Persia could only be perceived within the framework of bourgeois ideology at home in Europe. This is yet another demonstration of the ethnographic technique of mixing recognizability with strangeness, so as to allow her readers (and herself) to process the new knowledge with reference to the already-known. Moreover, this mixture offers another take on to the use of the present tense we saw earlier. This present prepares the reader for a confrontation with the visual material proper – the photographs that, just like the Vernet painting, present themselves a-temporally to the viewer.

Directly following the story of the Babi movement, Dieulafoy writes of her visit to a merchant in Zendjan, one of the richest Babis in town. Speaking to her readers and answering their unspoken question of why she actually went to his house, she writes:

> I accepted with pleasure, happy to enter into a reformed family. First of all I am surprised by the order that seemed to prevail in that house; I do not notice those numerous servants squatting, inactive, with a water pipe in their hand . . . The only wife and the daughter of the master of the house come to welcome me.

> J'accepte avec plaisir, heureuse de pénétrer dans une famille de réformés. Tout d'abord je suis surprise de l'ordre qui paraît régner dans cette demeure; je n'aperçois pas ces innombrables servantes accroupies, inactives, leur kalyan à la main . . . L'unique femme et la fille du khan viennent me souhaiter la bienvenue (Dieulafoy 1887: 84; 1989: 88).

Like the true bourgeois housewife she so obviously declined to be, Dieulafoy notes, surprised, that order rules in the house and that servants do not hang around idly. She establishes thereby a clear, albeit implicit distinction between this particular household of people who embraced the Babi beliefs,

---

[10] In the introductory chapter, left out of the volumes published by Phébus, Dieulafoy gives an account of her arguments with friends who tried to convince her that a bourgeois woman should stay at home instead of embarking on such dangerous travel. They called her *originale* which has connotations of oddness and eccentricity, effectively placing Dieulafoy at the margins of French society (1887: 1-2).

and other Islamic households where disorder reigned and polygamy was still in place. The close relation between order and monogamous marriage in which a woman fulfilled her duties as mother and wife resembles the ideals according to which French bourgeois women were supposed to live at the time.

In her study of bourgeois women in France in the nineteenth century, Bonnie Smith argues that servants and their behaviour conveyed important messages about the mistress of the house. Their conduct and restraint spoke to a woman's ability to run her household properly: "This reciprocity, this partnership between servant and mistress, perpetuated a traditional 'moral economy' within the household" (1981: 75). Smith focuses on the bond between economy and morality in this context. Others have added to this bond the often-overlooked intimacy between servant and mistress, an intimacy that inevitably accompanies the kind of work servants do.[11]

The same observation concerning a household properly in place and thus a working "moral economy" seems also to be extended in Dieulafoy's implicit note on the absence of polygamy, when she mentions "the only wife" of the master. Elsewhere, she speaks more directly to this issue. In fact, the core of Dieulafoy's criticism seems to be aimed at the institution of polygamy, "correctly considered as a source of vice and immorality" (1887: 87). At the very least, as a sign of moral disorder, polygamy inevitably contaminates the house as a whole – as the quoted juxtaposition of details suggests, where polygamy rules, servants are inactive, idly hang about in corners, and smoke water pipes. Where monogamy prevails, by contrast, order reigns and the mistress and daughter of the house act also as proper bourgeois hostesses who welcome the foreign visitor into their home.

It is striking in this context that the visit elicits only descriptions of the physical features and attire of the mother and her daughter. One would assume that there may have been compelling reasons for Dieulafoy to report on the conversation that she had with the two women. Yet such a report is wanting. Instead, descriptions of dress and facial appearance as well as remarks about beauty and comparisons with European women appear frequently, not only in Dieulafoy's travelogue, but also in travel accounts

---

[11] This intimacy frequently produced anxieties in the masters of the house. On servants as a charged site of European anxieties in the former Netherlands East Indies, see Stoler (2002: 133-37).

written by other women at this time. In some instances, this was a way, again, of locating the unknown within the known, thereby making it familiar. Thus, a particular item of apparel or hair style might work as a kind of déjà vu, recalling something similar at home, no matter how far-fetched in actuality the attempt to bring the two together might be (cf. Spyer 2000: 54). This mode of descriptive writing remains close to photography, and stays within the order to the primacy of visuality. As such, it can be considered another instance of ethnographic writing.

There is a third aspect to this privileging of description of outward appearance over rendering conversation. As Bonnie Smith proposes:

> Fashion formed a communication system among women, and even among men and women, a system that became the quintessential expression because it surrounded the female form itself (Smith 1981: 69).

Clothing, then, was a system to read and interpret, and French women travellers indeed interpreted the dress of Oriental women as a means both of expression and communication. Women travellers assumed they could "talk" to Oriental women and vice versa by means of dressing in a certain way. Description in this function is, then, a form of cultural translation.

In the middle of the text devoted to Babism, an image appears titled *Jeune fille babi de Zendjan* (figure 1). The text gives no information about the circumstances leading to the staging and taking of the photograph, nor are we told anything about this particular young woman. She has no name, but instead appears to stand in for a whole category of women, i.e. those who had been converted to Babism. We see her standing in front of a wall, a backdrop that highlights her presence, while at the same time closing her off from a dark background. Her attitude is resigned, her head averted, looking down. Her face is unveiled, although the white piece of fabric surrounding her chin seems to indicate that the unveiling is only temporary. As spectators we have apparently unlimited access to this young woman, although we might feel somewhat uneasy in the face of her reluctant pose. Why did she pose at all? Was she cajoled into posing?

Figure 1. Jane Dieulafoy (1887). *Jeune fille babi de Zendjan* in *La Perse, la Chaldée et la Susiane*. Paris: Hachette.

As in the previous photograph, the circumstances of the picture of Ziba Khanoum are not commented upon either (figure 2). But the photo is supplemented with a description. An Armenian woman had promised Dieulafoy to introduce her to the wife of hadji Houssein, a reputedly beautiful woman named Ziba, who was once part of the court of Nasir Ed-Din. What follows is Dieulafoy's first impression of Ziba.

> His wife deserves the reputation of beauty that she unanimously enjoys in Ispahan. One notices because of her short dress that she has lived at the court [where short skirts were fashionable, IB]. Is it to the heat or to coquetry that we must attribute the absence of a gauze blouse meant to lightly cover the bust of Persian women? I would not be able to decide on it, but I would envy the good

fortune of a painter or a sculptor who would be rather happy to have such a model pose before him.

Sa femme mérite la réputation de beauté dont elle jouit unanimement à Ispahan. On voit à sa toilette sommaire qu'elle a vécu à la cour. Est-ce à la chaleur ou à la coquetterie qu'il faut attribuer la suppression d'une chemisette de gaze destinée à voiler légèrement le buste des femmes persanes? Je ne saurais le décider, mais j'envierais la bonne fortune d'un peintre ou d'un sculpteur qui serait assez heureux pour faire poser devant lui un pareil modèle (Dieulafoy 1887: 268; 1989: 255).

The last remark harks back to the painting that triggered the beginning rhetoric, and at the same time, it has a slightly erotic tone, if only by proxy, since it is attributed to the artist. We see a woman depicted in what the photograph caption calls "tenue d'intimité". She seems to have just stepped out from a space hidden or closed off by a curtain. The female servant holding back the curtain almost blends into the background through the hue of her dress. She looks at Ziba who, in turn, looks away from the spectator. The bouquet of flowers that Ziba holds reinforces the impression that she poses for the image.

In part, the effect of posing has to do with the long procedure of taking a photograph in the early days of photography. At the same time, the fixation refers directly back to a common painterly tradition of depicting Oriental women, including the portrayal of servants who assist their mistresses in embellishing themselves and making themselves available for the spectator. This impression is further emphasized by the curtain as an implicit reference to the wearing of a veil or, in the servant's case, to wrapping one's body in long garments. The apparent unveiling of Ziba in the photograph hardly leads to the emancipation of women that Dieulafoy purports to favour, but instead visually underscores the availability of the body of Oriental women for Western spectators.

In her comments Dieulafoy expresses doubt about the manner in which Ziba is dressed and describes what the norm – or should we say, *her* norm? – supposedly prescribes: a gauze blouse covering the woman's bosom. Dieulafoy's rules for proper dress are transgressed and it seems to be in response to this transgression that she reverts to a fantasy about another kind of posing – that of the painter or sculptor's model. In addition to a displaced erotic fantasy, this remark also suggests an opposition between painting and

Figure 2. Jane Dieulafoy (1887). *Ziba Khanoum en tenue d'intimité* in *La Perse, la Chaldée et la Susiane*. Paris: Hachette.

photography. Artists might be happy to have a woman, beautiful and attired like Ziba, pose for them, but Dieulafoy does not see photography as fully equipped to fulfil the aesthetic requirements of representing the female Oriental body as painters or sculptors might do. Instead photography is meant merely to register an encounter, to preserve the presence before the camera. Benjamin claims, however, that the photographed portrait represents the last refuge for the cult value of the picture. It is in the hybrid genre of the human portrait that "for the last time the aura emanates" (1968b: 226). Unintentionally, Dieulafoy's representation of Ziba as an Oriental mistress draws precisely on this same tradition of representation.[12]

---

[12] For a discussion of the Orientalist tradition of representing women in paintings, see Kabbani (1986) and Nochlin (1983). Alloula (1986) has tried to correct representations of Oriental women with the ambiguous result of reinscribing stereotypes of Algerian women. For a critique, see also Chapter Six from Bal's *Double Exposures* (1996). Said (1978) provided the framework for many of these analyses, but his work shows a blatant blindness for gender aspects.

It is striking to see how quickly in Dieulafoy's text attention turns to the more intellectual aspects of the meeting. Immediately following the previous quotation, Dieulafoy – again barely hiding her surprise – observes:

> From my particular point of view, I have been above all struck by the vivacity of Ziba khanoum's spirit, by the gaiety of her character, the appropriate expressions she uses while talking and by the ease of her gestures marked by a certain nobility.

> A mon point de vue particulier, j'ai été surtout frappée de la vivacité d'esprit de Ziba khanoum, de la gaieté de son caractère, des expressions choisies dont elle se sert en causant et de l'aisance de ses gestes, empreints d'une certaine noblesse (Dieulafoy 1887: 268; 1989: 255).

Today, this expression of surprise may irritate as condescending, but it is important to notice the qualification "from my particular point of view". This phrase acknowledges the writer's own limitation with respect to what she already knows. In other passages, Dieulafoy reveals she is respectful of Ziba's opinions and asks her questions about the period of Ziba's life at the court of the Shah. The incongruity between text and image, however, lies in the contrast between Dieulafoy's respect for Ziba's mind and her unveiling of Ziba's body which, depicted in conventional Orientalist fashion, remains colonized in that it is made visually available for the Western spectator's gaze.

In a third encounter with women that Dieulafoy describes in some detail – in Aveh – the interest of the passage lies in the mutuality of the interpretation of alterity. Clearly the scene describes mutual assumptions about the appearance of the respective "other". The owner of a guesthouse where the Dieulafoys stay, invites his guests for dinner, with the explicit purpose of offering the farmers of the village an opportunity to look at the strangers. The women are especially excited "having learnt via our indiscrete soldier that one of the Europeans was a real woman" (ayant appris par notre indiscret soldat que l'un des Faranguis est une véritable khanoum [Dieulafoy 1887: 178; 1989: 162]). This remark foregrounds the fact that Jane Dieulafoy travelled in male attire in order to be able to move about more freely. Indeed, it is ironic that she disguised herself as the opposite sex, while at the same time she was opposing Persian women's disguise of themselves, that is, their practice of veiling.

The scene begins with a staging of the mutual voyeurism inherent in the ethnographic encounter. When she enters the women's quarter of the house "They all turned their gaze at me; I, for my part, reviewed generally this battalion of inquisitive women" (Tous les regards se braquent sur moi; et, de mon côté, je passe une revue générale de ce bataillon de curieuses [Dieulafoy 1887: 178; 1989: 163]). Although Dieulafoy is a spectacle, she is quick to turn the tables on her spectators – demonstrating that she remains in control of the situation, her discourse much like that of an officer inspecting his troops. Nor does she allow herself to be as overtly curious as the Persian women. Or rather, her curiosity is disguised as control.

The conversation begins with a discussion about marriage in Persia, as two children, aged eight and nine, are presented to her as each other's fiancés. Dieulafoy expresses her surprise regarding pre-arranged marriages and asks what happens if the spouses are not pleased with each other. It is obvious that Dieulafoy's standard of marriage is romantic love and therefore does not affirm marriage as contracted, for instance, as an economic agreement. Fatma, the mistress of the house replies: "They will divorce and remarry each for their part. Come here, Ali; the woman, I am sure, believes that you don't know how to read" (Ils divorceront et se remarieront chacun de son côté. Approche-toi Ali; la khanoum, j'en suis persuadée, croit que tu ne sais pas lire [Dieulafoy 1887: 178; 1989: 163]). The rapid succession of these two short sentences is highly revealing. The first replies crisply to Dieulafoy's stereotypical suspicion of arranged marriages – not so far removed from those contracted in France at the time. The second sentence makes explicit that the mistress of the house suspects the traveller of other stereotypes, of which ignorance is but one. In response to his mother's request, the boy fetches an almanac to demonstrate his reading skills. But Dieulafoy is not so easily distracted from her prejudices. She remarks:

> It seems to me that some parts of this work are written in an extremely licenti-ous language and, moreover, are giving advice which is hardly appropriate for the age of your children.

> Quelques parties de cet ouvrage m'ont paru traitées avec une extrême licence de langage et donnent, en outre, des conseils peu appropriés à l'âge de vos enfants (Dieulafoy 1887: 179; 1989: 164).

And just as the reader – at least this reader – is ready to feel indignation at such a patronizing attitude, the author turns around and saves the encounter by narrating again the mutuality of the cultural strangeness and its evaluation by the participants. Dieulafoy continues: "All the women looked at me with astonishment, then burst out laughing" (Toutes les femmes me regardent avec étonnement, puis éclatent de rire [Dieulafoy 1887: 179; 1989: 164]). The play on each other's received notions is ruptured by laughter, a laughter that temporarily and to some extent, dissolves power differences between the foreign visitor and the Persian women, allowing the latter to reaffirm their own position.

FATMA.

Figure 3. Jane Dieulafoy (1887). *Fatma* in *La Perse, la Chaldée et la Susiane*. Paris: Hachette.

When we look at the image that accompanies the text at this point (figure
3), it shows a portrait drawing of Fatma, the mistress of the house. As in the
earlier photographs, Fatma is depicted with her head turned away and her
face unveiled. When was this drawing made? Was it during the conversation
between Dieulafoy and the entire group of women? If so, why would only
Fatma be represented? We need the text to provide some clues. As in the
previous instance, the supplementarity is ambiguous. Far from illustrating the
text, more text is needed to understand the photograph. Hence, Fatma is
described in more detail in the text than the other women are.

> Fatma, the mistress of the house, must be twenty-five. Her head is covered with
> a white silk scarf, kept together under the chin with a turquoise; her hair, trim-
> med in fringes on her forehead, is thrown back on her back and divided in a
> multitude of little braids; a very light gauze blouse, slit on the bosom, leaves her
> breast almost uncovered; the dress, cut at the knees, is made out of silk from
> Benares. The other women are dressed in the same way.

> Fatma, la maîtresse de céans, doit avoir vingt-cinq ans. Sa tête est couverte d'un
> chargat de soie blanche attaché sous le menton par une turquoise; les cheveux,
> taillé en franges sur le front, sont rejetés sur le dos et divisés en une multitude
> de petites tresses; une très légère chemise de gaze, fendue sur la poitrine, laisse
> les seins à peu près à découvert; la robe, coupée aux genoux, est en soie de
> Bénarès. Les autres femmes sont vêtues de la même manière (Dieulafoy 1887:
> 178; 1989: 163).

Again, the peculiar relay of particularity and generalization characterizes this
passage as (proto-)ethnographic. All the women are dressed the same, but
Fatma is depicted in portrait form, just as she, not the others, has her portrait
made. As such Fatma becomes a *pars pro toto*, representing the totality of
women present. The text in the 1887 edition is printed around the image of
Fatma and supplements it by giving details about Fatma's clothing. The text-
image relation is ambiguous throughout the examples I have given, because
we cannot consider the photographs and the drawing as mere illustrations.
Given that neither is assigned absolute priority, the text is as much an illustration of the image as the other way around.

The description of Persian women goes hand in hand with their
registration through ethnographic devices. Both text and images are part and
parcel of heterogeneous attempts to create a domain of knowledge about the
"other". In this colonialist epistemology, photography as an instrument of

research plays a highly ambiguous role insofar as it is intended to elicit curiosity on the part of the beholder. This curiosity, in turn, turns photography into an instrument of further investigation – of penetration into the private spaces of Persian homes – and into a performance of the inequalities of power, most clearly manifest in the characteristic posing of Persian women. The curiosity that led the Persian women to invite Dieulafoy into their home, ends in their own Orientalist exhibition.

I emphasize that the role of photography in travelogues diverges from the text in an important aspect. The preoccupation with the unveiling of women's faces is apparent throughout the travelogue; in fact, all of the images of women contained in it play on this central theme. Within the text of the travelogue as a whole, the images might be said to function as punctums in Roland Barthes' sense of "this element which arises from the scene, shoots out of it like an arrow, and pierces me" (Barthes 1981: 26). Repeatedly arresting the spectator, each one of these images demands an intervention to establish meaning, to define what the conditions of its production were. As a result, the project of unveiling is ambiguous and signifies an inscription of difference in Dieulafoy's travelogue. On the one hand, unveiling corresponds with the requirements expressed in the *text* for an improvement of women's position under Islam, for their emancipation. On the other, the unveiling staged in the *photographs* and the *drawings* plays upon Western stereotypical representations of Oriental women in which their unveiling becomes the source of the desire to possess and dominate them. In short, unveiling here pulls the reader in two different directions as text and illustrations collaborate in working against each other. And they do so, across the fraught colonial, historical, political, and personal complexities of Dieulafoy's own position. Amongst others, she is situated as a French bourgeois woman – escaping her own bourgeois background – travelling disguised as a man in the Orient, as both a women traveller and herself a contributor to Orientalist knowledge production.

Returning to Benjamin's distinction between the more conscious, directed naked eye and the unconscious work of the camera, reading both the text and the photographs of Dieulafoy's travelogue we might be able to interpret what Dieulafoy's eye was itself unaware of. If we take her text as the reflection of her naked eye – as a motivated, directed impulse to "write about" – then the photographs may be understood as adding a level of perception the text does not offer. If the text represents an explicit desire for what Dieulafoy sees as the necessary emancipation of Persian women, the photographs at first glance appear to do the same. But, at another level, the photos add and feed into the fantasy of unveiling Oriental women. In this respect, the photographs act doubly: while maintaining and reproducing cultural and sexual "otherness", they simultaneously register the need for reform. Photography thus substitutes an unconsciously penetrated space with a space consciously explored by (wo)man, leaves the body of Oriental women indelibly marked by their difference.

Conclusion

In this analysis of ethnographic devices in the travelogues by de Gasparin and Dieulafoy, I have focused especially on moments of cultural translation. At those moments, when an audience is addressed, when a detail calls for further analysis, or when an exchange takes place, resulting in a "scene of production", it becomes possible to historicize – to situate – the ethnographic devices employed. Moments of translation, in other words, are those moments where the exchanges and interactive grounds for the production of knowledge about the other becomes available for interpretation. This, in turn, offers insights into the scenes out of which such knowledge subsequently emerged. Dieulafoy's insistence on her own position foregrounds this activity of cultural translation.

Clearly, both de Gasparin and Dieulafoy operate within the framework of a colonialist discourse, establishing conventional Oriental boundaries that separate them from the places through which they travel and the various inhabitants they encounter on the way. I have shown, however, that "disembedding" the historicity of the practices through which knowledge about the "other" and, in particular, women in the Orient, has been produced can also make us aware of the ways in which we, too, may be enticed to participate in such colonial constructions. At one and the same time, however, historicizing or reading the history of a textual and visual representation into the text may also reveal a moment of oscillation where history, as it were, may momentarily be remade or read "against the grain" –

which opens up the reading, asking it to resist stereotypical conventions, be they textual or visual.

PART II

MATTER IN AND OUT OF SPACE

FOUR

No-Man's-Land? Deserts and the Politics of Place

Deserts appeal to the imagination. Many paintings, photographs, and literary evocations of deserts speak to that appeal. The terrible beauty and the horrific power of their relentless barrenness constitute a provocation for rational man, eager to experience the sublime near-overwhelming power of nature in a landscape of real danger. However, like David Caspar Friedrich's *Monk* standing before a misty lake – the figure that has become the emblem of the Western imagination of sublimity – the primary condition for the sublime experience is solitude. And deserts, in spite of the imagination's products that urgently state the contrary, are not empty.

Deserts are imagined as empty – primarily, empty of people, of inhabitants – which renders them suitable spaces for colonization. A space that is thought to be void of inhabitants, like the moon, or like Palestine, is up for grabs. Recent history has tragically demonstrated what happens when people turn out to live in that space. The geographical expanses called deserts evoke two related responses: one is to consider deserts as empty, devoid of signs of life, and the other is to subsequently move in, conquer, traverse or colonize these spaces by setting up boundary markers. It is this double gesture that I want to analyze in connection with the politics of place. I will argue that empty deserts in need of boundary designations are fictions fabricated within a particular, Western, colonizing context.

This situation is also emblematic for the argument concerning boundaries that I am putting forward in this study. A boundary is a space that separates worlds of difference but is itself a world of difference: deserts are instances, precisely, of the notion that boundaries are not lines, limits, cuts through the inhabited world, but spaces themselves. Spaces, that is, in which people live, but also, spaces that people defend, attack, that nourish them and that they fight over; they are places of contestation.

If we consider representations of deserts, be it in visual or literary or, for that matter, theoretical form, one striking aspect such representations have in common is an unusual emphasis on materiality – a materiality foregrounded by means of personifications of nature. Deserts are beaten down by a relentless sun, by friend or by foe, depending on the interest of the contestants over the rights to inhabit the desert. It is due to the particular materiality – sand and stone – and the pictorially striking colours this matter offers to the eye – yellows, ochres, reds – that even the most dauntingly harsh desert retains a strong aesthetic appeal. However, these very material conditions of desert life also characterize the particular clashes between the imagination and reality in the contest over desert space as negotiable boundary.

A consideration of the materiality of deserts seems, therefore, an appropriate beginning to the second half of this study. For, paradoxically, matter appears simultaneously as both the bone of contention and the cause of the alleged emptiness that makes the contest redundant. As such, the desert can stand for an allegorical embodiment of boundaries as I have been discussing them here. In this chapter, through the analysis of visual, literary and theoretical presentations of deserts, I will question that emptiness, so that the desert can emerge as the negotiable boundary that it has been all along. I will show how emptiness is a feature of deserts only when, as is the case with boundaries in general, they are perceived from the outside.

The word "desert" evokes landscapes of a particular kind. For this reason my investigation will first focus on the idea of emptiness by way of a painting, *Le Désert* (Musée d'Orsay, Paris 1867) by the French nineteenth-century artist Gustave Guillaumet. But if imaginative cultural expression can be situated at one end of the scale of cultural production, theoretical discourse claims a place at the other end, that of rational reflection. Whether these discourses are so different from each other remains, however, a question. Therefore, I will proceed to interrogate Gilles Deleuze and Félix Guattari's notorious treatise on nomadology (1999 [1980]) in which the image of the desert figures prominently. If we take Deleuze and Guattari's point of view for granted, the nomad as a free agent occupies the desert in particular ways, but, as I will argue, only if we also want to comply with a semantic field connecting the other to the Orient. Deleuze and Guattari maintain specific ideas about a boundary separating the nomad in the desert from a sedentary population in the city: this is the second way of marking the desert as boundary I will investigate. A third way is foregrounded by the French New Novelist Claude Ollier who published a novel, *La Mise en scène* (1958) about a geographer charting white, empty spaces on his map of the Moroccan desert with boundary markers in the midst of Algeria's war of independence.

My argument thus engages various ways in which deserts have been imagined and rendered in different media and settings, but each of these renditions focalizes the desert from the outside. In order to question the politics of place thus envisioned, I will draw on Algerian author Tahar Djaout's *L'Invention du désert* (1987) and on an example of collaboration between a French artist born in Morocco, Titouan Lamazou, and a French photographer, Raymond Depardon who share a passion for the desert.[1] Both works foreground the desert as a place covered with palimpsestic traces of human histories and with flexible demarcations of lived spaces. Thus, deserts are exemplary places, inhabited and negotiated spaces, whose histories counter any illusion one might entertain concerning the eternal beauty of nature. In deserts, neither time nor space can be said to be unified, nor, for that matter, to stand still. In order to foreground this non-unifying character of deserts, I will proceed by means of short case studies, vignettes of the great variety of deserts as material instances of boundaries.

Desert as a Platitude

Gustave Guillaumet first exhibited his painting *Le Désert* (figure 4) to considerable success at the Salon of 1867 in Paris. Like all forms of success,

---

[1] While I was reading Emily Apter's *Continental Drift* (1999), I was inspired because of her repeated references to the desert in the work of Djaout and Ollier to read both authors. However, my interpretation of both works is at considerable variance with Apter's.

Salon-success may have been subject to the taste of the day, but it is worth looking a bit closer at the arguments for the acclaim. For example, Paul de Saint-Victor and Théophile Gautier lauded in particular the still life quality of the canvas. The French word for still life is *nature morte* – a terminological serendipity that suggests perhaps why the painting was appealing in the first place. Yet, this characterization might puzzle a present day viewer – or any viewer who *looks*, for that matter, instead of using the painting as a projection screen (Peltre 1997: 152). Because, if we look, what do we see?

Figure 4. Gustave Guillaumet (1840-1887). *Le Sahara, dit aussi le Désert.* Huile sur toile. Musée d'Orsay, Paris.

At first sight we are struck by the overwhelming flatness of the landscape depicted; a flat landscape covered in a yellowish, pale pink and blue light as if dawn had just announced a new day. In the foreground, right in the middle of the painting, lies a skeleton of an animal and because of its long neck, and the form of its hoofs and skull it is recognizable as a camel or a dromedary. Both animal species symbolize the desert, as the "ships" traversing the inhospitable sands of Africa or Arabia.[2] The metaphor, ship of the desert, speaks of isolation and emptiness, comparable to the ocean. In the

---

[2] See Khemir (2000) for a discussion of the tradition of dead camels in European paintings and photography as well as that of the mirage.

background, a small band of animals and human beings is doing just that: walking the desert as if floating on its surface, heading to a destination along a route that caravans have taken, thus connecting peoples inhabiting the deserts and its fringes in relations of trade.

Small groups of people in a vast landscape are instances of a conventional topos in Western landscape painting, suitable to render the scale of nature and the humbling expanse compared to which humans are tiny but – in the wake of the philosophy of sublime experience – masters nevertheless. In her discussion of the desert in her study of *Le Désert*, Christine Peltre interprets the small band of people in this painting as a "microscopic mirage" in a painting that otherwise shows the "expressive power of vacuity" (1997: 152). The use of the word "mirage" points to a specificity of the topos. Just like camels, mirages are a staple of the desert. Mirages underscore the emptiness of the desert as they give the impression of presence, but the presence is vacuous, vanishing into thin air. If we follow Peltre in her interpretation, the painting would foreground the perils of the desert: a limitless, desolate and deadly environment where ultimately even the best equipped animal dies.

Peltre's contention provides very plausible arguments for reading *Le Désert* along the lines she sets out. But the combination of Peltre's, Guatier's and de Saint-Victor's terminology keeps nagging me. The terms *nature morte* and *mirage* are a bit too suitable, not to this painting necessarily but to the idea of the desert articulated and sedimented through them. Her terms are pre-established notions that inform our way of looking, rather than notions that would emerge as a result of a look. For, why would we analyze the band of human beings and animals as a mirage in the first place? And why would we consider this flat landscape a still life, nature but then dead nature, as de Saint-Victor's genre term suggested? Both terms share an assumption not only of death and emptiness, but of flatness. One way to tackle the issue in question is, therefore, to take another look at the flatness of the landscape.

Le Désert calls forth flatness not just because, like all paintings, a two-dimensional representation of a three-dimensional world engenders such a characteristic. Flatness here has to do with a double and ambiguous meaning, as elaborated by Mieke Bal in her discussion of visual aspects in Proust's work. Flatness suggests an absence of depth and volume, a "mirage of depth" as Proust called it, but flatness also refers to the banal (1997: 2-3). She writes:

> The point is that, for Proust, art is, above all else, *flat*. Even the statues are two-dimensional, as is shown in the famous description of Françoise that doubly denies all "volume" to the servant (1981 Vol. 1: 57). Art is also flat in the sense of being banal. The literary aesthetics prevail over visual aesthetics, but the latter provide raw material for the former (Bal 1997: 20).[3]

And later, she quotes the following passage where the word "mirage" actually occurs:

> How often, when driving, do we not come upon a bright street beginning a few feet away from us, when what we have actually before our eyes is merely a patch of wall glaringly lit which has given us the mirage of depth (Proust 1981 Vol. 2: 435 quoted in Bal 1997: 86).

Proust, clearly, has been fed, along with countless others, by the topos of light as producer of flatness, as murderer of depth.

But still life, in spite of its French name, is not flat. As a recent analysis by Hanneke Grootenboer has clearly demonstrated, perspective in still life is a rhetorical ploy to push the flatness forward and give it a readerly depth (2005). She makes this argument in a study that begins with a quotation from Proust in which *nature morte* is explicitly associated with depth – in the philosophical as well as rhetorical sense. Grootenboer argues that perspective, that tool for a visual rhetoric of depth so thoroughly revisited by Hubert Damisch (1994) is bound up with vision itself. More importantly, perspective in still life painting deploys flatness itself – or rather, shallowness, which is not the same thing – as a tool to reach out and confront us:

> perspective establishes the conditions for vision and the visible, rather than for representation . . . We, as viewers, do not look into a pictorial depth that offers itself to us, but rather the objects are pushed forward by their shallow space and actively confront our gaze (Grootenboer 2005: 8).

According to this view, perspective distributes illusions of flatness and depth

---

[3] Bal's play on the French word for flat "plat" and "platitude" for banality is lost in translation.

in order to pre-ordain the kind of gaze we cast on things.

Peltre's assignation of the meaning "mirage" to the group of people and animals in *Le Désert* can now be interpreted otherwise. The mirage proposes depth and it does so in a way we have grown accustomed to when we look at a painting: a tradition of perspective. Depth is suggested, yet as a mirage, this depth is artificial. Depth is not "there", just like the people and animals are not there when we take them to be no more than a mirage. The mirage, then, acquires a double meaning in the painting: paradoxically it accentuates the flatness by suggesting depth, but it does so by means of foregrounding artifice.

As I already indicated, flatness has a second meaning, referring to the banal, the commonplace. Projecting traditional topoi as a form of lazy looking is no more than deploying commonplace. Taking this second meaning of flatness into account in the interpretation of *Le Désert* radically alters our previous perceptions. As long as we see the commonplace qualities of the desert depicted and accept the people and the animals in the distance as a mirage, we can consider the desert as emptiness. But once we let the pictorial strategy sensitize us to this artificial flatness, we are enabled to reject this platitude. This rejection opens up the image to a reversed strategy of looking. We can now foreground the small band as beings that are alive, so that the painting obtains other qualities. What was flat before, now acquires "real" depth. The stillness of death, figured in the camel skeleton as well as in the term *nature morte*, stands in contrast with obvious signs of life: a group of people and their animals walking the desert. The desert is not at all empty, it is *our interpretation* that renders it empty – or not.

Once we bring the small group of people back to life, the second question regarding *Le Désert* can be answered: why would De Saint-Victor qualify the painting as a still life? The full quote about *Le Désert* is worth reading:

> Still life painting if there ever was one. Imagine the painted nothingness, the emptiness sketched, a perspective of sky and sands unfolding as far as the eye can see, up until the red-hot iron bar that harshly closes the horizon.

> Tableau de nature morte s'il en fut jamais. Imaginez le néant peint, le vide dessiné, une perspective de ciel et de sable déroulée à perte de vue, jusqu'à la barre de fer rouge qui ferme durement l'horizon (De Saint-Victor quoted in Peltre 1997: 152).

Terms indicating an empty space abound: nothingness, emptiness, endless views. The passage clearly demonstrates the interests the qualification *nature morte* serves: it actively empties the image of life. There is nothing the eye can latch onto save the lifeless carcass in the foreground.

The connection between still life and emptiness of life is no coincidence; in fact, this connection must have informed the invention of the term itself. Indeed, in his path-breaking work on still life painting, Norman Bryson has argued that absence of human beings is one of still life's characteristics (1990: 60). What is more, the metaphorical collapse of representation of, on the one hand, small and everyday objects such as breakfast tables – or even more singular objects such as a cabbage and a slice of melon – and, on the other, the vast expanse of desert space, is not de Saint-Victor's alone. Philippe Jullian has asserted a particular connection between paintings of deserts and still life paintings (1997). The connection is, of course, based on the motif of death itself. As Jullian argues,

> like the skulls which baroque painters put beside jewels and flowers to symbolize the impermanence of human life, the desert was a constant reminder of ever-present death (Jullian 1977: 100).

Emptiness as produced by a perspective that humbles the people and aggrandizes space, and the contrastively large skeleton, so prominently displayed in the middle of the painting, bring home this message of death with unambiguous insistence. But once again, this interpretation – and thus de Saint-Victor's characterization of *Le Désert* as still life – is only possible on the condition that we negate human presence. De Saint-Victor thereby confirms the stereotypical tradition of interpretation.

If a focus on death does nothing but repeat the stereotype of the empty desert, what might the opposite, a focus on life, contribute to a different understanding of desert space as a negotiable boundary? We don't have to do away with all aspects of de Saint-Victor's argument, if we consider Bryson's introduction of another crucial element of still life painting – that of hospitality and conviviality. Human beings as such may be absent from still life paintings, but their actions and, indeed, their sociality are represented: what they offer their guests is the subject of the painting (Bryson 1997: 17-59). The laws of hospitality require that the guest be brought food and provided with shelter (Derrida 2000). In the most absolute sense, hospitality is about making space for the other, even if she is anonymous, or unknown. By virtue of its barrenness, desert space makes hospitality even more keenly necessary – indeed, a matter of life and death. Connecting hospitality to the practicalities of life in the desert, anthropologist Marceau Gast (1983) contends that survival in the desert depends upon social integration, on the existence of an infinite number of relations no one can do without. It is this kind of hospitality, attending to the other and to the unknown, which is practiced in the desert, yet it is also this aspect of the desert that tends to be forgotten, that remains unseen, overruled as it is by conventional images of emptiness that we bring to its representations.

Reframed in this way, de Saint-Victor's assertion that *Le Désert* is a still life painting opens up two contradictory strains in his reasoning. The first one would comply with a stereotypical reading of Guillaumet's canvas, emphasizing the absence of human beings and therefore dismissing the band of people as a mirage. The second, in line with Bryson's analysis, suggests that, rather than representing objects without human presence, still life painting is *about* hospitality; in the latter case, the band of people is a presence that requires attention. The painting of *Le Désert* is then an emblem of both the stereotypical and of the critical edge this painting makes possible; moving beyond stereotypes whose power it also recognizes, this reading facilitates a look that attends to the issues surrounding the desert as a geographical expanse. It is with this double reading in mind that I now move to a piece of theoretical discourse on the desert.

Deserts and the Oriental Other

When it comes to deserts, no theoretical piece of writing will turn out to be more influential than Deleuze and Guattari's evocation of such spaces (1992). In his well-known critique of the nomadology thesis in *Mille Plateaux*, Christopher Miller dismantles a central claim of that thesis, namely, that nomadology is non-representational and non-anthropological (1993). Miller points at Deleuze and Guattari's heavy borrowing from anthropological sources and the extensive use they make of anthropological statements. If, as Miller claims, Deleuze and Guattari's nomad thought is in fact "arborescent", it is rooted in a "violently representational, colonial ethnography" (Miller 1993: 13). While Miller's claim may be slightly overstated, it offers a useful entrance into the complex thought of the philosophers' view. The term "colonial ethnography" clarifies what, for me, is at stake: a paradoxical bond between colonialism – with an assumption of emptiness – and an ethnographic desire for encounter, as discussed in the previous chapter.

The desert is such an emblematic case because it qualifies this colonialist assumption with Orientalism – a mode of thought I have extensively discussed elsewhere.[4] This colonial ethnography shows itself in all its ramifications in Deleuze and Guattari's use of Orientalist sources and their subsequent replication of this discourse (Miller 1993: 30-31). Whereas Miller mentions this Orientalist aspect toward the end of his article, he does not elaborate on it. I would like to formulate a critique of Deleuze and Guattari's framing of nomadology by indicating how the desert functions in their discourse, and how it informs their politics of place. As I will argue, whatever else they put forth, the desert in Deleuze and Guattari's discourse becomes crucially connected to a set of references that create a semantic field in which the Orient is other.

In the chapter on nomadology, deserts are prime examples of "smooth space" and as such opposed to "striated space". Smooth space is negatively defined by lack of what constitutes its other: smooth space signifies "a field without conduits or channels", the latter being signs of striated space. Smooth space consists of "non-metric, acentered, rhizomatic multiplicities" (Deleuze and Guattari 1992: 371). Deserts fit the bill particularly well according to Deleuze and Guattari's sources, because "there is no line separating earth and sky; there is no intermediate distance, no perspective or contour; visibility is limited" (1992: 382).[5]

Even though deserts thus seem to represent smooth space *par excellence*, Deleuze and Guattari admit that oases pose a problem in their classification,

---

[4] See in particular my study of Orientalism in eighteenth and nineteenth century France (2004b) and the volume *After Orientalism*, devoted to a critical engagement with the legacy of Edward Said (Boer 2004a).

[5] For a full discussion of smooth versus striated space, see Chapter Fourteen of *A Thousand Plateaus* (474-500). Tim Cresswell has discussed smooth and striated space primarily in relation to the nomad as an urban phenomenon (1997). My discussion of deserts results in a different take on the position of nomads.

because they are like "fixed points" (1992: 371). Not part of the desert, and rather its opposite – oases are places with a fixed location. This space

> closes off a surface and "allocates" it according to determinate intervals, assigned breaks; in the smooth, one "distributes" oneself in an open space, according to frequencies and in the course of one's crossing (Deleuze and Guattari 1992: 481).

In spatial terms then, striated space divides a surface, whereas smooth space involves distribution across a surface that can vary. Oases, clearly, are striated spaces within the smooth space of the desert. They are the places where the presence of water makes agriculture, and thus sedentary life, possible. In a very visible way, oases mark the difference between smooth and striated space because of irrigation channels, signs of cultivation, palm trees, and houses. According to Deleuze and Guattari, all these elements represent striated space. But in their location and function *within* the desert, such striated spaces undermine the very notion of the desert as smooth space. For, not only are oases themselves striated; they divide and structure – and thus striate – the desert itself.

Differences between smooth and striated space also are manifest in social formations. Nomads, as a war machine, roam the smooth space of the desert whereas state apparatuses, as sedentary social formations, organize striated space. Clashes between the two social formations inhabiting opposing spaces are inevitable, because these spaces are incompatible (Deleuze and Guattari 1992: 380-81). The clashes that occur are border conflicts. But such conflicts can only be understood in this way on condition that boundaries are seen as dividing lines, not spaces themselves. In other words, if I may slightly overstate my case for the sake of clarity, these clashes are pre-determined as occurring in a completely dichotomized spatial arrangement of Deleuze and Guattari's own making.

The example of the distinction between smooth and striated space shows that binary oppositions rule nomadology. War machines are opposed to state apparatuses and, analogous to this distinction, so are, in a rendering of Dumézil's ideas, magician-kings to jurist-priests, despots to legislators; finally, the obscure, violent and fearsome is contrasted with the clear, the calm and the regulated (Deleuze and Guattari 1992: 351-52). In spite of the authors' warning that these oppositions are "only relative", what we are left with is the idea of deserts as smooth spaces, populated by war machines, magician-kings, and despots who are obscure, violent and fearsome. As a consequence of the density of references in their book, the "politics of quotation" that importantly informs *Mille plateaux* makes it difficult, if not impossible, to disentangle this image from the philosophers' thesis.[6]

I will use one example to clarify my point about the set of references that connect the desert to a semantic field in which the Orient is other: the Orient as the site of struggle between state apparatus and war machine. It might seem paradoxical to designate the Orient as such, because at the same time it is quite often mentioned as an instance of desert-like smooth space (Deleuze and Guattari 1992: 379-80; 384-85). But the Orient as a smooth space is at a disadvantage compared to the West, as Deleuze and Guattari claim. The West is victorious because in the Orient the components of the state are more disconnected, disjointed,

> necessitating a great immutable Form to hold them together: 'despotic formations', Asian or African, are rocked by incessant revolts, by secessions and dynastic changes, which nevertheless do not affect the immutability of the form (Deleuze and Guattari 1992: 385).

In a truly Marxist vein, the Orient is deemed unable to ever free itself through revolution from these despotic formations. "Immutable", "despotic", and politically unstable, the Orient is what it has always been and will always remain in the Western imagination.

Elsewhere, I have analysed the ways in which despotism has functioned as a boundary marker in Western representations of the Orient since the early eighteenth century (Boer 1995-1996; 2004b). In these representations, despotism represents the limited government, always alluring to "good" and sound government systems, such as republics or monarchies. The aim attributed to despotism's rulers is to instil fear among their people; the despot governs without laws and is at best whimsical in his conduct. The philosophical imagination discussed in this chapter, appears to be

---

[6] The concept of "the politics of quotation" is developed in Bal (1996: 195-223).

fundamentally indebted to these traditional views.[7]
Throughout the history of cross-cultural representations, this figuration of the despot can be recognized. As I have argued, this figuration is the West's ambivalent projection and desire. Violence, obscure motives, and fearsome behaviour cling to him, lawlessness characterizes his government, and his point of view sustains and multiplies his power. In spite of Deleuze and Guattari's project of transforming some key topoi of Western thought, then, their imagination of the desert cannot help but fall back on the legacy that feeds it.[8]

After first distinguishing state-form in the West and the Orient along lines of interconnectedness or disjunction, the Orient is even further split in a second instance when the desert turns out to be, undeniably, a space, not a line. As Deleuze and Guattari maintain:

> The great empires of the Orient, Africa and America *run up against* wide-open smooth spaces that *penetrate* them and maintain gaps between their components . . . : the oriental State is in direct confrontation with a nomad war machine (Deleuze and Guattari 1992: 385; emphasis added).

If we remain with the Orient as an example, it is a disjointed state form, a despotic formation that is forced to battle continuously with a nomad war machine at the edge of smooth and striated space. Hence, the Orient contains both: state-form and nomad war machine, smooth and striated space. This persistence questions the distinction itself.

The desert is the great plain, and the nomad war machine roves around this smooth space. Thus, it also concurs with Orientalist perceptions of the only possible state forms in the desert-like regions of the Middle East, North Africa and Asia, that is, unchanging despotic formations, forever and immutably other to the West. As a consequence, it will be difficult to detach the desert, as Deleuze and Guattari use the notion, from its Orientalist connotations, in spite of its varied geographical locations. But what is more to the point here, the desert of nomadology is empty, or rather, emptied out.

---

[7] For a sustained analysis along these lines of monarchy and the republic compared to despotism, see Montesquieu *De l'Esprit des lois* (1927 [1748]). For a recent investigation of despotism, see Alain Grosrichard (1979) and my criticism of both (2004b).
[8] Whereas the despot is ambivalently gendered, the nomad in *Mille plateaux* is firmly male, in spite of attempts to gender nomadic subjects as female, e.g. by Braidotti (1994, critiqued in Chapter One).

By emptying the desert, a classic gesture of primitivism according to Miller, this desert becomes a space where boundaries are inexistent (1993: 25). For, boundaries only occur where smooth and striated space meet, but do not merge. Of course, this specific understanding of boundaries is a result of the dichotomies that run through Deleuze and Guattari's analysis. As I will show in the following cases, deserts are boundaries only insofar as they are negotiable spaces, although borders do exist within the desert itself for those willing to see them. And such boundaries, because they are negotiable, have a history; they are not "natural", in spite of what our geography books have us believe. Often, these boundaries are, or contain, traces of histories, thus constituting inhabited space, a lived space of human practices.

How Empty Spaces Get Their Name

On the back cover of its 1982 edition, Claude Ollier's novel *La Mise en scène* is called a "colonial novel of adventure" and "a detective novel", "but also an astounding *documentary* on a withdrawn region of the Muslim Berber world" (1982 [1958]; emphasis added). While this combination of qualifications is apt to arouse suspicion regarding its truth claim ("documentary"), I am particularly sensitive, here, to the qualifier "colonial". For, as I have suggested above, the concept of desert appears to invoke the emptiness that moulds its referent into an object fit for colonial appropriation. As it happens, in Ollier's novel, the leading character is a geographer – a representative of the discipline that bestows regions a colour according to their "colonializability". The novel was published in 1958 and was the first novel ever to be awarded the Prix Médicis. Its literary success was bound up with its particular style, informed by the aesthetic of the "New Novel". One of the major characteristics of this literary movement was a thorough questioning of the conventions of realism, particularly in relation to the observing subject, which many New Novels staged in dramatic ways.[9]

In Ollier's novel, geographer Lassalle sets out to chart a blank space on the map of the Moroccan Atlas mountains. As was pre-ordained by his professional training, Lassalle considers the empty space as both inhabited

---

[9] Such authors as Nathalie Sarraute and theorist Alain Robbe-Grillet explored the relationship between observation and description, as well as observation and (aggressive) action. See, for example, Sarraute's *Tropismes* (1939) and Robbe-Grillet's *Le Voyeur* (1955).

and unknown, present yet absent because not represented on the map. He prepared himself through extensive study:

> Standing before the map . . . Lassalle imagines describing to himself the itinerary, as he has done every evening for some time, on the same map and the documents imparted to him by the Society: maps and sketches based on previous explorations, surveys of the future track, description of the principal obstacles, with photographs in support, and above all, studies of the topography of the Imlil basin, particularly valuable, because Imlil and its surrounding high mountain ranges, right South of Assameur, are invisible on the ordnance survey map, lost somewhere in the centre of a large unmapped zone.

> Debout devant la carte . . . Lasalle s'imagine décrire lui-même l'itinéraire, comme il le fait chaque soir depuis quelque temps déjà, sur la même carte et sur les documents que lui a communiqués la Société: plans et croquis établis au cours de précédentes reconnaissances, levés de la future piste, description des principaux obstacles, photographies à l'appui, et surtout, études sur la topographie du bassin d'Imlil, particulièrement précieuses, car Imlil et ses hautes chaines environnantes, en plein sud d'Assameur, sont invisibles sur la carte d'état-major, perdues quelque part au centre d'une vaste zone non cartographiée (Ollier 1982: 56).

In a dense integration of tenses, Lasalle muses in the diegetic present how he has been picturing to himself (in the recent past) what his surroundings will look like (in the future) during his exploratory work. By looking at the map, he is able to produce a mental map of a particularly rugged, desertic and mountainous part of the Atlas region, characterized as "lost" and "unmapped". Two years before, a colleague of Lassalle attempted what he is now to finish: to fill in the blank spaces on the map, because a road needs to be constructed for the exploration and subsequent exploitation of a mine.

Before moving into a further analysis of *La Mise en scène*, I propose to think through these observations in terms of spatial theory. In a well-known study, social geographer Edward Soja has developed the notion of the "trialectics of spatiality", as a departure from the binary notions prevailing in geographic discourse (1996: 8-12). What he calls Firstspace concerns the concrete materiality of spatial forms, with things that can be empirically mapped. Secondspace is conceived space, the domain of representations and images (1996: 10). The dualisms set Firstspace up against Secondspace, that is, objectivity versus subjectivity, material versus mental, and real versus imagined. What Soja calls Thirdspace reflects the thirding of spatial dialectics, the lived practice of mapped space, by Henri Lefebvre (1991). Even though Soja's Thirdspace remains somewhat vague, it is possible and fruitful to reformulate the gist of *La Mise en scène* in spatial terms.

When Lassalle looks at the map, it shows him what should be "there": villages, mule paths, dry riverbeds, and mountain ranges, all of them signs on the map. This map represents Firstspace. Lassalle scrutinizes the map and the other material provided by the Society, and imagines himself describing his itinerary through the landscape represented by the map. In other words, before embarking on his expedition he already projects the retrospective account he will be able to give. The projection of Lassalle's reading of the map into mental images can be called Secondspace.

However, what a map shows are signs, dots representing villages, but not the people inhabiting them: Lassalle charts the road leading to a mine, yet considers this track only a minor intrusion into the lived practice of space of the people owning the land. As it happens, he will need interpreters and guides since he does not speak the language of the region. In fact, in terms of Soja's terminology, *La Mise en scène* on the whole might be interpreted as a failure on the part of Lassalle to read Thirdspace.

Lassalle prepared himself for this project in certain ways appropriate to his professional identity – he studied surveys, maps and photos. But he comes wholly unprepared in other ways. He has not invested any of his time in the people inhabiting the region. An encounter can only take place in the present anticipated in the quoted passage. A captain in the village from which he departs informs Lassalle about the people of Imlil:

> You'll find the people of Imlil very sympathetic. Highly independent in character, of course, like all the tribes from the high ranges, distrustful even, very irresponsive once they suspect you of wanting to meddle in their business but, by contrast, likeable and hospitable when you have gained their trust.

> Les gens d'Imlil sont très sympathiques, vous verrez. Très indépendants de caractère, bien sûr, comme toutes les tribus de haute montagne, méfiants même, très fermés dès qu'ils vous soupçonnent de vouloir vous mêler de leurs affaire, mais en revanche aimables, hospitaliers, quand vous avez gagné leur confiance (Ollier 1982: 53).

This speech harbours all the major aspects of the ethnographic encounter as we have seen it function in the previous chapter. Hospitality is the meeting place, the site where encounter becomes possible. It is the opposite of colonial appropriation. The mentioning of the related and accumulated notions of independence and distrust, irresponsiveness and suspicion in this speech contain a subtle threat, followed by well-meant advice of how to reap the benefits of a positive attitude. Actually, the captain provides Lassalle with a model of benevolent colonial rule: once he gains the trust of Imlil's inhabitants they will be likeable, but when he interferes in their affairs he will be distrusted. Lassalle's problem turns out to be his ignorance of the language; he neither speaks nor understands Arabic let alone the Berber language spoken by the people he will encounter. In view of Assia Djebar's thoughts on her use of French against the acoustic backdrop of Arabic and Berber, this ignorance is especially meaningful. It turns Djebar's polyphonic language into a depleted, limited language, which is univocally that of the colonial power. Hence the book cover's characterization of the novel as "colonial".

On his way to Imlil, and to his great fortune, Lassalle encounters Ba Iken, an inhabitant of Imlil, who guides him to Asguine from where he will conduct his survey. With his impeccable French, his grey-blue eyes and his profound knowledge of the region, Ba Iken is the perfect go-between, representing the in-between in terms of language as well as (racial) appearance. Like an ideal local informant helping the ethnographer, he informs Lassalle about local relations, family ties and the surroundings of the village. However, in other respects Ba Iken seems to hold back crucial insights, a reticence that initiates the novel's suspense – the motor of detective fiction, that other characterization on the cover.[10]

These withheld insights concern the mysterious murder of a young woman and the death of a geologist named Lessing. Both events have taken place just before Lassalle's arrival; both are surrounded by speculation. Because Lassalle is focalizing the events, the reader is presented with his speculative, uncertain interpretation of the events only. Lassalle might be a good reader of maps, but a good interpreter of the people of Imlil he is not. And how could he be, without access to the language yet informed by pre-established knowledge, shaped by geographical visualizations?

---

[10] Many New Novels deploy generic allusions to detective fiction to make their point on the artificiality of fiction. See, for example, Robbe-Grillet's *Les Gommes* (1953).

As it turns out, Lassalle meddles with the affairs of the inhabitants in two ways: he inquires incessantly into the dead girl and Lessing, while simultaneously investigating the best route for the future track to the mine. In both processes, Lassalle neglects local conditions and lived practices. His attempt to fill in the blank on the map runs parallel to exploring the unknown circumstances of both deaths. Death – we recognize the topos of still life and mirage. The combination of intrusions suggests that charting the map is also an act of violence that brings danger. Ba Iken, of whom Lassalle grows ever more suspicious, is his sole source of information. One telling instance of this epistemic limitation and dependency concerns an encounter with Idder, a man living in the village. Ba Iken acts as a translator not just for Idder's words, but for his concerns as well. In a significant passage that ponders the conception of boundaries as lines involved in the act of mapping, and the consequent intrusion upon inhabited territory, the act of translation is represented in a way that alerts us to this inevitable cultural aspect of translation:

> – He wants you to know. He doesn't want to leave before.
> – Well, okay, what does he want from me?
> – He is saying that yesterday and today, you crossed his land, down there, on the other side of Asguine.
> – Yes, I have seen him. He even attempted to quarrel with Ichou.
> – Right, and then he says you had your "demarcation" in your hand.
> – My demarcation?
> – Yes, your map, your plan . . . And so he believes that you will have the track cross his piece of land and he is furious. He wants to know nothing about . . .
> While Ba Iken is explaining, the man continues to point his index-finger in the direction of the plot, there . . . then several times over, he passes his left hand over his throat . . .
> – Don't worry, Ba Iken concludes. He has this habit of yelling.

> – Il dit que tu dois savoir. Il ne veut pas partir avant.
> – Bon, eh bien, qu'est-ce qu'il me veut ?
> – Il dit qu'hier et aujourd'hui tu es passé sur son champ, là-bas, de l'autre côté d'Asguine.
> – Oui, je l'ai vu, bien sûr. Il a même cherché querelle à Ichou.
> – Bon, alors il dit que tu avais ton "bornage" à la main.
> – Mon bornage ?
> – Oui, ta carte, ton plan . . . Alors il croit que vous allez faire passer la piste sur son terrain et il est furieux, il ne veut rien savoir . . .

Pendant que Ba Iken explique, l'homme continue de brandir son index en direction de la parcelle, là-bas . . . puis il passe sa main gauche, à plusieurs reprises, sur sa gorge . . .
– Ne t'en fais pas, conclut Ba Iken. Il a l'habitude de crier comme ça (Ollier 1982: 160-61).

In this act of cultural translation, Idder comes across as a particularly quarrelsome figure, yelling and screaming, making aggressive gestures. Note there is a great ambivalence here. The gesture of passing his hand over his throat can be as much a threat as an expression of fear for himself, indicating that Lasalle's geographical conquest threatens his, Idder's, welfare. Ba Iken attempts to normalize the situation by pointing out that screaming is Idder's habit. Representing the local inhabitant as a slightly hysterical over-actor is one way to reassure the Western geographer.

What is not taken into consideration – and Lassalle's continuous focalization doesn't allow for it – is the question whether Idder's complaints are justified. Someone is trespassing upon Idder's land with a map in his hand. With great insight in the different kinds of spaces – resonating with Soja three spaces – Idder interprets the map as a boundary-making device. The kind of boundaries that maps produce is that of geography's Firstspace, the line that only separates one space from another, consisting of no real space in itself. This kind of boundary does, indeed, threaten Idder's existence within the space that is thus denied. Hence, Idder has every reason to suspect Lassalle of stealing his land.

Lassalle cannot see what Idder's problem is. The man's anger is fully mistaken in Lassalle's opinion. The geographer tries to reassure the two men:

– But Ba Iken this is a misunderstanding! First of all, nothing has been decided. Besides, the track may very well avoid his land . . . may go around it at the edge of the hillock and pass a little higher. Tell him he has nothing to fear. Moreover, if we would ever chip some meters of his piece of land, we would pay him a compensation.

– Mais c'est un malentendu, Ba Iken! D'abord, rien n'est décidé. Et puis, la piste peut très bien éviter son champ . . . le contourner à la sortie du mamelon et passer un peu au-dessus. Dis-lui qu'il n'a rien à craindre. Et puis, si jamais on rognait quelques mètres de son terrain, on lui verserait une indemnité (Ollier 1982: 161).

The estimation of the conflict by Lassalle shows a different picture: not the threat of loss of land, but a misunderstanding that can be solved through a change in the track's route or financial compensation. Conforming to the colonial attitude, the possibility of serious adaptation to the local situation is not even considered. If the map so decides, a few square meters can simply be taken, as long as some money changes hands.

As a consequence of the clash with Idder, interpreted by Ba Iken, Lassalle becomes more and more suspicious. His suspicions extend beyond Idder's complaints about his land: without much proof Idder gets connected to the death of the young woman and Lessing's death as well. In a rather grotesque reversal of the situation, Idder is being criminalized by Lassalle who invests him with an aggression that was evoked by Lassalle's behaviour in the first place. In the wake of suspecting Idder, Lassalle also grows to doubt Ba Iken's words and deeds.

On a symbolic level, *La Mise en scène* posits the coincidence of two dead bodies and the act of mapping by a representative of colonial presence. Thus, the capture of the land is connected to two dead bodies through a process of filling in the blanks. Yet filling in the blanks is what Lassalle is ordered to do, as he, and his superiors, believe the land to be empty. His map – Firstspace – showed him a blank and therefore in his imagination – Secondspace – there is no such thing as ownership of the land. This is a colonizer's comfortable assumption of emptiness, not recognizing Thirdspace, the lived practice of space and place. Not for a moment does the notion of blanc, hence, of emptiness, seem to be challenged, in spite of the obvious and, here, hostile assertion of inhabitation.

Lassalle's failure to interpret Thirdspace inevitably brings him into conflict. He remains deeply suspicious, despite several invitations from inhabitants of the Imlil basin, despite his dependence upon Ba Iken who interprets for him, and despite some men saving his life during a torrential rainstorm. And these doubts prevent him from any real contact with the people he meets. Encounter becomes impossible. Idder complains about Lassalle's intrusion on his land, pointing out that existing boundaries should be respected. Lassalle considers the empty space on his map as smooth space, to echo Deleuze and Guattari's terminology, in order to render it into striated space. But space was already striated, albeit not according to Lassalle's interpretation. In a gesture repeating and reinforcing the colonialist practice, Lassalle moves about looking for the most advantageous track, without recognizing ownership, boundaries or the histories of the land. For him, "blanc" land is itself a boundary, the one between civilization and its opposite. Hence, he not even considers the possibility that the space he disposes of is negotiable.

An Exploded Sense of Desert

Tahar Djaout, a young Algerian author assassinated in 1993 during the Algerian civil war, is perhaps most insistent in his search for the desert.[11] Djaout's narrator traverses deserts, speculates about them in geographical surroundings that have nothing to do with deserts, and uses the desert metaphorically in a variety of ways. He also writes the history of a famous historical teacher of Islam. And yet, the result is not an image of the desert as the Western imagination has it. Instead, this narrator offers an exploded sense of coming to grips with a phenomenon.

The male narrator in Djaout's novel *L'Invention du désert* (1987) has been asked to write the history of the Almoravids, a medieval dynasty that, from their land at the borders of the Sahara, subjected the whole of North Africa. But instead of concentrating on the history of the Almoravids as the narrator was told to do, he gives in to his fascination for the figure of Ibn Toumert. Ibn Toumert was a reformer in the twelfth century, a Berber from Morocco who had travelled to Mecca for the pilgrimage or *haj*. Attracted by his strict adherence to the Koran, he gained a following on his way back. Carrying nothing but a walking stick of olive wood, Ibn Toumert became the scare of all those who had become lax in following the laws of Islam. Under his spiritual leadership, considered a *Mahdi* by his followers, the Almohad dynasty replaced the Almoravids (Hourani 1992: 84-85). A *Mahdi* is a spiritual leader who is himself under guidance. Since the early days of Islam, there is a powerful belief that a *Mahdi*, "he who is guided", will stand up and restore justice in a world that has gone astray. In the course of his narrative, the history of the people from the desert coming to power begins to mingle

---

[11] For an extended text of mourning on the brutal assassinations of Algerian intellectuals during the civil war, see Djebar (1995).

with the narrator's own history, a fact acknowledged from the beginning: "My (hi)story, according to all appearances, is in danger of transforming into biography" (Mon histoire risque, selon toute apparence, de se transformer en biographie [Djaout 1987: 17]).[12]

In a large city in the North, recognizable as Paris, the narrator works on his manuscript in the midst of winter. Likening winter in Algeria, his fatherland, to his present surroundings leads to a peculiar semblance as well:

> But winter here is a winter of empty pavements, mercilessly straight. No space for those small hills with shrubs where dead birds hide out. There is so much frost under the skin and so much loneliness behind closed windows. Sometimes white shadows, mealy-mouthed, pass by, women wrested from the mirages of a city drier than the driest of deserts. One can try to torture one's unconscious to give birth in it to an oasis with its rustling of palm trees and its lazy birds, you find yourself powerless, entangled in the speckles of a cold whiteness – oh! not this other whiteness: in the surroundings of Ouargla, land sown with salt as if it had snowed in the furrows.

> Mais l'hiver ici est un hiver de pavés chauves, impitoyables de rectitude. Sans place pour les monticules buissonneux où se fourvoient les oiseaux morts. Il y a tellement de gel sous la peau et de solitude derrière les fenêtres closes. Des ombres blanches, douceureuses, passent parfois, femmes arrachées aux mirages d'une ville plus aride que le plus aride des déserts. On a beau torturer son inconscient pour y faire naître une oasis avec ses bruissements de palmes et ses oiseaux paresseux, on se retrouve impuissant, empêtré dans les mailles d'une blancheur froide – oh! pas cette autre blancheur: aux environs de Ouargla, terres ensemencées de sel comme s'il avait neigé dans les sillons (Djaout 1987: 13).

Djaout's discourse is so metaphorical the translation cannot do justice. The pavements of the city are qualified as "bold" (chauves), a personification that is then elaborated in terms of personality, by means of words such as mercilessness and intransigence or straightness (rectitude). The city has a skin, a personifying element that establishes continuity between the outside

---

[12] The French word "histoire" does not differentiate between story and history. For a similar procedure to integrate a personal history with the history of peoples from the desert, see Memmi (1977). Of an altogether different character is the estimation of Jean-Charles Humbert when he speaks without notable irony about the Sahara's encounter with history: "In 1900, the Sahara encountered History: French troops, in marching charge and under gunfire had just entered the oasis In Salah for the first time, last stop towards the final occupation of the Sahara" (1996: 5; translation mine).

with its frost and the inside with its metaphorical frost of solitude. The sentence that introduces the figure of the feminine also makes the comparison between the social and the physical deserts explicit. The city leaves no space even for the insignificant details (small hills with shrubs on it, where dead birds linger) of the North African landscape. With an exclamatory, perhaps nostalgic "oh!" the narrator presents even a salt desert as preferable because less frosty than the city. As a metaphorical desert, the Northern city exudes whiteness, a whiteness that is cold. Within these cold surroundings, imagining an oasis is virtually impossible. Explicitly, the desert's salty whiteness is very different from, doubtlessly preferable to, the ice and frost so prominent in the North.

Thus the relation between North and South is elaborated in various ways facilitated by metaphoricity: both contrasts and similarities are at play. The geographical desert as a place is compared and then contrasted with the metaphorical desert of the Northern city. Both show whiteness, but whiteness of a different kind. North and South become connected in other respects as well. The narrator travelled to the North, to France, "a little Eden", like many of his fellow countrymen. He is the mediator, like every other migrant, between paradise and daily life in Algeria. The writer carries his project in his head "like those urns in which Indians, according to their migrations, transport the bones of their ancestors" (Ma tête est semblable à ces outres où les Indiens transportent, au gré de leur migrations, les os de leurs ancêtres [Djaout 1987: 26]). The metaphor generates a metonymy: like a literalized synecdoche, here the writer's urn contains the history of the Almoravids, the history of the South.

Initially, the narrator had moved to the North in order to write this history, but clearly he needs to go South to finish his project. Piecing together his information, remembering a pulverized dynasty, is not just a matter of writing in cold cities, as he ascertains, but also of traversing the very same geographical expanses Ibn Toumert negotiated (Djaout 1987: 26; 40). Language and geography converge; writing becomes geography conceived as Thirdspace. And, as the metaphors in the passage quoted above already intimated, the desert with its salt becomes the "salt of the earth". For, unlike many others who travel the desert to escape or seek unknown sensations (Henry 1983), the narrator needs the desert, that reputedly barren space, as nourishment for his intellectual work:

> It is rather a way for me to look at the interior, because since time immemorial the desert has inhabited and enlightened me. A lantern lighted in my breast that demands to be fed incessantly.

> C'est plutôt une manière pour moi de regarder vers l'intérieur, car le désert m'habite et m'illumine depuis des temps indéterminés. Un fanal éclos dans ma poitrine et qui demande à être sans cesse alimenté (Djaout 1987: 27).

Traversing the desert is a need for the narrator to reach within himself. Without it, he would probably not be able to write the story of Ibn Toumert. In view of the tradition of conceiving the intellect in terms of light, most obvious in the Western concept of enlightenment, the metaphors of light and nourishment can be interpreted as integrating physical and intellectual well-being.

The desert encountered by the narrator is a very different place from the desert Ibn Toumert travelled. Assembled in a taxi speeding at 130 kilometres per hour along the roads towards the South of Algeria, accompanied by a singing voice from a cassette, the passengers encounter a road sign every now and then, an oasis, or stop at a hotel with a swimming pool. Due to a thorough restructuring of the desert's economy, tourists flock to the remotest places and nomads become sedentary: the desert's endlessness is conquered (Gast 1983; Massey 1994: 125-45; Conley 1998).

Yet, this is but one appearance of the desert; it also shows itself in all its barrenness:

> The landscape is nothing but a lure, a pre-ordained void where shadow itself is absent: a succession of barely real dunes that can bypass one another or sag under the influence of an unexpected wind. At times, at intervals that undoubtedly are very long, we see skeletal, solitary stalks, single markers that restore some reality to a disincarnated landscape.

> Le paysage n'est qu'un leurre, un vide décrété où l'ombre elle-même est exclue: une succession de dunes à peine réelles qui sous l'effet d'un vent inopiné peuvent s'enjamber ou s'avaler. Nous voyons, à des intervalles temporels qui sont sans doute très longs, des stipes squelettiques et solitaires, seuls jalons qui redonnent quelque réalité à un paysage désincarné (Djaout 1987: 30).

Staring out of the taxi at a landscape that bears a striking resemblance to Guillaumet's painting *Le Désert*, all sorts of dangers are evoked by the narrator. As a lure, the desert might pull you in, never to set you free again. One might die in the desert, adding one more skeleton to the ones already present, or lose one's sense of time. These are mere speculations, although they appeal to the sense of uncanniness of the imaginarily empty space.

In Djaout's *L'Invention du désert* however, the desert is not one, but many. It may be empty on first sight, but traces disclose how the desert has been inhabited. Take Tehouda, a town founded in dust. A town of which the narrator tells us that "Tehouda is not a historic place, it is not a place in any sense. Tehouda doesn't exist" (Tehouda n'est pas un lieu d'histoire, elle n'est même pas un lieu tout court. Tehouda n'existe pas [Djaout 1987: 31]). It does not exist, the narrator claims, because there is no road sign pointing to it, no commemorative plaque inscribing its history in the present. Yet it is the site of the history of the Maghreb.

But one can hardly call Tehouda a non-place in Marc Augé's terminology (1995). In Tehouda, small mausoleums of saints, partially covered by sand, tell the stories of Okba, and of La Kahina, seventh-century chieftainess and resistance fighter against the Romans (Apter 1999: 59). These are the stories that make for crucial histories of the desert: Tehouda is at the crossroads of various histories onto which the narrator's own history is added. The absence of writing is at the same time an evocation of the palimpsestic writings that make up the place.

Hence, in a movement back and forth between Firstspace and Secondspace the desert reveals and covers up histories; traces become visible and disappear again. This suggestion of endless palimpsests is also an evocation of a particular meaning of boundaries. Borders are flexible in such surroundings because every marker will eventually vanish in a physical sense, yet might be remembered for generations to come. And still, as he asserts "the whole history of the country [the country of birth of the narrator] is a history of land-surveying" (Djaout 1987: 121). Hence, there is a continuous push and pull between marking the land, as we have seen in Ollier's *La Mise en scène*, and the narrator's realization that territory is not demarcated, cannot be marked in any precise and definitive way. In my view of the desert as boundary and boundary as negotiated, hence, lived space – in other words as Thirdspace – the impossibility to mark the space is precisely what constitutes it as functional and productive boundary space.

Deserts, then, might be moving phenomena, metaphorical or not, residing in Northern cities, in the narrator's head, or in the tundra of regions even further North (Djaout 1987: 123; 134). Likewise, Ibn Toumert, errant reformer of former times, is moving. A traveller across time and space, Ibn Toumert materializes in Paris, walking the Champs-Élysées, his senses bombarded by advertisements, nude pictures, and scarcely clad pedestrians. His world is turned upside down. Even when he meets his fellow country-men in the Parisian neighbourhoods of Barbès and Goutte-d'Or, neighbourhoods with a large North African population, or perhaps especially then, he is aware of his different status. A status that sets him apart not just from the French but, in a sense, from humanity as a whole, "because to be an immigrant does not mean one is not living in a country that is not one's own, but one is living in a non-place, outside any territory" (Car être immigré, ce n'est pas vivre dàns un pays qui n'est pas le sien, c'est vivre dans un non-lieu, c'est vivre hors des territoires [Djaout 1987: 53]).

In the process of writing, the narrator's difficulty in "locating" the history of the Almoravids runs parallel to the difficulty of locating "the" desert. He asks himself: "Are the Almoravids somehow behind this? The desert invades me. [It] ferries me across in its malleable wanderings" (Les Almoravides y sont-ils pour quelque chose? Le désert m'envahit. Me transborde dans ses errances malléables [Djaout 1987: 61]). His response is more travel across other deserts, among them deserts in Saudi Arabia, Yemen and Aden. In a process of travelling across these deserts – both the geographical phenomena mapped as Firstspace, and the metaphorical instances of deserts, Secondspace – the trialectics of spatiality enable the narrator to craft ever-closer connections between his personal history and the histories he puts in writing. It is in these crucial connections that Thirdspace is being articulated.

The narrator's story is part of a chain of stories about the desert extending back to his great-grandfather. This ancestor told the story of his pilgrimage to Mecca to his mother; she in her turn passed the history on to her son. When her son grows to maturity, he sets out to visit Saudi Arabia, Yemen and Aden. Arriving in Djedda he finds himself to be a follower of his great-grandfather and of Ibn Toumert. The narrator is about the same age as Ibn

Toumert was when he passed Djedda on his way to Mecca; his great-grandfather had made such a long journey across the North African desert landscapes that he arrived in Djedda too late for the *haj*. He had to wait a full year for the next period of *haj*. This ancestor is the narrator's link to Ibn Toumert; he is conducive to the narrator in his understanding of his own history and that of Ibn Toumert, of a modern world to which Ibn Toumert belongs as much as he is part of an older world (Djaout 1987: 71; 76).

Ibn Toumert accompanies the narrator in the latter's own pilgrimage and as a descendant of his ancestor pilgrim:

> For a similar journey, I would have loved to have a head vibrant and pure like my ancestor; I would have loved Ibn Toumert to accompany me not as a book to be written, not as the piss smell of old documents, but as an unrestrained burst of blood that pushes me to defy the sun, that crams me with the ruses of warriors while the desert encircles me with its traps.

> J'aurais tant aimé avoir pour un voyage pareil la tête vibrante et vierge de l'ancêtre; j'aurais aimé qu'Ibn Toumert m'accompagne non pas comme un livre à écrire, non pas comme une odeur pisseuse de vieille documentation, mais comme un sang incontinent qui me pousse à défier le soleil, qui me bourre d'astuces guerrières lorsque le désert m'encercle de ses pièges (Djaout 1987: 76).

The narrator's desire for purity, a virgin head like a tabula rasa, cannot be fulfilled, as he very well knows. Within his head – the urn containing his history – he carries the elements necessary to complete the story of Ibn Toumert and, through him, the story of the Almoravids.

These two histories mingle with the narrator's history. Perhaps they can only be told because of the imbrications with a personal history. Together, they bring forth images of the desert as a multiple, inhabited, palimpsestic geographical and metaphorical place. Djaout's project can thus be read as a project to inhabit the desert with histories wherever they are, inhabiting them as lived spaces. Indeed, as contemporary visual artists also intimate, historicity and Thirdspaceness go hand in hand. Time and space inhabit the desert, which consequently is far from empty; far, that is, from being available for colonization.

Inhabited Tracks: Deserts as Lived Spaces

Ollier's geographer was so obsessed with the track he was to design that he could not see the field inhabited and cultivated by Idden. However, tracks can also be signs of life and interconnected histories within the space of the desert, as we will see in the art of photographer Raymond Depardon and Morocco-born artist Titouan Lamazou. Their joint project, commissioned by the Fondation Cartier in Paris, came about on the occasion of an exhibition on deserts (Depardon and Lamazou 2000).[13] The resulting series of seventy-two works are intimately collaborative: Depardon made photographs onto which Lamazou subsequently added drawings. Depardon considers the drawings as "second interpretations", invoking a temporal dimension in the production and interpretation process while also foregrounding the interpretive nature of photography.

While making the photos, Depardon was well aware of the second interpretation to come. Indeed, he anticipated them. Deliberately, he left the image a bit empty to give room to Lamazou for his drawings, a gesture clearly appreciated by Lamazou. As the latter asserts, "it was more simple to intervene by drawing on photos that were pure and empty like the desert, than on images with people on them" (2000: n.p.). We recognize the by-now familiar motif of emptiness. Lamazou sees the similarity between deserts and photos in their common emptiness and purity, based on their lack of people. Which is not to say that this is the case with each photograph.

One of these pictures, for example, has an inhabitant of the desert in the foreground, half-length, and so sturdily enveloped in protective clothing against sand storms that it is hard to see whether this figure is represented from the front or the back, let alone whether it is a male or a female figure. Due to perspective, the half figure of the human dwarfs the mountains that cut the image in half, in the middle ground. Over this black and white photograph Lamazou has drawn the outline of a prostate ram – the animal Abraham sacrificed in Izaak's stead – in ochre, the predominant colour of the desert. The intriguing question whether the artist also considers this an empty image – a view that the composition would almost allow! – will have to be

---

[13] This publication provides information about planning, collaboration and production of the works. The catalogue does not contain page numbers.

left aside for now, although the answer is of importance. What interests me here is that his contention makes it possible for me to add onto his "second" interpretation, and thus tie some of the strands of my argument together.

Figure 5. Titouan Lamazou et Raymond Depardon (2000). *Carnet de voyage du desert*. "Sahara" (Tombouctou, Mali). Dessin sur une photographie de Raymond Depardon. Paris: Collection Fondation Cartier pour l'art contemporain.

Were I to follow the process of production of this work, I would start with the photo (figure 5). The photo shows a desert landscape with barely perceptible elevations and a sand dune. Most prominently, however, are the deep tracks in the sand curving from the foreground towards the left. A vehicle apt for transportation in desert environments, like a truck or a four-wheel drive, must have produced those tracks. The angle of the photo is such that it creates the impression that we as spectators are inside the truck, looking through the rear window and watching the tracks just drawn in the sand. Thus, the tracks can be interpreted as an indication of movement or travel – be it of people inhabiting the desert or of tourists. At the very least, we can see those tracks as a sign of human presence, however empty the desert might seem.

In a number of other works, trucks occur prominently. In one, a skeleton of an overturned rusty old truck figures in the centre of the photograph, with only a small palm tree blown sideways by the wind in the background. Over this, the artist has drawn a sketch of a young human face, a bit to the left of the truck, and again, in ochre, as if to recall and commemorate the driver who may have died when his truck was blown off balance. On the next page, the incongruous, tiny gas pump is almost hidden by the drawn outline of a page-filling truck. The subsequent page in the catalogue shows a tiny truck in the photograph itself, as well as a driver inside a truck, with the rear-view mirror visible – and over this image a decorative flowery pattern and a somewhat abstract, perhaps animal-like outline is drawn.

To return to the work reproduced here, through the indentations in the sand, the desert's space becomes quite literally striated and will remain so for a long time, until the sand covers the tracks. On the basis of this image I submit that the desert, in contrast to Deleuze and Guattari's dichotomizing qualifications of it, is a space where a continuous negotiation takes place. Various peoples cross the desert, make use of it – or abuse it as Ollier's *La Mise en scène* showed. Consequently, it is never empty. Nomads and state apparatus do not meet at the edge, a border where desert and cultivated lands or city dwellers come into contact. On the contrary, deserts are covered by tracks, borders and other kinds of demarcations that are not lines but form spaces.

As Marceau Gast has argued, in the language of the Touareg, many words and terms designate the desert (1983). The variety of terms have to do, among other things, with the presence or absence of water, of pastures and the dimensions of the desert. Hence, what might look smooth from the outside is in fact a varied landscape in which all sorts of flexible demarcations are present, which draw and redraw spaces through time.

Lamazou's drawings considered as interpretations further compound this density. Through these drawings, and in figure 5 in particular, the interpretation acquires more complexity and adds more layers onto our previous observations. Over the tracks on the photo, Lamazou drew a tent in sandy colours. Note that the tent is *on* the tracks, not next to them. Through the outlines of the tent, we can still see the truck's marks. It is this placing of the tent that leads us to read the tent and the tracks *together*, despite their apparent contrary connotations. This togetherness is not harmonious. The tent is drawn, deliberately it seems to me, in defiance of the laws of perspective. The truck's tracks, by contrast, are almost paradigmatic of those laws: wide apart at the bottom of the picture, they come together as they recede into the distance. However, they deviate from the straight itinerary by veering sharply to the right, which takes the vanishing point out of the field of vision.

The dis-harmonious integration of photograph and drawing evokes both modern means of transportation and flexible forms of housing, as it also deploys the modern and the traditional means of expression, photography and drawing; here tradition and modernity doubly interact in the desert's space. As I have argued with respect to Djaout's *L'Invention du désert*, tracks, visible or not, connect various and varying histories: personal histories link up with the history of peoples, of religious beliefs, of men and women living in the desert, wherever the desert might be located. Because the tent is placed over the tracks, the tracks become inhabited twice over: by the perhaps foreign but supposedly geographically alert driver of the truck as well as by the supposedly indigenous tent dwellers. In the light of these conditions, Lamazou's assertion that a photo of the desert without people is more pure and empty cannot hold, and it must be taken with an ironical grain of salt. The desert was always already inhabited.

In this chapter, I have argued for the recognition that the desert is not empty. In spite of the radical thrust of the theory it allegedly feeds, Deleuze and Guattari maintain a stereotypical idea of the desert flavoured with Orientalist connotations that characterize the Orient as other. Their place of enunciation is firmly Western. Claude Ollier's novel is a good example of a clash of perspectives, staged in the clash between the characters. Lassalle's failure to read Thirdspace prevents him from seeing and acknowledging the other perspectives he encounters. This is one meaning that we can assign to the novel's title, *La Mise en scène*.

Lasalle's perspective of the desert, just like that of Deleuze and Guattari, is effectively subverted by the many deserts conjured up by Tahar Djaout. This author also brings forth a change in perspective: it is only from the outside that the desert seems empty, for those who do not read the signs of presence.

From the inside, every trace tells a history; in the desert empty space does not exist. And when the truck driver and the tent dwellers run into each other, when the mechanically reproducible photograph and the unique, vulnerable drawing meet, negotiation can get underway. Only in that sense can the desert with its material specificity – of which Lamazou's ochre is a trace – come to stand for a more general notion of boundaries. For the boundaries that they are: spaces, not lines. Only then can the lines that cross them become meaningful signs of inter-cultural activity; indeed, of encounter.

FIVE

Just a Fashion? Cultural Cross-Dressing

On Sexiness Today

Figure 6. "The Secrets of Love". Diesel advertisement (March 1996). In *Elle* (Dutch edition). Permission by Diesel S. P. A. and *Elle*.

Just a fashion? If fashion is as innocuous and ordinary as we tend to assume, it wouldn't do to debate, in a book on the cultural construction of boundaries, something as frivolous as the Rudolf Valentino look-alike turned female fortune-teller, used to sell Diesel Jeans shorts by means of the message of love (figure 6). Just a fashion? Then, there is nothing to worry about concerning this modern woman (figure 7) reclining on fur. Fashion tells us – as in Buñuel's late masterpiece *Belle de jour* starring the queen of perversion, Catherine Deneuve (1967) – that we can safely mix signs from different cultural domains, and indeed, cultures, in the glamorous clothing of the 1996-97 winter fashion.

Such reassurance is also conveyed by means of the accompanying text to the image, which states:

> Sleek, ankle-length skirts and dresses, tantalizing slits and shiny ornaments. The attitude of Yves Saint-Laurent's muse Catherine Deneuve mixed with Bianca Jagger's and Jerry Hall's glam rock. Gold is OK, fake fur is chic and lurex no longer a superfluous luxury.

Figure 7. "Belle de Jour" (September 1996). In *Elle* (Dutch edition), 110-111. By permission of Cornelie Tollens and *Elle*.

The images of these two ads, however, propose more than the latest in fashion and merit close analysis. *Belle de jour*, Luis Buñuel's well-known film is but one of the possible intertexts invoked in the title and text accompanying the photo. Other references are at play as well, such as common expressions. Take for example the references to the beauty of the woman in the photo, as in *belle comme le jour*, meaning "to be a divine beauty". Interestingly, belle de jour also has a specific botanical meaning. Bindweed, a genus of plants characterized by their twining and vine-like branches and stems, has flowers that are in bloom one day only. Like the sinuous lines of a twining plant, whose flowers quickly fade but seduce as long as their short lives last, the model's undulating form refers to a body, twisting and turning, displaying the precious beauty, distant and mysterious, of a Catherine Deneuve, or in the more outgoing versions, of a Bianca Jagger or a Jerry Hall.

The combined intertexts of Buñuel's film and botany draw attention to the sinuous lines of the model's body. In that respect, I want to point out yet another intertext, namely the image's resemblance to the ways odalisques were depicted in Orientalist painting. This Orientalist intertext is notably visible, even emblematized in the serpentine line of the body. We recognize this line, and the ensuing eroticism, in paintings of the nineteenth-century Orientalist tradition, for example in Jean-Dominique Ingres' *La Grande odalisque* from 1914 (Ockman 1995). Heavy ornaments furthermore characterized the Orientalist tradition – as echoed in the excessive jewellery the model wears.[1]

Dressing as the Belle de jour, then, is a way to enter the world of movie stars and fashion models, but also of other connotations cultivated by Orientalism, such as laziness, passivity, and perversion. Highly gender-specific, both traditions are muses fit to stimulate men's inspiration, and both employ highly cultured references to the Orient mixed freely with nature. An example for Western women? Just a fashion? One message is clear, a message concerning identity. What such ads say upfront is, what matters in your appearance is not what you are, but what you want to be, or even more, it is not what you want to be, but what you want to become, temporarily,

---

[1] For labor conditions in the globalized fashion production process, see Naomi Klein (2000: 202-29).

ambivalently, as a fiction. In this chapter I will examine some implications of
this fictionality.

Contemporary Odalisks

In the *Diesel* ad, a Diesel Magic Ball will tell you everything about the No.1
mystery for mankind since the Big Bang, that is, the secrets of love. This
strictly modern cliché of the eternal importance of love obscures historicity
and, subsequently, geographical and cultural specificity, even in such a time-
bound phenomenon as fashion. Our Rudolf Valentino look-alike, evoking a
star whose very name is already a sign for love and who would have send
women swooning in earlier days, has been able to conjure an image in his
crystal ball. We see a young white woman, playing innocent, yet her hands
holding on to dangling strings of white beads or pearls, strings that might
surround her uncovered belly anytime to send her into the gyrations of a belly
dancer. And what is it that this Orientalized gender-bender, cross-dressing as
a woman, flaunting headscarf with beads, polished nails, and exuberant
jewellery, yet maintaining his two-day beard, is asking us to see? His or her
power to not only conjure the white beauty with her belly ready to turn
Oriental, but also, given his or her eyes seductively cast our way, to conjure
our own image in the mirror of the crystal ball sexiness.

What can be the rationale of this emphatic mixing of Occidental and
Oriental signs? The product to be sold, the blue jeans – the uniform of
Western hipness – is utterly Occidental. This simultaneous attempt to lure us
into buying jeans and the allusion to fortune-tellers suggests that the
globalized capitalism from which such ads spring has a stake in cultural
mixing. The fortuneteller, a profession traditionally associated with Roma
and hence, from within Western geographical vagueness, with the Orient, is
conventionally female, dirty and deceptive. Here, the figure cannot be
determined to be single-gendered, nor to possess only one cultural identity.
Sexual seduction and theft – in other words, financial seduction – are overtly
merged. But whatever the first association coming to mind, the mix of
Occidental and Oriental clichés, of sexual and mysterious, female and male
seductions, is clearly meant to be striking. This overt Orientalism at the end
of the twentieth century points to the problems and complexities of cultural
cross-dressing.

Cultural cross-dressing elicits fantasy. Whatever else it does, it refers to the *as if* situation of fantasy, dreams, and fiction, where everything is possible. The fortune-teller dresses *as if* he were a woman, *as if* he was Oriental, and the artifice of that fiction is part of the message. There is no attempt to obscure the deception – which, for that reason, is not deceptive at all. On the one hand, the *Belle de jour* flaunts the latest fashion, produced in the fashion capitals of the world, which still happen to be Milan, Paris, London, or New York. On the other hand, she poses *as if* she is, also, by virtue of her fashionable wear, and in spite of her emphatic whiteness, Oriental.

Cross-dressing implies an act in which one consciously and for a period of time takes up a particular form of dress. The term *cultural* cross-dressing, then, conveys a sense of freedom from boundaries. It suggests that the beauties in the pictures, but also the persons who can buy such beauty, are free to transgress the boundaries erected and maintained by the culture of capital. One is free to transgress boundaries. One can bend gender roles but also cultural roles. To be just as playful, yet fixed. To be attractive, but only for one's other. These crossings appeal to onlookers enticed to identify with roles, not realities. By using the term cultural cross-dressing I wish to stress the fact that here, in the examples I am looking at, the seduction and its double deception – to make you feel you can play the role, for your own fun, but primarily to attract your other, male, Western, or otherwise other – is directed toward the assumption of a culturally constructed model of a very specific, recognizable because age-old kind, namely the Orient.

As Roland Barthes has argued long ago, in the heydays of structuralism in cultural analysis, fashion is a highly developed system (1967). This system functions in a capitalist world economy and thus proves to be an example *par excellence* of globalized production and consumption. I use fashion here to address the rigid dichotomy on which the anti-globalization movement structured its opposition to globalization. To be sure, fashion is primarily economy-driven. But, steeped as it is in financial structures, the fashion system precisely elaborates that structure by posing questions of identity formation and cross-cultural representation.

In concurrence with Barthes, I do deliberately call it a "fashion system", a sign system that can be analyzed semiotically in the ways it displays relations to class, gender, and ethnicity. It is that particular combination of power inequities that makes fashion relevant beyond the simple economic terms that rule it. What makes cultural cross-dressing relevant is the pertinence of questions about inequalities of power not only in terms of finances, although the combinations of economy and gender, ethnicity and age further strengthen the economic side of things. In this article I will develop a cultural analysis of the fashion system that is not limited to a simple binary opposition between global and local. Rather, I will consider the boundaries erected and maintained by fashion to be a space in which negotiations take place. The questions that precede all others are: who speaks for whom, what modes of cultural cross-dressing are privileged over others, and what are the implications of that privilege?

In fashion today, those questions are urgent, yet rarely foregrounded. Of course, fashion houses dictate trends – even trends such as "anything goes" – and designers decide about colours and fabrics. We may scream and rebel against the modern day despots of fashion but enough willing victims of the craze for Gucci shoes one year and Comme des Garçons suits another, keep the cheap labour in the free trade zones of Southeast Asia going, and the laws of fashion in place. To give an example: the Belgian top-designer Dries van Noten, who is known for his love of fabrics, and saris in particular, draws his inspiration from different parts of the globe. India is his muse one year, Africa the next, and Istanbul the year after. But in an interview he declares that he is interested "not [in] the purely Indian or African, but [in] the mixing of ingredients". He does not want to produce clients who are "living illustrations" or clones of the designer. Instead, he states: "I sell options to people, no lifestyle" (Van der Haak 1996: 14). But, as the verb "to sell" in this sentence foregrounds, these options are not entirely free of charge.

Mixing ingredients and selling options may sound like the liberal message of the United Colours of Benetton: an unproblematic yoking of separate elements, temporarily grafting one piece of clothing onto another (Apter 1999: 19). Yet, this hybrid form is a far cry from the hybridity Homi Bhabha advocates. In Bhabha's influential view, "hybridity" becomes "an active moment of challenge and resistance against the dominant cultural power" (Bhabha paraphrased in Young 1995: 23). This raises the issue of the usefulness and the burdens of the concept of hybridity in cultural analysis.

In his book *Colonial Desire* Robert Young traces the genealogy of hybridity. Cautious to avoid unwanted associations in a discourse meant to counter these, Young insists that

> Hybridity . . . shows the connections between the racial categories of the past and contemporary cultural discourse: it may be used in different ways, given different inflections and apparently discrete references, but it always reiterates and reinforces the dynamics of the same conflictual economy whose tensions and divisions it re-enacts in its own antithetical structure (Young 1995: 27).

As Young insists, the problem of recycling concepts is akin to the politics of quotation. Reiterative practice is not harmless – it can be said that "it always reiterates and reinforces" those ideological tenets that underlie the creation of the concept in the past. The same holds for visual quotation. Therefore, it is important to perceive what happens in the visual discourse of cultural cross-dressing, as an instance making use of hybridity, in the tensions it evokes and the ambiguity it implies. This critical urgency also implies the need to understand the history of such phenomena in our present. A short detour will show how and why cultural cross-dressing needs to be contextualized historically.

Turqueries and Masquerades

Cultural cross-dressing is not a new phenomenon. In fact, it has a rather long history, bound up with power structures of class and gender even before ethnicity. I would like to turn to some early examples of cultural cross-dressing, and demonstrate the relevance of this theoretical term in the analysis of mid-eighteenth century paintings of women, upper-class women, dressing up *as if* they were Oriental. All three are part of *turqueries*, paintings of a fantasized Orient. The first two are by Carle Vanloo: *Sultane prenant du café* (1755) (figure 8) and *Deux sultanes travaillant à la tapisserie* (1755) (figure 9). The third is by Jean-Marc Nattier, *Sultane sortant du bain, servie par des esclaves* (1742) (figure 10). All three paintings give ample reason to suppose that they are "about" the Orient – see for instance all the by now familiar Oriental details – and therefore depict women *as if* in the Orient (for more on the Vanloo paintings, see Boer 2004b).

Figure 8. Carle Vanloo (1755). *Une Sultane prenant du café*. Paris: Musée des Arts Décoratifs.

The genesis of *turqueries* has often been explained by historical factors, anecdotal in kind. The visit by an Ottoman embassy, Said Pasha, to Paris in 1742 functions in those explanations as the point of departure for a true fashion craze to have oneself painted in Oriental dress.[2] To be sure, there is no reason to doubt that this visit might have functioned as a catalyst in promoting a fascination with otherness. But I would add that the contemporary media were instrumental in distributing particularly inflected accounts of Said Pasha's visit, his entourage and the presents he brought with him, accounts in which this fascination was offered to the French public. Pierre Martino mentions issues of the *Mercure* entirely devoted to that visit, and the publication of little pamphlets to keep the Parisian population up -to-date (1906: 97-103). However, the linear, deterministic relation between

---

[2] Such historical explanations have been foregrounded by Pape (1989), Breukink-Peeze (1989) and by Martino (1906).

Figure 9. Carle Vanloo (1755). *Deux sultanes travaillant à la tapisserie.* Paris: Musée des Arts Décoratifs.

an incident such as an embassy visit and a structural phenomenon such as the rapid proliferation of pictorial representations of women dressed as Oriental women is not satisfactory. Nor does it explain why today's savvy players in the field of fashion would still deploy such strategies.

The reason for my discomfort can be described in terms of the relation between text and context. In the interpretation mentioned above, the context functions as a given and determines the meaning of the event, thus establishing a one-to-one relation. Moreover, the term context, as an abstract noun, does not encourage an examination of agency and subjectivity, nor of the historical specificities of *acts* of contextualization. Jonathan Culler (1988: ix) has pointed out that interpretive strategies determine a certain context. Context is a text as well. It is produced and needs to be clarified as much as events (see also Bryson 1994). Culler offers an apt alternative term: "framing". This term is a verb and thus facilitates the analysis of activity, agency, and subjectivity. It gives us a better grasp of the activity of contextualization and of the agency involved, the partiality of interpretations based on it, and the ambivalence that the verb "to frame" harbours. Therefore, instead of analyzing cultural cross-dressing as a static phenomenon, I want to elaborate on the ways it operates in a system of exchange, as a dynamic process. My framing centres on fashion, cross-dressing and the shifts in roles they imply.

As Daniel Roche has indicated in his study *La Culture des apparences* (1989), the phenomenon of an Oriental fashion could only operate in a system of exchange where after the mid-eighteenth century a rapidly growing number of publications on clothing, costume, and what came to be called *fashion* developed. Cultural cross-dressing, therefore, is firmly embedded in relations of production and trade, of circulation of imagery and, to use Roche's term, of a culture of appearances. In this culture of appearances, dress was a way to distinguish among people and to distinguish oneself. As a mark of what Bourdieu has notoriously termed *distinction*, dress can be interpreted as a sign system (1989).[3] Colours, fabrics and ornaments functioned as signs to indicate and maintain social relations within their particular hierarchies. These were never rigidly fixed. Rather, in terms of my analysis of boundaries, they were always negotiable, yet not self-evidently mobile. With the advent of fashion, conventional codes of dress were modified, while fashion also installed the fear of confusion of class indicators and social values. It is in the tension between distinction and convention, in other words, between the desire to be distinct and the fear of not belonging, that cultural negotiation can take place.

The notion of cross-dressing appeals to the fear of confusing categories as well as to the desire to distinguish (one-self). As the dictionary indicates, to cross-dress or trans-vest means to clothe across, i.e., in violation with custom. In their well-known study *The Tradition of Female Transvestism in Early Modern Europe* (1989), Rudolf Dekker and Lotte van de Pol indicate how female cross-dressers were seen as disturbances of the existing arrangements between the sexes. Women dressing as men tried to escape the limitations

---

[3] I differ here from a more strict interpretation by Joanna Entwistle (2000) about fashion as a sign system.

Figure 10. Jean-Marc Nattier (1742). *Sultane sortant du bain, servie par des esclaves.* London: The Wallace Collection.

that society imposed on them. All the women in Dekker and Van de Pol's study were lower-class women, who, according to contemporary trial reports, by dressing as men "dressed *up*", that is, they tried under false pretence to pose as socially "higher", as men with all the advantages of masculine roles.

When we look at the examples of cultural cross-dressing both from today's fashion ads and from the historical paintings, Dekker and Van de Pol's study raises some questions. How to interpret the issue of class, as the women posing on the paintings under scrutiny here were upper-class women? If dressing as a man is considered "dressing up", how is cultural cross-dressing to be interpreted in distinction from gender cross-dressing?

Cross-dressing has also been analyzed in the context of the carnivalesque (Russo 1986; 1994) and the masquerade. These terms are not automatically the most appropriate ones for the variation of transvestism I have termed cultural cross-dressing here. Cultural cross-dressing, it is easily apparent, differs in some important respects from masquerade. As Terry Castle analyzed in her book *Masquerade and Civilization*, the masquerade, in its English eighteenth-century context, developed rapidly at the beginning of that century into a very popular and heavily criticized phenomenon. She states that

> the masked assemblies of the eighteenth century were in the deepest sense a kind of collective meditation on self and other, and an exploration of their mysterious dialectic . . . The pleasure of the masquerade attended on the experience of doubleness, the alienation of inner from outer, a fantasy of two bodies simultaneously and thrillingly present, self and other together, the two-in-one (Castle 1986: 4-5).

Castle's emphasis is on the notion of self, which, in masquerading, remained elusive and inaccessible as a way to devalue unitary notions of the self in ever-changing disguises. Masked and disguised, crowds gathered in public spaces such as the Haymarket where balls were organized. The masquerade attracted higher and lower classes, men and women. It was unsurpassed in providing a site for intermingling and possibilities for transgression – both socially and sexually. This aspect illuminates, incidentally, the connection between the masquerade and the carnivalesque. This connection resides in the radical reversal of seemingly fixed social and gender roles, but also in an inevitable return to the original situation.

The antithetical element that is present in both the masquerade and the carnivalesque nevertheless moves within certain limits. Castle asserts that masqueraders did not dress either as themselves or as people like themselves, but always required an antithetical element that was nevertheless limited by class boundaries (1986: 75). Castle's statement only holds to a certain extent since this limitation is precisely what elicited cultural cross-dressing. The antithetical element would be expressed in the reversal of class characteristics or, failing those by lack of distinctiveness, ethnic backgrounds.

As costume historian Aileen Ribeiro shows in *The Dress Worn at Masquerades in England* (1984), upper class English ladies would remain within their class boundaries, using ethnic diversity instead. They would, that is, masquerade as sultanas, not as lower class Turkish women. Hence, certain reversals were possible over and against the preservation of other class-related features. Higher classes would dress as shepherds, women as pirates, men as Dianas. But once cultural boundaries were crossed, class remained in place. The exotic costume was the most popular subspecies of the so-called fancy dress, related in particular to those national or ethnic groups evoking romantic associations. In the masquerade, the Orient was represented prominently in a profusion of sultans, sultanas, Janissaries and Circassian princesses.

When the question of politics arises, however, Castle is quick to dismiss the relevance of a critical perspective of the kind I am advocating. Castle even interprets the disguise in exotic costume, quite naively in my view, in terms of a utopian projection and discards motifs focusing on power differences quite easily.

> Granted, one might see in foreign costume a mere displacement of imperialist fantasy; the popularity of the masquerade coincided after all with the expansion of British imperialism, and the symbolic joining of races could conceivably be construed as a kind of perverse allusion to empire. Yet, at a deeper level, such travesties were also an act of homage – to otherness itself. Stereotypical and inaccurate though they often were, exotic costumes marked out a kind of symbolic interpenetration with difference – an almost erotic commingling with the alien. Mimicry became a form of psychological recognition, a way of embracing, quite literally, the unfamiliar. The collective result was a utopian projection: the masquerade's visionary "Congress of Nations" – the image of global conviviality – was indisputably a thing of fleeting, hallucinatory beauty (Castle 1986: 61-62).

This passage begins, tellingly, with the word "granted", thus opening itself up for contradiction. Although Castle is surely right to decline any simplistic accusatory note of imperialism, what she calls utopian I would prefer to see in terms of desire. But what kind of desire this entails may not be so clear. There is something, after all, which can be called imperial desire, which is a far cry from the unambiguous embrace of otherness suggested by the phrase "visionary 'Congress of Nations'".

A few features of the masquerade will have become clear by now. These features are relevant for a closer understanding of cultural cross-dressing as partly similar, partly distinct from masquerade. Masquerades operate by the grace of mass gatherings whereas cultural cross-dressing, at least in the paintings as well as in the fashion ads, seems to point at more individual choices. Van Noten sells options, he says in *Elle*; and the paintings concern domestic scenes, not public festivities. Choice is, of course, also an issue in a masquerade but its more obvious goal would be the play with different costumes for the sake of being seen by large groups of people.

Moreover, masquerades vary greatly in their choices. One could be a Harlequin at one occasion and a Sultana at another. Most importantly, and with reference to the concept of boundaries, Castle's argument that one rubs shoulders with the other, rendering homage to the other in a visionary congress of nations, presupposes an *outside* perspective on the mass of masqueraders. Individual masqueraders did not collaborate to nicely distribute different costumes so as to create a utopian vision: this can only be perceived once the masqueraders gathered as a larger group.

Furthermore, masquerades were parties, meant for amusement, in which cross-dressing was a form of play. What interests me here, however, is not the element of play as such, but the implied questions of power involved in this play. To ask: who has the liberty to play? Who represents whom and why? The carnivalesque and the masquerade in their antithetical characteristics turn the tables on the rich and powerful, but whose tables are turned – and by whom? – when women dress as if they were Oriental women? Who is playing around with cultural roles and who exactly is being played *with*? My word choice is deliberate here, invoking the various connotations of "playing around" and "playing with" in Western culture. In other words, these questions readjust the focus, stressing aspects that Castle dismisses too hastily: the relations between self and other as they are perceived within hierarchies, and the ways in which they are engendered within a sociocultural context.

One might think that the play with cultural roles is obvious, because, in the three *turqueries* shown in the old master paintings, the women who are represented are clearly Western women. The same can be said of the fashion ads. But here, the concept of framing comes in handy, for I think that the effort to simply read "the Occident" in the paintings is as unavailing as the failed attempt to read "the Orient" in them. The point, by contrast, is precisely to confuse categories, not unlike the Valentino look-alike and his ostentatious masculinity under the headscarf. Hence, no sense of categorical purity in the interpretation of cultural cross-dressing can be obtained. Yet, it is equally striking that some details might again militate to give us this impression.

I am thinking for instance about details which occur in the titles. Nattier's *Sultane sortant du bain* is also known as *Mademoiselle de Clermont at the Bath*; Vanloo's *Une Sultane prenant du café* acquired the addition "represented with the traits of Madame de Pompadour" (Rosenberg and Sahut 1977). Names of Western women do not exactly match the impulse to interpret the women in the paintings as Oriental. Nevertheless, rather than offering decisive answers as to whom and what is represented, the title changes do tell us something about the accrued histories of interpretation.

These added titles, supplements in the Derridean sense, only foreground the need to emphasize not only the Oriental but also the Western roles and identities that are being played. Illustrative of this apparent interpretational aporia was a response of a friend of mine to whom I showed these images of cultural cross-dressers. In what seemed a knee-jerk reaction he remarked: "They are not supposed to represent harem women, are they?" The ambivalence he expressed – saying "harem" in the form of a question with a negative slant – reflects exactly what I will try to argue in the rest of this chapter. "Question" is the operative word in my friend's response. For the representations of cultural cross-dressing do put into question fixed notions of cultural identities and posit instead the exchange I have been foregrounding throughout this book: a situation of negotiation.

Reading either exclusive Orientalness or pure Westernness in the paintings is difficult to achieve. Instead, the resulting ambiguity serves to maintain a fine line – or should I say, rather, a space? – between two possibilities, equally unsuitable. On the one hand, the representation of European women posing as Oriental women, and on the other, a complete conflation of Oriental and Western signs. These two options are equally inappropriate because, as the fashion ads already demonstrated, cultural cross-dressing has to reveal itself *as such*, while simultaneously perpetuating the illusion and desire to "be" an Oriental woman. In truly post-modern fashion, the fiction is overt while the desired fictionality is offered as available. Rather than the wholesale endorsement of the other identity, it is the *desirability* to "be" this other woman that is absolutely necessary.

But not just any other kind of other woman: the representation of French women as black women is to my knowledge non-existent, at least with respect to eighteenth-century representations. The tension between these two poles – of the disclosure and maintenance of illusion – brings about the play, but also the ambivalent dialogue present in the paintings. Therefore, I propose to take as the theme of the representations neither cultural cross-dressing revealing itself as such, nor the perpetuation of the illusion, but to read the depictions of cultural cross-dressing as intersecting sign systems in which a situation of negotiation is emblematized.

Exchanging Information, Negotiating Power

To illustrate my point let us look at the two Vanloo paintings, *Une Sultane prenant du café* and *Deux sultanes travaillant à la tapisserie*. Madame de Pompadour commissioned Carle Vanloo, a very fashionable painter in France in the mid-eighteenth century, to execute the two paintings, so-called *dessus-de-porte*, for her room in Turkish style in the Château de Bellevue. The relation between the two paintings is emphasized in both their function and their subject matter. The *dessus-de-portes* were commissioned as pendants. Traditionally, pendants were two paintings, often portraits, which were related in their representation or were meant to indicate a mutual bond. The subject matter of the two canvasses is related in the repetition of various elements – most notably the flowers, the window whose function as boundary-constituting we remember from the first chapter of this study, and, crucially for my purposes here, the negotiation going on between the women in both paintings.

The window seems to be the same in both paintings, although it is taken at closer range in *Deux sultanes*. The window functions as the principal source of light in both. Its presence indicates the division between the outside world and the interior scene that we as spectators perceive, and that was constitutive of Bouraoui's young girl's world (1991). As it did there, albeit in a more cheerful fashion here, the window functions as a framing device, seemingly over-determining the message of domesticity. Because the window is explicitly included in the scene, it emphasizes even more our awareness that the scene is taking place inside, and that we as spectators have been allowed in.

Yet another issue is addressed by the window in combination with the flowers in the pendants. In *Une Sultane prenant du café*, the woman seated on the right side wears flowers on her headdress, so emphatically that their upward position is slightly ridiculous and clearly serves the purpose of emphasizing their presence. Moreover, a vase containing flowers is placed on the windowsill. Although the flowers are natural elements, in both instances of their use in the painting they have been cut and brought in from the outside. As we all know, cut flowers quickly fade, especially when not put in water but on someone's head. They fade almost as rapidly as the flowers of the bindweed called "Belle de jour" discussed before. Reminiscent of seventeenth-century vanitas still lives, of which we have seen other evocations in the discourse on deserts, their wilting beauty might reflect back upon the person wearing the flowers on her headdress in the painting.

As it happens, one of the persistent stereotypes about women in the Orient occurring in Orientalist literature is that their beauty quickly fades because of the frequent baths they take. And, once we enter the realm of Orientalist stereotypes, cut flowers also signify artificiality because they are subject to cultivation, as the still life-like arrangement of the flowers in the vase suggests. The relation with still life painting is reinforced in the combination of different flowers in the vase, a common place established through Dutch still life painting of the seventeenth century (see Bryson 1990; Grootenboer 2005). This association becomes even more Orientalist once we realize that tulips and the tulip fever that was raging in the seventeenth century – an early instance of the emptiness of capitalism – originated from Turkey.

The position of the vase in the windowsill, inside, but next to the window, directs our gaze to the ornate panes of glass that constitute the boundary demarcation, hence, the dividing screen between inside and outside that separates as well as connects. Moreover, the vase posed right there focuses our attention on the flowers as cut, hence their cultivated state. By metonymic extension, it also points to the "cultivatedness", hence, the artificiality, of the person wearing the flowers on her headdress. This element of cultivation is repeated and further developed in *Deux sultanes*. Here, the transposition of the world beyond the windowpane is elaborated even more artificially, in the work that preoccupies the women, the flowers in the tapestry and the flower and leaf motives on the dress of the woman on the right, as well as in the cushions and the drapery. In this companion piece, flowers have spread out everywhere, manufactured with such insistence that the fact that these scenes are depicted in paint adds another layer to the artificiality.

Again, we can learn from Proust when it comes to understanding the importance of artifice. In the first books of *La Recherche*, it is the family's friend Charles Swann who functions as the master of the first, emphatically indirect artistic education the hero receives. It is Swann who suggests to the grandmother that Marcel should be given presents of "several 'layers' of art" (1981 Vol. 1: 40). By this he means photographs, not of the Chartres Cathedral, but of Corot's painting of the Cathedral. The irony is as thick as the artificiality itself. But the truth beyond the irony is also obvious: cultural education is based on reproductions, reiterations of clichés that instil expectations in us concerning what seems normal, relevant, and attractive, including, as I am discussing here, "exotic". In general, I want to suggest that both paintings pose the question of inside versus outside in terms of that of culture versus nature. In this respect, they differ from Bouraoui's distinction, where inside and outside are opposed as confinement and freedom, albeit not without complications (1991).

But windows, as we saw there, are transparent; they produce space as much as separation. Strikingly, here, the situation of negotiation depicted in both paintings questions this apparent set of rigid oppositions. In *Une Sultane* an arrested moment is depicted – not any moment, however, but the exact point in time at which an exchange takes place. By means of the title, an element of parergon that enhances the legibility of the painting, we are alerted to this particular situation. The verb *prenant* is ambiguous. To take a coffee means both to consume it and to accept it. The latter, more literal meaning is activated here. The negotiation is represented in the steaming cup of coffee, handed to the sultana by the black woman. This arrested moment is transformed into a moment of contact by the look that passes between the two women, and their half-open mouths that dramatize the exchange of words. Perhaps "Voici Madame", "Thank you, my dear", as one imagines a dialogue of offering and acceptance in polite French society would sound.

Coffee, introduced in the 1660s by the ambassador of the Ottoman sultan, had become a fashionable commodity in French eighteenth-century society, albeit only for its upper class consumers (Martino 1906: 348). Meanwhile it maintained at least a part of its "outside", exotic and inaccessible property for the French population at large. Yet, there is another quality of coffee that I would like to highlight in the context of my discussion here. As Edward Lane has indicated in his description of the modern Egyptians, coffee needed careful preparation, both of the beans that required roasting and of the coffee itself (1978 [1836]: 138). With reference to Lévi-Strauss' distinction between the raw and the cooked, coffee can be considered not a raw item, but a highly refined, "cooked" commodity (1964). Thus, in its very refinement it also signified the absorption of exotic otherness as the highest form of civilization.

Then, there is the cup itself. The coffee cup is a container, and as all containers it embodies the qualities of its content, here, both inside qualities (hosting a refined cultured commodity) and outside qualities (a culturally alien element imported to France). It was also a delicate form of French craft, the fabrication of fine china that made French Limoges china famous. As a container, the coffee cup can be aligned with the window, because each points at the difference between inside and outside, culture and nature. In that respect, the invisible division between the two women – the very distinction they are depicted as being in the process of negotiating! – becomes visible as well. Being closest to the window, so close that the shrubs outside might be taken to be her shadow or reflection, the black woman would seem to be firmly placed in the realm of nature, on the edge or even outside the cultivated space depicted. The white woman, by contrast, sits with her back to the drapery, firmly anchored in the realm of cultivation.

The display of white and black women together in paintings has a long tradition, a tradition that was particularly vivid in eighteenth- and nineteenth-century France. In this tradition, perhaps most famously represented by Manet's arguably ironic commentary upon it in his *Olympia* from 1865, the roles for both were defined in antithetical ways. The black women were mostly depicted as servants – and if not clearly depicted, still interpreted as such. The white women were represented as mistresses – whether or not also mistresses of invisible gentlemen in the sexual sense of the word. The black women were represented as active, busy to display and adorn their mistresses, as we can see in Nattier's painting *Sultane sortant du bain*. Here, to dress and adorn one white woman, it takes as many as six black women. The title calls them slaves. It seems significant that this entirely Orientalist scene distinguishes not only between white mistress and black slaves, but within the group of black women, depicts the one woman in charge of displaying the towel and hence, the physical contact with the white woman, as clearly whiter, less emphatically black than her colleagues. This is how differences and intersections of class and race were marked as oppositions.

In a departure from this binary scheme, I would argue that, at least in *Sultane prenant un café*, the black woman occupies a somewhat mobile position. Not only is she active and speaking; while the sultana is confined within the seclusion of the imaginary harem, the black woman has, given her position in the composition, an ability to move between inside and outside spaces. She is part of the interior scene, but she has entered the Orientalist space created in this room from the outside, at the very least from the kitchen where the coffee has been brewed.

In *Deux sultanes* the negotiation seems less obvious except for the look the two women exchange. They seem more equal, both dressed up as Oriental, both racially white. Yet, the gestures of the women are significant. The woman on the right leans forward, extending her hand, while her legs are bent as if to reinforce the argument she tries to convey to the woman on the left. The latter is in a position to listen. She sits more relaxed, while holding the needle of her tapestry work. Interestingly enough, in the engraved version of the painting by Jacques-Firmin Beauvarlet, the title is changed to *La Confidence*. This new title makes explicit the sense of intimacy between the women, for the word *confidence* in French is used in the sense of being confidential with someone and usually intimates erotic secrets.

The significance of the change in the title is that it foregrounds the nature of the exchange: one woman confiding in another. Inspired by Nancy Miller's work on women writers and the tying of knots as a way of writing for women (1988: 125-62), I would like to suggest that the speech of the woman on the right is reworked at the same moment. This is done by way of the knots the woman on the left ties on the tapestry. For, she is the only one holding a needle.

Cross-Dressing the In-Between

This reworking and questioning of the nature-culture opposition, by way of positing negotiation as a consistent pattern in the paintings, leads me again to consider Madame de Pompadour as herself the cultural cross-dresser in these particular paintings. In the representation of Madame de Pompadour as sultana, it is significant that the painting is a *dessus-de-porte*, marking the boundaries between this room where she "is" a sultana and other spaces where she has other functions, other identities. This interpretation turns the division of spaces into a rigid demarcation. But as I have argued, I am more interested in the function of boundaries as allowing negotiation. In the former interpretation, we can say that the Orient is brought home to France as an imaginary space. Yet, in the framework of the latter, we might perhaps see de Pompadour's cultural cross-dressing as inspired by a different motivation, which is the desire to overcome strict demarcations in function and power.

When we take a look at the position Madame de Pompadour had as the official royal mistress at the French court of Louis XV, it is clear that she occupied a role that was both fixed and transitional. In comparison with the queen, related to the king by force of an arranged marriage, the official mistress derived her position from his desire. But to maintain her status, which according to Chaussinand-Nogaret was marginal and central at the same time, she had to continually stimulate the king's desire. As soon as he would lose interest, the next mistress would take her position:

> Thus a disequilibrium is created between the queen and the mistress: for the one indifference and respect, for the other love and influence . . . A distribution of roles, a specialization of functions therefore exists between the women of the king. The queen embodies order, legitimacy, orthodoxy, and immobility. The mistress, on the contrary, is pleasure, movement, and creation (Chaussinand-Nogaret 1990: 16).

Madame de Pompadour can therefore be seen as the embodiment of in-betweenness, occupying a provisional space between the king and the queen. In that light it is striking to see her represented as a sultana, the highest

position of a woman in the harem of the sultan. While this was the top
position, it was not fixed. Any woman in the harem could become a sultana, a
function that does not imply the demarcations between queen and mistress at
the French court. The legitimacy embodied by the queen – emphasized in her
official function of bearing the royal heir – is displaced onto the sultana, who
bore the sultan's children. Moreover, the sultanas often played an important
part in the political power play of the seraglio in which the positioning of
their children in the line of succession was but one aspect of the intrigues.[4]

Madame de Pompadour's informal, political powers at the French court
were widely recognized. Ultimately, in her guise as sultana, the suggestion
that this painting makes possible is that her political role could result in the
actual access to power. Therefore, the ostensible appeal of Madame de
Pompadour's acting out her desire by representing herself as the
personification of the desirable (for the male gaze) is supplemented with the
effort to overcome the strict demarcations in function and power. This is an
instance of the productivity of boundaries once they are conceived of as
spaces for negotiation.

Until now we have looked at details in the representations of cultural
cross-dressing that indicated and questioned distinctions between inside and
outside, between culture and nature. Returning to Nattier's painting *Sultane
sortant du bain* these distinctions and their problematizations are also played
out on the body of the white woman depicted. If we follow the direction of
looking in the image, all gazes focus on the woman who supposedly was M[lle]
de Clermont. It is as if the "slaves" look up to her in awe of her beauty. The
figure that interests me most is the woman to the right of M[lle] de Clermont's
legs, the one I earlier indicated as being "less black" than the others. She
looks intently at a piece of fabric she is holding to dry M[lle] de Clermont's
feet, part of the process of getting her dressed. She looks at the fabric and not
at the object of all the other looks.

By means of her gaze she is presented as the bearer of narrativity. By her
focus on this narrative element in the painting, the fabric about to be used in
action, she emphasizes the process of dressing. This is not just any action,
however. Dressing, in the context of dressing up as Oriental, is also a self-

---

[4] For analyses of the political role of the sultana, see Shaw (1976: 170; 191; 193-94; 204), Mernissi
(1990) and Peirce (1993).

reflexive element. It foregrounds, in other words, the possibilities to take up "dress". After a bath one can decide how to dress and thus decide to dress as Oriental, temporarily assuming a different cultural identity. In this sense, the painting winks at Judith Butler's theory of gender performativity. This theory was initially misunderstood as stating that gender and sex are just like dresses one can choose in the morning. In her introduction to *Bodies that Matter* (1993), Butler redresses this misunderstanding of her earlier book *Gender Trouble* (1990).

All but one of the looks are directed to Mlle de Clermont and so is ours as spectators. The woman who is the bearer of narrativity and of self-reflexivity returns our gaze, however, and thus compels us to consider what is going on in the painting. That is, she invites us to reconsider our easy assumption that this is the Orient displayed before our eyes.[5]

Nattier's painting poses the question of fixating and fixed notions by explicitly referring to the *process* of dressing and taking up an identity. As I have argued before, the interpretation of cultural cross-dressing is necessarily based on a wavering in-between, where the negotiation of different roles and positions takes place. The point *Sultane sortant du bain* makes, is that agency matters – both for the cultural cross-dresser ánd for the spectator looking at a scene of cultural cross-dressing. This agency is where the very negotiation of boundaries takes place.

Revisiting Boundaries

I would like to conclude my argument in this chapter with a few brief considerations on the importance of the concept of cultural cross-dressing and the boundaries this practice poses and transgresses – indeed, poses in the very act of transgression. It summons the particular conception of boundaries as spaces, not lines. In her successful and widely read study *Vested Interests: Cross-Dressing and Cultural Anxiety* (1992), Marjorie Garber states that there can be no culture without the transvestite, because the transvestite marks the entry into the social order. One of Garber's examples is Flora Tristan, who, in order to gain access into the House of Lords, cross-dressed as a Turkish man (Garber 1992: 314-16). In order to resolve a situation where

---

[5] For a slightly different analysis of this painting, Pollock (1999: 287-94).

women were not allowed, Tristan cross-dresses in a double sense, as a man and as a Turk. Appropriating the representation of a cultural "other", she, of course, pulls at the loose thread where the fabric of gender roles can begin to unravel. But Turkish dress is utilized here as a mediating third "place", the space of representation, as Garber – following Lacan – calls it. However, I am not as optimistic as Garber about the automatic effects of cultural cross-dressing and its possibilities for play.

My hesitation centres on "cultural otherness" as a means to another end. It is very hard to see how cultural otherness can find a space other than its stereotypical manifestation, unless we theorize it and problematize the concepts that naturalize those stereotypes. Moreover, it is necessary to realize that cultural cross-dressing is deeply implicated in unequal relations of power, where the cultural "other" does not call the shots and has little or no recourse to influencing the process of being represented. Cultural cross-dressing, therefore, is not reversible. This asymmetry is inherent in the practice.

In order to elaborate this aspect of power inequality and take it back to contemporary debates on self and other, let me continue the ongoing discussion of boundaries. As I indicated in the introduction to this study, boundaries have a tendency to be perceived as anonymous and to supersede the individual, as geo-politician Michel Foucher (1991) has argued. Dividing spaces and groups of peoples, yet no one's possession, the anonymity of boundaries is guaranteed by naturalizing impulses that strengthen their stable and immobile qualities. Those naturalizing impulses, I argued before, help to make the activity in the *construction* of boundaries disappear from sight, i.e. the act of boundary-making itself becomes invisible. With the help of the play with boundaries in cultural cross-dressing, we can see why the question of boundaries has been directed toward the definition of what a boundary is and where it is located.

Boundary-questions of *what* and *where* reinforce fixity, anonymity, and the apparently differentiating powers of boundaries as unquestioned tools for social distinction. Cross-dressing appears to unfix what people are, but the stereotype it appeals to needs to be fixed for this temporary unfixing to be possible at all. Boundaries, including those between people and the way they dress, naturalize the eminently cultural domains that separate people according to conventional categories. This view of boundaries limits possibilities for interpretation and operates as a reductive instrument for those interpretations.

Against this fixing view of boundaries, I propose instead, that boundaries are not stable, but mobile, and a space of negotiation. I see them as instances of a space in which different and contrasting visions, more often than not unequal in terms of power, come into play. This is what happens emphatically in cultural cross-dressing. There and, as we can now see, elsewhere as well, boundaries are negotiated in a process that does not stop with the provisional designation of a boundary. The boundary is arbitrary in character, temporary and changeable. The next chapter will make this eminently clear.

This necessary detour through the notion of boundary leads back to the mixing of ingredients that fashion designer Dries van Noten talked about and to the post-modern commonplace of a world without boundaries. I respond to such claims with "if only that were true!" Such a vision is either wildly utopian or abusively deceptive, thinly covering the capitalist interests that globalization as a catch-phrase embodies. If hybridity is indeed taken as a form of bricolage, not a form of breeding and bleeding, if it is only a mix to your liking, not a fatal racial manipulation, then we might ask whether it is worthwhile to spend time analyzing fashion or cultural cross-dressing. But if, by contrast, we take seriously Gayatri Spivak's statement that "radical alterity requires imaging", then we might as well scrutinize those images critically and carefully consider what negotiations take place, if any (1996).[6]

Take for example a well-known ad of United Colours of Benetton, showing three hearts titled *White, Black, Yellow*. At the heart of the matter, the ad proposes, we are all equal; no boundaries, no negotiations are necessary – just step into the parlour of sameness. For a fashion house selling clothes as markers of difference, this is more than disingenuous. But hybridity as an active moment of challenge and resistance against the dominant cultural power does retain and urge a focus on the political, as Homi Bhabha contends. With this focus in mind and cultural cross-dressing

---

[6] For an extended analysis of postmodern fashion and the place of women in the history of textile, see Spivak (1999: 337-52).

as the complex and dynamic process I have been analyzing, I want to turn to my last example.

Figure 11. HIJ advertisement (spring 1995). By permission of *We Europe*.

The Dutch company for men's fashion HIJ (indicating the third personal pronoun masculine in Dutch) launched a campaign in the spring of 1995 (figure 11) in which a series of 6 black men were depicted for the promotion of shirts. While the Dutch concern about the growing numbers of asylum seekers entering the country was at its provisional high, the promotional campaign for shirts did not cause a single ripple. No comments in the press. When I asked my students what this campaign was about, other than mere clothing, they responded that it must be connected to rap music or to the growing interest in Aboriginal art or to a Third World awareness in general.[7]

---

[7] The company used to have separate stores for HIJ (him) and ZIJ (her), until the company merged the two into WE in 1999. For the connections between rap, masculinity and black men, see Andrew Ross (1998: 71-78).

Note the link with the Benetton advertisements that also promote cross-cultural relations and environmental concerns. Half of the photos in the campaign were similar in content to the HIJ photograph of the black man in figure 11: men wearing shirts, the patterns of which were repeated on their faces. The other half showed black men bared to the skin except for some beads and feather ornaments around their ankles and wrists that "dressed" them. They were carrying shields, open circles in which the shirts were hung in such a way that they functioned quite coyly as modern-day fig leaves. The overall image of the campaign was "men as warriors". Warriors who were in dire need of a reconstruction and rehabilitation of their masculinity, which was to be attained through black men as a sign.

This clever device might be interpreted as a form of ethno-marketing, targeting a consumer public of young black men. But what struck me most was the literal excess of the message, the overflow of the print of the shirts onto the face of the men in the imagery. Whereas clothing is removable and positioned on the body, the print indicates a form of inscription *onto* the body that has much more serious implications. The signifiers of racial, ethnic and cultural boundaries will, of course, not carry over onto the men buying the shirts in this instance. For potential buyers the shirt will be a detachable piece of clothing, the paint on the faces of the black men will stay where it "belongs". The new, probably white masculine warrior will make do with the shirt.[8]

Fashion, in this way, produces, promotes, and recycles powerful images of otherness as enviable and "imitatable" models. They appeal to a sense of the authentic, of a genuine otherness, as attractive. In what fiction theory would call a wilful suspension of disbelief, fashion makes this cultural cross-dressing the most "normal" thing in the world. In this sense, fashion is perhaps the most "authentic" of post-modern cultural expressions. Without wishing to dismiss its vital and integral role in the fashion system, I am highly critical of some forms of cultural cross-dressing. My critique concerns precisely the kind of images of otherness presented with such frequency and self-evidence that they receive an authenticity that completely lacks any

---

[8] It might be clear from my analysis that I am at odds with Pacteau's otherwise fascinating interpretation of Jean-Paul Goude's photos of Grace Jones (1994). What is detachable there according to Pacteau, the black skin, is exactly what cannot be detached in the HIJ ad.

awareness of the political implications of the fundamentally contradictory character of cultural cross-dressing.

However, on the basis of the meaning of boundaries that I have been developing in this book, I believe, perhaps naively so, that it is possible to become sensitized to the mechanisms at work in this practice; these mechanisms include possibilities for negotiating the inequalities of power, and undermining the naturalizing impulses that strengthen them by taking the functioning of boundaries into account. Then, but only then, the dictum "Just a fashion" will have run its course. Fashion, that is, will no longer be a whimsical phenomenon of the day but something that, in its very artificiality, will show its hand as, paradoxically, the most deeply entrenched form of authenticity that contemporary, post-modern culture has produced.

SIX

Border Fetishism: Negotiable Authenticity

Authenticity and Framing

What, indeed, can authenticity mean in the post-modern world of travelling and crossing boundaries? In order to understand the double materiality and artificiality of cultural artefacts as themselves constituting a boundary, I will approach this final aspect of boundaries by means of the old, upper-class habit of collecting art. Two collections will be explored. A novel by the French author Georges Perec (1936-1982), *Un Cabinet d'amateur: Histoire d'un tableau* (1979), narrates the life and history of collector Hermann Raffke, a German-born wealthy brewer in Pittsburgh. His collection culminates in the painting "Un Cabinet d'amateur", depicting Raffke seated in front of his favourite canvasses.[1]

I will contrast this collection featured in a fictional account with the private museum Insel Hombroich in Neuss, Germany, which houses the collection of Karl-Heinrich Müller, a German real estate mogul. Located in a secluded marshland area, modern-built structures contain the objects of Müller's collection, originating from different parts of the world. Whereas Perec describes Raffke's collection in detailed accounts of value, market considerations, and signs of authentication, an account that conveys the

---

[1] In order to distinguish between the novel and the painting with the same title, references to the painting will be in quotation marks. All translations are mine, unless otherwise indicated. My thanks to Philippe Déan and Rachel Boué for introducing me to this wonderful novel.

intimate connection between image and wording as well as between commodity fetishism and the aesthetics of high art, Insel Hombroich seems filled with disclaimers of any association with the market and forges instead a tight link between nature and culture. Shorn of the common markers of value and money, the objects displayed in Insel Hombroich carry no titles or references to artists, year of production or donors. This absence signals a disruption. In the modern world, museum display has invariably used words to accompany, or frame, the visual artefacts on display. This is such a standard practice that the absence of words appears a disruption of a cultural code. Insel Hombroich turns such obvious hallmarks of museum display on their head – thereby begging the question how this disrupted word-image relation influences the museum's visitors, its artworks' spectators, in their interpretational processes vis-à-vis the works displayed.

The fetishism involved in collecting is a widely analysed phenomenon (see Elsner and Cardinal 1994). In my analysis of the two collections however, my main focus is not the investigation of the fetishism involved in collecting itself, although much could be said about Raffke's motivation for his feverish collecting or the ways in which Müller's collection acquired its hybrid character. Rather, I seek to confront the two collections with each other in their interaction with readers and viewers and trace the fetishism of authenticity that surfaces, accompanies and structures that interpretational process. Authenticity is the tenacious preservation of a boundary for its own sake. For, as I will argue, it is in the obsession with authenticity that the function of boundaries comes to the fore. Thus, this fetishism of authenticity, I will argue, is the most intense form of the production and protection of boundaries, a form that illustrates the point as well as the risk of boundaries as such.

Authenticity is primarily an issue of visibility as an index of presence.[2] Each in their own particular way, the interpretation of readers and viewers of these collections is directed toward the material objects that function as fetishes in the two collections – the painting "Un Cabinet d'amateur", the unidentified objects in the museum Insel Hombroich – such that the sheer

---

[2] This is why, in the previous chapter, I alleged that fashion, as a domain of cultural cross-dressing, is such an emblematic practice that betrays the mechanisms of the construction of authenticity – of authenticity *as* construction.

presence of those objects, the encounter with them and the knowledge that ensues from this encounter, is foregrounded, albeit differently in each case.[3] And indeed, "the irreducible materiality" of the fetish object, as Pietz characterized one of its salient aspects, presupposes that the fetish is "there", materially present, if ambiguously so (1985: 7). This materiality – as well as its ambiguity – makes this fetishism an appropriate instance of cultural practice on which to end this section of my book, and the book as a whole. At the same time as being "authentically" material, however, absence or lack is just as much a part of the fetish. Characterized by a seductive incompleteness, as an unfulfilled promise that repeatedly draws the desiring beholder within its sway, the fetish as *objet chargé* acts upon those who behold it and holds them in its grip. "To be sensuous is to suffer", as Marx put it, in the sense of being acted upon (Marx quoted in Pietz 1993: 144; Cf. Spyer 1998) and it is the power of "Un Cabinet d'amateur" and Insel Hombroich's unidentified objects to evoke the double presence/absence of the fetish. Both are implicated in the interpretational processes elicited by the two collections and operate in highly specific ways in each.

Collections establish particular ties with visibility and invisibility and this visual component is crucial to fetishism. Through the question of visibility, fetishism comes to stand for the materiality of boundaries. The boundary between visibility and invisibility itself incarnates the more general sense of boundaries, constructed and made visible, or projected upon visible elements of geographical space, such as mountains and rivers. Boundaries, as the discussion of the fetishism of authenticity will suggest here, are representations of representations. And this is, not incidentally, also the definition of collections. My interpretation of the two collections highlights how both complicate the issue of the representation of representation, thereby ultimately forcing readers and viewers to perform their own productive look. In that process, fetishism surfaces as a phenomenon *of the border*, that is, as an inherently unstable, hybrid, and mobile phenomenon, invested with contradictory desires. Desires, moreover, that imply a violence performed to the objects and a detachment, a removal that tries to repress this violence.[4]

---

[3] On collecting see Mieke Bal (1994) and James Clifford (1988).
[4] For "border fetishism" specifically see Spyer (1998). Mieke Bal (1994) discusses the violence in fetishism both in Freud and Marx.

In what follows, I discuss first Perec's novel *Un Cabinet d'amateur. Histoire d'un tableau* (1979) named for the painting at its heart. This novel – and the collection of which it is the fictional account – raises the issue of authenticity in a dizzying mirage of faking. Thus, the novel foregrounds the artificiality of authenticity itself. Next, I will analyse Insel Hombroich's refusal to invoke the conventional markers of art historical and museological authority. The museum thereby seeks to foreground the authenticity of art. Its refusal to frame artworks is thus an attempt to enhance their "purity" as art. I will conclude by offering some reflections on the significance of framings, and modes of framing and un-framing.

Contested Presence

The narrative of Georges Perec's short novel starts conventionally enough. Its first words present the title of the fictive painting, and the first event told is its display:

> *Un Cabinet d'amateur*, of the American painter of German origin, Heinrich Kürz, was shown to the public for the first time in 1913, in Pittsburgh, Pennsylvania, in the framework of a series of cultural manifestations organized by the German community of the city at the occasion of the twenty-five years of the reign of Emperor William II.

> *Un cabinet d'amateur*, du peintre américain d'origine allemande Heinrich Kürz, fut montré au public pour la première fois en 1913, à Pittsburgh, Pennsylvanie, dans le cadre de la série de manifestations culturelles organisée par la communauté allemande de la ville à l'occasion des vingt-cinq ans de règne de l'empereur Guillaume II (Perec 1979: 9).

This opening sentence also inaugurates several boundaries: between the Old and the New World, Germany and the US; but also of the pre-war German empire and the war soon to begin; as well as, more subtly, that between the "authentic Americans" in Pittsburgh and the German immigrés. The latter boundary, of course, is the most tenuous one.

A rich collector of art, Herman Raffke, of German descent and the owner of several breweries in Pittsburgh, had commissioned the young painter Heinrich Kürz to paint his portrait, representing him seated in his collector's room in front of his favourite paintings. As the opening sentence patiently exposes, the first exhibit of this painting titled, like the novel itself, "Un

Cabinet d'amateur", is part of a series of cultural events organized by the German community of Pittsburgh, on the occasion of the 25th anniversary of the reign of Kaiser Wilhelm II. Amidst a caricature evocation of all the patriotic manifestations a cultural minority can possibly come up with, the rather modest exhibit of Kürz's painting attracts a growing number of spectators, increasing by the day.

What made "Un Cabinet d'amateur" as a painting so extraordinary? More than a hundred paintings representing all the genres and schools of European and North American art "are assembled on the single canvass and reproduced with such accuracy and meticulousness that we would be able to discern them all with precision" (Plus de cent tableaux sont rassemblés sur cette seule toile, reproduits avec une fidélité et une méticulosité telles qu'il nous serait tout à fait possible de les décrire tous avec precision [Perec 1979: 17]). The painting therefore demonstrates a double veracity, or authenticity: it exhibits both the mastery of the artist – capable of reaching a degree of veracity and exactitude that drew the admiration of an ever growing audience – and the extensive possessions of the amateur of the arts, the collector amidst his collection. Thus, the painting is inserted in a long tradition in which collections of paintings and other objects are made visible.[5]

Raffke's proud display of his collection of many objects within a single painting raises the question what a collection is. Roger Cardinal defines a collection as "a concerted gathering of selected items which manifest themselves as a pattern or set, thereby reconciling their divergent origins within a collective discourse" (1994: 71). This is a rather static image of a collection. By contrast, Bal (1994) argues that a collection cannot be considered to have a beginning until something of a collection already exists. Only in relation to other objects can any given object be assigned a meaning: like the best of stories, and indeed, like Perec's novel itself, the beginning of a collection necessarily occurs in media res. The collection's meaning will change with the addition of new objects, which retroactively redefine the whole range of objects to which they have been added.

---

[5] For examples of this tradition, see Peter Bacon Hales's article in a special issue on rethinking the Introductory Art History Survey of the *Art Journal* (1995). In a recent study, Manet van Montfrans has elaborated on the connections between *Un Cabinet d'amateur* and the pictorial tradition of the genre (1999: 287-373).

Collecting also has, of course, a cultural specificity. Collecting in the West, as Clifford maintains "has long been a strategy for the deployment of a possessive self, culture, and authenticity" (1988: 218). Thus, collecting in this sense requires norms and values to channel the desire that fuels it. The desire to possess and collect requires transformation into a meaning-making desire, a desire that selects, orders and classifies. As soon as desire fixates itself on a single object, "good" collecting turns into fetishism. Susan Stewart suggested this distinction, contending that "the boundary between collection and fetishism is mediated by classification and display in tension with accumulation and secrecy" (Stewart in Clifford 1988: 219). According to this view, any collector willing to show his possessions to others escapes the fetishism that compels secrecy.

But Krzysztof Pomian contests this division between classification and display, on the one hand, and accumulation and secrecy, on the other. For him, the withdrawal of an object from the circulation of commodities in which it has previously functioned results in alternating movements of the object in its own right and the collection at large, displayed one time and kept under lock and key on other occasions. Pomian's understanding, then, of a collection is the following:

> a set of natural or artificial objects, kept temporarily or permanently out of the economic circuit, afforded special protection in enclosed spaces adapted specifically for that purpose and put on display.

> tout ensemble d'objets naturels ou artificiels, maintenus temporairement ou définitivement hors du circuit d'activités économiques, soumis à une protection spéciale dans un lieu clos aménagé à cet effet (Pomian 1987: 18).

What interests me about Pomian's arguments is how he connects the themes of invisibility and visibility with that of a collection. He points out that a paradox reigns in the circumstances of a collection. On the one hand, collections are positioned outside the economic circuit, and on the other hand, in this very capacity, they enjoy special protection. In Marxist terms, the objects have an exchange value without having a use value.

Moreover, occupying a position outside of economic circulation does not necessarily mean that the objects have become invisible forever. Pomian cites examples of tombs, temples, and other locations where objects were kept that might be paraded around on special occasions or visited by pilgrims. Sacristies of cathedrals hold collections of relics such as those believed to be body parts of saints, pieces of the Holy Cross, and so on, which are seen in public only on special occasions. Thus, the objects fulfil a role as intermediary between those who behold them on specific occasions and their more general invisibility and inaccessibility. It is the potential – not the actual visibility, the material truth of the object – that guarantees its authenticity.

Writing of late antiquity, however, Peter Brown insists on the carefully constructed tension between distance and proximity; this tension both underwrote the experience of pilgrimage, and ensured that *praesentia*, or the physical presence of the holy, was the greatest blessing that a late-antique Christian could enjoy (1981: 86-88). For, even in the physical presence of the saint's relics or the culminating moment of the pilgrim's arrival, visibility and accessibility was once again deferred, replaying in this way on a minute scale the distance, delays, and yearnings of pilgrimage or, as Brown observes:

> the art of the shrine in late antiquity is an art of closed surfaces. Behind these surfaces, the holy lay, either totally hidden or glimpsed through narrow apertures. The opacity of the surfaces heightened an awareness of the ultimate unattainability in this life of the person they had travelled over such wide spaces to touch (Brown 1981: 87).

Brown here insists on the *in*visibility that hides the holiness of the object, an invisibility that is in tension with, but also guaranteed by, the visibility of the object that harbours the holiness.[6]

In his discussion of collecting, Pomian seems to depart from the distinction made by Walter Benjamin between the cult value of objects and their exhibition value with the latter held to be characteristic of the age of mechanical reproduction (1968b: 223-25). Cult value "would seem to demand that the work of art remain hidden", whereas the exhibition value points at the extraction of objects from their cult settings and their presentability to a wider public. In this shift from cult value to exhibition value, the work of art, through processes of mechanical reproduction,

---

[6] See also Mondzain (2004) for an in-depth analysis of holy objects and the question of visibility.

emancipates from its parasitical dependence on ritual. Perec's novel contests this trade-off.

Rituals of Imitation

Instead, the novel relentlessly questions the very possibility of authenticity, or, in other words, establishes an unbridgeable gap between art as imitation and art as authentic. In *Un Cabinet d'amateur*, the rich collector Raffke displays his wealth, acquired through the process of working his way up, American-style, to become the owner of breweries in Pittsburgh. As his autobiography shows – posthumously published by his sons – once his financial position was comfortable Raffke dedicated himself to collecting paintings. If, following Clifford, the desire to possess has to be transformed by regulatory practices into "good" collecting, Raffke fulfilled his role by having thirty advisors work for him to guide his taste, an expertise for which he himself lacked confidence. The one painting he acquired without the aid of advisors was "Un Cabinet d'amateur" by Heinrich Kürz, meant to be the pinnacle to a long process of collecting. Therefore, this painting synecdochically represented his entire collection. But synecdoche was clearly not enough. The painting was also in charge of representing the entire collection iconically.

Long stored in Raffke's house, the painting left this safe haven to be put on view, but only for a very special occasion of national identity: the twenty-fifth anniversary of the reign of Kaiser Wilhelm II was an opportunity for Raffke to show he was of German stock. This resonates with Pomian's special occasions indicated to display objects that are normally kept hidden, and the obvious larger-than-life implications for the meaning of this event. Kept outside of the economic circuit under normal circumstances, the painting's exhibition at this event marks an effect not be missed. In Pomian's terms, once put on display at this special occasion, "Un Cabinet d'amateur" not only functioned as an intermediary between the viewers who, much like pilgrims, come in ever larger numbers. It also made visible what this painting represents but was otherwise remained hidden: Raffke's collection.

As I mentioned earlier, the painting depicts Raffke seated in front of his possessions and shows a hundred paintings representing all genres and schools of European and American art. The catalogue, anonymously published, draws attention to three particular paintings featured on the canvass of "Un Cabinet d'amateur": a Renaissance painting from the Italian school representing a Visitation of the Virgin Mary on the left wall; on the right wall a still life by Chardin, and on an easel in the right-hand corner a most unusual painting by the German-born Adolphus Kleidröst, titled *Portrait of Bronco McGinnis*. Bronco McGinnis, claiming to be the most tattooed man in the world and, as such, on display at the International Exhibition in Chicago, turned out to be a fraud, when upon his death it was discovered that only the tattoos on his chest were authentic.

Clearly, these three paintings together harbour the issues of authenticity and the fetishistic valuation of it, which the novel sets out to question. Italian Renaissance painting remains the most prestigious school of painting – itself divided in regional and local schools – and especially prestigious when religious painting is the subject. Chardin's still lives, *natures mortes* to recall the terminology discussed in Chapter Four, are equally notorious as "French". The third painting is a German one, thus integrating Germany into the canon of great painting. But, while German art obviously comes to play on the nationalism of the German immigrants, it is this piece that, authentic in itself, depicts a fake.

Authenticity is also the organizing principle of the exhibition. An ingenious set-up of the exhibit doubles the painting in its representation – the room was organized following the set-up in the painting. That is, "Un Cabinet d'amateur" was depicted on the back-wall, Bronco McGinnis' portrait was placed on an easel in the right-hand corner, and the other paintings in the room were hung exactly in the same position as they appeared on Kürz's canvass. This doubling effect excited the spectators, as they could compare the original paintings and their miniature forms, so scrupulously reproduced by Kürz.

Paradoxically, then, authenticity is presented as a matter of imitation. Moreover, the doubling was given yet a further twist, as the catalogue text observes with admiration:

> And there, they will have a marvellous surprise: the painter placed his painting in the picture, and the collector, seated in his room sees on the back wall, in a direct line with his look, the painting representing him while looking at his collection of paintings, and all those paintings reproduced anew and so on,

without losing any of their precision in the first, second, or third rendering until nothing more remains on the canvass than infinitesimal traces of the brush.

Et c'est là qu'ils auront une merveilleuse surprise: car le peintre a mis son tableau dans le tableau, et le collectionneur assis dans son cabinet voit sur le mur du fond, dans l'axe de son regard, le tableau qui le représente en train de regarder sa collection de tableaux, et tous ces tableaux à nouveau reproduits, et ainsi de suite sans rien perdre de leur précision dans la première, dans la seconde, dans la troisième réflexion, jusqu'à n'être plus sur la toile que d'infimes traces de pinceaux (Perec 1979: 22).

As soon as the spectator enters the room of this exhibition, she hence enters into a virtual hall of mirrors – while the reader reading about this undergoes the same effect. "Un Cabinet d'amateur", exhibited as its own double, is reproduced ad infinitum on the canvass itself, thereby drawing viewer and reader into complex interactions with its fetishistic qualities.

These qualities involve a desire for authenticity and vision as confirmation of a presence, something that is deferred ad infinitum.[7] The desired authenticity, depicted as presence, is represented in its impossibility. The painting develops into a locus of attention similar to places of pilgrimage, compelling special measures to ensure its protection. Guards had to be positioned at the exhibition door to keep the mass of viewers from completely overrunning the room. Only twenty-five viewers were admitted at a time and after fifteen minutes they are made to leave. Many of them returned time and again, engaging in what might best be described as a ritual of inspection.

The two main reasons for the sensation "Un Cabinet d'amateur" elicits are obvious: its effort to attain absolute veracity and its inclusiveness. These two reasons are mutually incompatible, however. There was no moment when the work was finished while the painter was simultaneously painting the canvas. But as a depiction of a collection it is a possibility. In this line of reasoning, the painting can be read as a documentation of Western art as it represents the major schools and genres of art. "Un Cabinet d'amateur", then, functions as the ideal of an encyclopaedic desire (Magné 1989: 193-206). But this desire is anchored in and through the claim to veracity that the painting puts

---

[7] This mise en abyme structure of *Un Cabinet d'amateur* has been pointed out by others as well, see Burgelin (1988: 205-07), Ballestero (1996: 164-72). For mise en abyme, games, and ludic structures, see Motte (1984: 50-60).

forward. The room itself proposes a reality effect (Barthes 1986), of course, by reproducing the painting in all its details, yet the spectators attach more meaning to the paintings reproduced in ever smaller representations on the canvass proper:

> The favourite game of those maniacal observers, who would return several times a day to examine systematically every square centimetre of the painting, and who displayed a wealth of ingenuity (or audacious acrobatics) to try to better see the upper parts of the canvass, was to discover the differences existing between the various versions of each of the represented works, at least up to the level of their first three reproductions, most of the details thereafter evidently ceasing to be clearly discernable.

> Le jeu favori de ces observateurs maniaques, qui revenaient plusieurs fois par jour examiner systématiquement chaque centimètre carré du tableau, et qui déployaient des trésors d'ingéniosité (ou d'audacieuse acrobatie) pour tenter d'aller mieux regarder les parties supérieures de la toile, était de découvrir les différences existant entre les diverses versions de chacune des œuvres représentées, au niveau du moins de leurs trois premières répétitions, la plupart des détails cessant évidemment ensuite d'être distinctement discernables (Perec 1979: 25).

Viewers attempt through the means of jeweller's magnifying glasses to discern the smallest details, and, by forming virtual human pyramids, try to perceive in minute brush strokes the umpteenth reproduction located high on the painting.

The exhibit leads to a temporary and unprecedented boom in the sale of optical magnifying instruments, and to a craze Pittsburgh never witnessed before: what the spectators to their astonishment discover is that reproduction is not complete; imitation only refers to the original but never exactly reproduces it. The lesson in looking for the truth is harshly disturbed:

> One could have thought that the painter had had his heart set on executing the copies each time as faithfully as possible and that the only perceptible modifications had been imposed upon him by the limits themselves of his pictorial technique. But it did not take long to see that, on the contrary, he had forced himself to never strictly copy his models, and that he seemed to have taken a malicious pleasure in introducing time and again a minuscule variation: from one copy to another, persons, or details disappeared, changed places or were replaced by others.

L'on aurait pu penser que le peintre avait eu à cœur d'exécuter chaque fois des copies aussi fidèles que possible et que les seules modifications perceptibles lui avaient été imposées par les limites mêmes de sa technique picturale. Mais l'on ne tarda pas à s'apercevoir qu'il s'était au contraire astreint à ne jamais recopier strictement ses modèles, et qu'il semblait avoir pris un malin plaisir à y introduire à chaque fois une variation minuscule: d'une copy à l'autre, des personnages, des détails, disparaissaient, ou changeaient de place, ou étaient remplacés par d'autres (Perec 1979: 25-26).

The painter, as this passage goes to demonstrate, establishes a cleft between imitation and authenticity, a gap that thwarts the cultural assumptions underlying the fetishism of authenticity. Kürz's malicious pleasure frustrates the viewer's desire for reality and exactitude; his reproductions are never exact copies of the originals as if to point out that repetition always comes with a twist. Consequently, the instruments, such as magnifying glasses, which help decide upon the accuracy of reproductions, turn against the spectator in the form of distorting mirrors as if they mock the viewer's expectations.

Nevertheless, or maybe because of new details continually discovered in the copies, the curiosity of the visiting crowds is constantly fuelled. Spectators make listings of differences between the various copies and attempt to find a justification for them, because, of course, they must have a meaning. One meaning nobody seems to want to accept is that the painting problematizes representation and presents itself as such. This inevitable outcome and the concomitant frenzy it creates, finds its resolution in an act of violence and wilful destruction. A visitor throws a bottle of ink against the canvass and "Un Cabinet d'amateur", together with its "originals", is withdrawn from the exhibition.

Death Wish to Cult Value

This act of destruction is itself an imitation. Among the literary works that stage the desperate attempt at mimetic perfection considered as equivalent of beauty, and the subsequent destruction when the attempt necessarily fails, both Balzac's and Zola's novels on the subject have retained critical attention of a philosophical kind. What, these novels seem to ask, is art compared to "life"? And the answer appears to lead to death (e.g. Didi-Hubermann 1985).

After this act of destruction, "Un Cabinet d'amateur" is returned to its prior safe haven and hidden again from the public eye. All that is left for the public is an article published by a certain Lester Nowak, titled "Art and Reflection" in which the painting is described in its mirroring qualities. Just as I have done before, Nowak places "Un Cabinet d'amateur" in the tradition of paintings with the same title representing collections and their collectors. The mirror is in fact the only remnant for the public to contemplate: after the collector's death "Un Cabinet d'amateur" disappears along with the morbid wishes expressed in Raffke's will. His body, preserved by the best taxidermist of his time, was clothed in the same dressing gown that he wore in Kürz's painting, seated on the same chair, and lowered into his tomb. The tomb itself replicated on a reduced scale the exhibition room with the painting by Kürz occupying the back wall, and to the right of this – instead of *Portrait of Bronco McGinnis*, dismissed as a fake because the model was fake – a full-length portrait of Hermann Raffke himself, made some forty years earlier during a visit to Egypt. The corpse was set up facing the paintings and the tomb was sealed.

One might think that the fetish qualities of "Un Cabinet d'amateur" were entombed together with the body of the painting's owner, an owner whose own emotional investment and bodily attachment to the painting extends beyond his own demise. These fetish qualities are necessarily double: they comprise presence and absence, a desire for authenticity and full visibility and, at the same time, their continual deferral as each miniature painting produces the next, ad infinitum. As I have suggested, the painting attained this fetish status in another context where the painting's exhibition and its presence and visibility to the public opened up the space for the fetish to emerge. Yet, notwithstanding its cult-like entombment, bringing it back to cult value in a Benjaminian sense, "Un Cabinet d'amateur" enjoys a remarkably long after-life as fetish produced in the painting's absence although repeatedly signified by markers of its persistent presence.

A few years after Raffke's death, a first auction of his collection takes place and, much to the disappointment of potential buyers, none of the paintings reproduced in "Un Cabinet d'amateur" appears in the auction catalogue. Their interest had been whetted by the posthumous publication of Raffke's autobiography, containing a listing of all his acquisitions together with details about the date and circumstances of the paintings' acquisitions, and often including the price he had paid. A second impulse for the potential buyers had come in the form of a *catalogue raisonné* of Heinrich Kürz's work, published after his death in a railroad accident in 1914. Since the original of "Un Cabinet d'amateur" had been put to eternal rest with Raffke's body, this catalogue's author, Lester Nowak, took great pains to supplement the five other known paintings by Kürz with the unlikely number of some fourteen thousand preparatory sketches of his masterpiece.

Nowak's catalogue erects a monument of presence in the absence of the original by providing the authentication and provenances of the painting represented on the canvass of "Un Cabinet d'amateur". Simultaneously, this urge for attribution is mocked for its desire to attach the correct, and where possible, renowned, names to the paintings:

> The two major revelations of this study concerned the *Annonciation aux Rochers* and the *Chevalier au Bain*. Basing himself on the numerous similarities existing between the *Annonciation* and certain details of the *Vision de Saint Eustache* at the National Gallery (the deer, the mottled dog, the small greyhound) and of the *Légende de saint Georges* at the Santa Anastasia (the two dogs next to Saint George) and of the *Annonciation* at the San Fermo in Verona (the wings of the angel and the piece of landscape above him), Nowak effectively showed with near-certainty that the work could be attributed to Pisanello.
>
> Les deux révélations capitales de cette étude concernaient l'Annonciation aux Rochers et le Chevalier au Bain. Se fondant sur les nombreuses similitudes existant entre L'Annonciation et certains détails de la Vision de Saint Eustache de la National Gallery (le cerf, le chien tacheté, le petit lévrier), de la Légende de saint Georges de Santa Anastasia (les deux chiens près de saint Georges) et de l'Annonciation de San Fermo de Vérone (les ailes de l'ange et la découpe du paysage au-dessus de lui), Nowak démontrait en effet que l'œuvre pouvait, avec une quasi-certitude, être attribuée à Pisanello (Perec 1979: 94).

We are moving closer to cultural practices of the fetishism of authenticity here. The authentication is based exclusively on motives, in a dizzying game of cross-references. As is well known from recent discussions, conventional art historical practices of tracing provenance and establishing attribution have direct links to the production of the value and importance of the art works. Here, this practice put "Un Cabinet d'amateur", now with its constitutive elements, back into circulation. In short, Nowak's labour keeps "Un Cabinet d'amateur" present and visible, and, in so doing he subjects it to market mechanisms.[8]

A second auction takes place in 1924 and, based on Nowak's meticulous work, many paintings fetch prices unheard of until then. The reader of Perec's novel, however, is caught off-guard – just as much as all the eager collectors and distinguished museum curators who had been vying with each other to secure the masterpieces of Raffke's collection for their private collections and institutions – when a few years later a letter by Raffke's nephew Humbert arrives. Humbert, the organizer of the auctions, delivers a disturbing message. He reveals that most of the paintings sold at the second auction were false and produced by himself.

Raffke had found out that the paintings collected during his first few trips to Europe were false, a discovery that compelled Raffke to avenge himself by turning the tables upon a world of art sellers and buyers who pride themselves on their expertise. He used every one of his subsequent journeys to Europe to assemble and forge evidence in order to authenticate the works his nephew Humbert Raffke, an accomplished pasticheur, produced. Nowak was in on the plot as well. But the key to Raffke's diabolical, yet playful, scheme resided in "Un Cabinet d'amateur":

> The cornerstone for this patient mise-en-scène, of which every stage had been carefully thought out, had been the realization of "Un Cabinet d'amateur", on which the paintings of the collection, displayed as copies, pastiches, and replicas would very naturally look like copies, pastiches, and replicas of *real* paintings.

> Le clé de voûte de cette patiente mise en scène, dont chaque étape avait été très exactement calculée, avait été la réalisation du *Cabinet d'amateur*, où les tableaux de la collection, affichés comme copies, comme pastiches, comme répliques, auraient tout naturellement l'air d'être les copies, les pastiches, les répliques, de tableaux *réels* (Perec 1979: 124-25).

Humbert Raffke, alias Heinrich Kürz, proved his talent in misguiding whoever wanted to believe in the truth of the painting, thus neglecting the many ways in which it had shown itself to be a representation.

---

[8] For conventional approaches to attribution, see, for instance, the debates surrounding the Rembrandt Research Project, discussed in Bal (2003a).

Perhaps, one should have been more aware of a small detail in Raffke's will, which was enacted in the set-up of his dead body facing "Un Cabinet d'amateur", in the tomb. Whereas in the 1913 exhibit "Un Cabinet d'amateur" was displayed with the *Portrait of Bronco McGinnis*, in the tomb the fraudulent tattooed exhibitionist had been replaced by that of an equally fraudulent collector – the portrait of Raffke himself, or as we now realize, Raffke's portrait of himself.

At this point, when the reader is already severely destabilized by Raffke's tricks, the novel takes one last turn, which serves final blow to the reader's reliance on authenticity, visibility, and presence for its concluding lines:

> Diligent verifications undertaken quickly showed that most of the paintings of the Raffke collection were indeed false, just as most of the details of this fictitious story are false, a story conceived for the mere pleasure and thrill of pretence.

> Des vérifications entreprises avec diligence ne tardèrent pas à démontrer qu'en effet la plupart des tableaux de la collection de Raffke étaient faux, comme sont faux la plupart des détails de ce récit fictif, conçu pour le seul plaisir, et le seul frisson, du faire-semblant (Perec 1979: 125).

The elaborate mise en abyme structure in *Un Cabinet d'amateur*, which mirrors and doubles the collection in an endless proliferation, entices the reader to hold on to signs of presence that attempt to cover up crucial absences. And then, in a final gesture of contempt for the values it has been staging, and with authorial sovereignty, the narrative reveals its own fake status and explodes the notion of presence in showing how we "forget" or suppress the lack that underscores the fetishism in our interpretational process.

Touring Absences

Such an elaborate discourse on authenticity, covering up the lack of it, is entirely absent in the museum Insel Hombroich. This institution's attempt to achieve authenticity resides in its refusal of discourse altogether. Yet, it evokes responses that nevertheless focus largely on presence and the visible. This is emphasized in admiring newspaper articles, such as in the *Münchener Abendzeitung*, which called Insel Hombroich "the most beautiful private museum in Germany", and the *Herald Tribune* naming it the "Atlantis of a collector", or the French critic Pierre Restany exclaiming it to be "an earthly paradise" (all quoted in *Zeit Magazin* 1990: 44).

Figure 12. Thomas Riehle (1996). *Insel Hombroich.*

One of the major attractions of the museum is its location. Its motto is "Kunst parallel zur Natur" (Art parallel with nature), an indication of the general setting and environment of Insel Hombroich. Modern buildings, designed by the sculptor Erwin Heerich, are located in a landscape of wildflowers, poplars and willows in the bend of a small river. Karl-Heinrich Müller, owner of the collection, prefers to speak of Insel Hombroich as an encounter or an event, rather than a museum. This encounter between art and nature, inside and outside, is articulated in the lack of guards, climate controls, and other overtly protective measures. The doors of the museum buildings are always open, thus exposing the objects to the influences of heat, cold, humidity, and aridity. The collection is displayed in a mix of materials, objects, and paintings. Categories such as "Western" or "ethnographic" art, "high" and "low" art, or periodizations, dissolve in what comes across as a rather random placement of objects.[9] Familiar markers and categories have also disappeared and so have, in a still more radical manner, all references to artists, titles, and dates. Indeed, the result is quite an encounter.

Now, the walking tour can begin – although no preset itinerary has been established by the museum. Armed with a map on which the various pavilions are indicated, the (generic) visitor wanders through this bucolic landscape. A brick structure rises like a tower in the lowlands and upon entering the empty space, the visitor is forced to become a listener. Once inside, there is nothing to see, but the heavy door that falls shut behind you sends waves of sound rippling through the space equipped with wonderful acoustics. It brought one critic to speak in *Avenue* of a cleansing experience, peaceful and almost religious, because of the monumental quality of the "modern cathedral" (Klinkenberg 1989: 70).

Other pavilions contain parts of Müller's collection such as the so-called Labyrinth. Here, in a maze-like structure, the eye meets a bewildering arrangement of furniture that appears Japanese, collages that seem to date from the early 1920s, as well as paintings, vases, objects, sculptures from who knows where and when. The familiar movement of the head and eyes to

---

[9] I am deliberately using the term "object" despite its problems as pointed out by Clifford (1991). The art-artifact divide would have raised even more serious trouble (but see Duncan [1995: 5]), which I will discuss later in this chapter. The term "object" is used to be able to address arrangements that vary in materials, period, and cultural contexts.

the small labels indicating artist, title and year of production is interrupted, because there are none to be found. No help in determining what you are looking at, no sense of common context, no educating gesture – and isn't that what museums are supposed to offer? Left behind with the conventional guiding principles of museum visits thoroughly shattered, the reliance on other interpretative frameworks becomes a matter of some urgency.

In my deliberate use of tentative terms such as "looks like", I try to suggest that the absence of common markers indicating periodization or cultural context does not lead to their complete dismissal, since the visitor used to their help tends to invoke them mentally anyway. Yet these markers remain uncertain and, as a result, they are hardly helpful. As an example of this disorienting absence of textual markers, I want to take a look at some rooms of the Labyrinth to show what additional strategies are at work in the museum.

Figure 13. Thomas Riehle (1996). *Insel Hombroich.* "Graubner room".

In what I call the Graubner room (figure 13), the spectator encounters an arrangement of sculptures and paintings carefully displayed in a bright space. The paintings have a certain softness to them, looking like mattresses, as a filling has been inserted between the cloth and the frame. All these monumental canvasses are covered with whirls of colour, one of the colours dominating in each. Fiery red, blue-purplish, green or brown: thanks to their strong colour and despite their softness, they hang like forceful statements on the wall. Lining the room on three sides, the paintings intersect with sculptures that stand together in loosely grouped arrangements. Torsos and heads carved in stone, slender on their pedestals, they convey both delicacy and robustness. Insofar as the questions concerning the origin and creator of the sculptures have lost much of their relevance, other aspects acquire more importance in making sense of what we see.

The hieratic character of the sculptures reinforces the verticality of the paintings, yet their protruding surfaces go together with the sculptures' three-dimensional qualities and spatial arrangement. Both paintings and sculptures show softness *and* harshness despite the different materials from which they are made. Materials, texture, and colours, in their relationship to each other, provide means of interpretation in the absence of obvious textual markers. For instance, the colour whirls on the canvasses led me to think of Monet's repeated rendering of the water lilies in his garden pond in Giverny, and his famous studies of the Japanese bridge, painted in different seasons, techniques, and shades of colour. The connection to Monet is not accidental. A garden modelled after Monet's garden at Giverny, is part of the landscape enveloping the pavilions. Moreover, the colours in the room refer to the four elements of fire, earth, water, and air, and therefore to everything that can be made out of their various combinations. Even though I could consider the works one by one, what is emphasized in the Graubner room is not the individual work of art but the dynamic relationality at play between different works. With relationality I also mean to point to forms of "intertextuality"; to the different connections, coming about as one wanders from one room in the Labyrinth to another.[10]

Just before the passage in the middle, on the left wall (see figure 13), there

---

[10] For introductions to this concept, see Kristeva (1980) and Bakhtin (1981).

is a painting that seems to act almost as an intermediary. It indexically refers the spectator to a room with collages, similar in form, while simultaneously maintaining a relation with the Graubner room sculptures in its vertical and horizontal lines. Parallel to the room with collages, another one is furnished with a wooden chest, two chairs, a porcelain vase with an arrangement of twigs, and a sculpture of a monk-like figure. It struck me how this quiet scene of objects resembled the Graubner room in the play of lines, and how the fiery red of the canvasses there sensitized me to the flamed surface of the wooden chest. If it weren't for the slight elevation on which the two chairs were placed, foregrounding the museum character of the display, I might have thought myself in a private space.

This possible confusion is foreclosed in the next room, where the museum is very much present again. Smoothness of surfaces is replaced by ruggedness, both in the paintings and the sculptures there, drawing the attention to texture and material. The paintings have a sculpted surface, because of the granular quality of the paint, a granularity repeated in the sculpture itself. In colouring too, paintings and sculpture show a connection and a contrast to the strong colours of the room with furniture and the Graubner room.

Intertextuality and Frameworks: Absence as a Fetish?

A first tour of the Labyrinth that took the absence of textual markers seriously, provided some of the strategies a spectator might use in making sense of this space's exhibited objects. Texture, material, and colours, for instance, do present ways to perceive the objects not in and of themselves, but instead in relational terms. Expectations about educational and informational gestures – normally furnished to visitors by museums – are effectively undermined. Insel Hombroich bans a passive "aha" *erlebnis*, responsive only to what markets and media have already declared worthy of attention. Rather, the museum urges the spectator to develop an active and interactive attitude to what one sees. No single viewing experience – for example that of confirmation that a work is indeed produced by the famous Kurt Schwitters, Rembrandt, or Matisse – is privileged at the expense of others.

Instead, this display, or rather, this environment I gladly qualify as interactive, activates the visitor into supplementing the missing information. It asks the spectator to make explicit what would otherwise remain implicit. As a result of prior encounters with art and the information about it, even if textual markers are absent, viewers are not suddenly bereft of all forms of textuality, although, as I will show, some of the responses to the museum seem to indicate just that. In fact, spectators draw on frameworks which are mediated in and through language, be they of a less obvious nature.

Frameworks, however, beg the question of framing, i.e. of what the relationship is between a work and its context. Derrida (1987: 37-83) has shown how the issue of deciding what the work (*ergon*) or the frame (*paregon*) is, cannot be so easily resolved. Names, dates and other identificatory markers do frame the work, although they are neither part and parcel of the work nor completely separate from it. As Derrida argues:

> A parergon comes against, beside, and in addition to the *ergon*, the work done [*fait*], the fact [*le fait*], the work, but it does not fall to one side, it touches and cooperates within the operation, from a certain outside. Neither simply outside nor simply inside (Derrida 1987: 54).

Hence the parergon operates at the border of a work in a supplementary fashion, always revealing a lack inside the work (1987: 42-43; 59).

In an important addition, Jonathan Culler has extended Derrida's argument into a consideration of the role of the critic whose presence is inseparable from historical knowledge and does not take context as a given:

> Context is not fundamentally different from what it contextualizes; context is not given but produced; what belongs to context is determined by interpretive strategies; contexts are just as much in need of elucidation as events; and the meaning of a context is determined by events. Yet when we use the term *context* we slip back into the simple model it proposes (Culler 1988: ix).[11]

In short, the interpretive strategies of the critic are foregrounded, shifting the emphasis from the presumably clear-cut fashion in which work and frame, in both a broad and narrow sense, were separated, toward a reflection on the strategies one employs.

---

[11] Within the framework of art history and literary theory, the discussion of context has been taken up by Mieke Bal and Norman Bryson (1991). See also Bal (1991) and Bryson (1994).

Perhaps, then, I have too hastily assumed in my comments above that a viewer makes the otherwise implicit interpretational practices explicit and that the museum undermines a passive response. Taking the arguments by Derrida, Culler, and others into consideration, theoretically at the very least, another possibility presents itself. If textual markers were to be considered as belonging to the work, completing it and motivating certain interpretative frames, their absence opens up possibilities for the operation of the fetish in a range of differing ways. That is, confronted with a lack in the work, interpretation cannot be finalized by labelling the work "properly". Instead, the lack or absence itself emerges as a constitutive part of the fetish.

At this point the reader will remember that in Perec's novel, the presence of all the signs of authenticity was a condition in which the fetish was able to emerge and, even when the fetishized painting was itself absent, the presence of its markers made a continuation of its fetishized status possible. In Insel Hombroich, we encounter a different, indeed, perhaps opposed situation as the works are present, but the signs of their authentication are not.[12]

Some of the critics' responses I invoke here assume that the absence of textual markers does lead to forms of visual innocence, to a non-textual response. At the end of the day, then, this response fetishizes the objects even more, emphasizing their purity and beauty, whereas the violence of their detachment from their context of origin is forgotten. The criteria underlying the responses are those of Western art. For example, in the Dutch newspaper *De Volkskrant*, art critic Ineke Schwartz contends regarding Insel Hombroich that: "Here only the laws of aesthetics and harmony count . . . [Müller's] collection is a hymn to the beauty of form and colour" (1995: 8). In similar terms, Joachim Peter Kastner asserts that the objects displayed benefit from their placement in a natural surrounding:

> The artistic phenomena, embedded in eloquent nature, leave a strong impression. Ideally, they lead the spectator back to the roots of perception, when light and colours, space and bodies, movement and sound were experienced "pure", as such (Kastner 1992: n.p.).

Pure perception is enhanced by eloquent nature, foregrounding beauty of

---

[12] Other signs of authentication are present of course, such as the tickets one buys at the entrance or the map to guide the visitors.

form and colour. The direct connection between the objects exhibited, analyzed as works of art, and the senses struck by their beauty precludes a critical response in these assessments.

If perception of the admittedly beautiful objects in ideal terms is "pure", what kind of elements would contaminate this "pure" response? Surely nature does not count as a source of contamination, but market considerations along with the conventions of the art historical and museum curatorial world do seem to be considered as such. Would contamination consist of not going along with the play of light and colours, space and bodies, movement and sound *only*? Compelling as the objects in Insel Hombroich are, they raise certain questions that are relevant in view of the following remarks about the mixing of objects.

Knowing where the objects in Insel Hombroich come from and by whom they were made, the critic in *De Volkskrant* allows for their intermingling, but under certain conditions, as part and parcel of a hymn to the beauty of form and colour. She claims:

> Therefore, *Iranian neolithic* objects from tombs do not clash with canvasses by Graubner or Corinth. *Here, Japanese* wooden printing-blocks and small *eighteenth century Chinese* glass vases are as much art as the tapestries by Eduardo de Chillida or costume designs by Matisse (Schwartz 1995: 8; emphasis added).

It seems as if Iranian neolithic objects – traditionally referred to as "artefacts" – are allowed close proximity to objects of "art", classified as belonging to a different domain of value and appreciation – because they do not clash in beauty of form and colour. Some of the quality of objects such as de Chillida's tapestries or Matisse's costume designs rubs off on Japanese printing-blocks and Chinese glass vases and thus renders them into art. But they become art only in the here and now of this particular display.

Kastner has a similar response to the joint exhibit of what had formerly been separate between museums for "Western" and "ethnographic" art. In his view, objects attain an a-historical and geographically non-specific status:

> The artefacts exhibited here exemplify what determines the entire island as an esthetic event. In this space, they do not seem to be a string of collector's pieces, but differently accentuated processes (Kastner 1992: n.p.).

Differences in time and cultural origin hereby recede. As indicated in the footnote, Kastner focuses in his appraisal on the common denominators that join artists in their efforts and processes of creation, because artists everywhere have struggled to master the working of light and colour, the movement of bodies and so on. In the name of similitude, differences are definitely relegated to the background.

James Clifford has argued with respect to the controversial 1984 Primitivism show at the Museum of Modern Art in New York, that exhibits which attempt to overcome the differences between "Western" and "ethnographic" art are riddled with problems along the aesthetic-anthropological divide (1988: 188-214).[13] In this debate, centring on aesthetics, he posits that the objects were exhibited as a-historical and without cultural context. Art became a category able to transcend time and culture, and able to strike us by its beauty alone. Focusing on anthropological considerations, on the contrary, would mean being explicit about the cultural contexts, histories of collecting, and colonial situations linked to imperialist endeavours.

The celebration of aesthetic pleasures is easily demonstrated in Schwartz's and Kastner's response to Insel Hombroich, and my own interpretational strategy of relationality might fall under the same spell. Affinities and resemblances of material, texture, and colour, quite easily fetishize these very aspects. Objects from non-Western cultural contexts become acceptable as art in the West only after shedding their anthropological contextualization, and it is this crucial understanding that a focus on presence might obscure (Price 1989: 60 quoted in Hart 1995: 144). It is by force of anonymous presence that these objects can enter into the same status as objects obviously categorized as Western. A look at the visitor's map however shows this not to be the case, as a trade-off between complete anonymity and cultural specificity becomes visible. The following description is that of the Labyrinth:

---

[13] See also Karp & Lavine (1991) and the debate surrounding the "Magiciens de la terre" exhibit of 1989 at the Centre Pompidou and the Musée de La Villette in Paris. See for example special issues of *Art in America* (1989), *Les Cahiers du Musée national d'art moderne* (Martin et al 1989), as well as Coombes (1994), and Spivak (1993).

In the building "Labyrinth" various domains of the collection are represented.
By a wilful staging they were brought into dialogue by Gotthard Graubner . . .
Khmer sculptures and Chinese figures of the Han period are in correspondence
with paintings by Gotthard Graubner. Pivot-wise exhibited in the Labyrinth are
subcollections of the early China of the Han, Tang, and Ming periods, Khmer,
as well as of the 20th century. Works exhibited are by Lovis Corinth, Kurt
Schwitters, Hans Arp, Jean Fautrier, Francis Picabia, Fritz Schwegler and
Raymond Hains (Visitor's map 1995).

As a gesture toward the visitor's desire for specificity, the map only goes
halfway. Names of major artists, Western, but not further specified, are
coupled with equally general appeals to connoisseurs of Chinese historical
periods. Regions, broadly defined, serve as rough indications.

Obviously, the intermediary position the map tries to negotiate will never
satisfy either side of this divide. In the museum Insel Hombroich, the fetish
as a phenomenon of the border uneasily straddles the aesthetic-
anthropological divide. Objects identified as Western art can merely coexist
with objects identified as non-Western by suppressing what W.J.T. Mitchell
called "the violent yoking" of what is other and what is considered most
modern (1986: 191 quoted in Bal 1994: 107). Because of this violence that
accentuates presence, absences inherent in the fetish are neglected.

A Final Tour d'Horizon

Strolling along the pavilions and pastures that make up Insel Hombroich, and
taking in the effects of its motto – Art Parallel to Nature – the encounter calls
forth various responses. These may vary between celebrations of beauty,
hardly questioning what the museum proposes, and more critical attitudes. I
was comforted in a certain respect by Bernhard Korte, the landscape architect
of Insel Hombroich, whose remark on landscaping I wish to extend to the
museum as a whole: "Insel Hombroich is tended as if it is not cared for. The
wilderness is desired, the naturalness is artificial" (Klinkenberg 1989: 70-71).

This comment brings back the ending of Perec's novel with its jubilant
expression of wilful faking. A critical attitude then might focus on the make-
believe and pretence that plays such an important role in that novel and also,
we can now see, in Insel Hombroich. If we consider the museum through the
lens of Perec's pleasure in make-believe, it becomes a task of some relevance
to investigate the cultivated combination of naturalness and artificiality as

they guide and subvert interpretational practices. Thinking along the lines laid out by Perec, one realizes that no display of whatever object is natural, nor will any display expose its full artificiality.

Taking both naturalness and artificiality into account, as well as their combination as an "authentic" construction – a wilful making of authenticity – a critical attitude motivates one to include what is present and absent. This attitude perhaps criticizes the fetishization of either presence or absence at the exclusion of the other. Instead, it attempts to investigate how both are addressed in a continuous movement. If indeed this movement of the fetish is traced, the viewing event of Insel Hombroich becomes a self-reflexive and layered experience. Just as the final lines of *Un Cabinet d'amateur* in fact ask us to reread the whole novel and trace its fetishistic appeal as a construct, with authenticity as the lure, we might peer on our maps of Insel Hombroich and decide to revisit what it is that brought about our wonder and awe, and which then nudges us to trace *its* fetishistic appeal.

I began this book with the case of a classical topos: the woman at the window. Hers was an absolute boundary, one she was forbidden to transgress. But as my analyses have shown, boundaries exist by virtue of their transgressability. And with transgression – legitimate or in contraband – the possibility of negotiation is opened up. Even in the absolute, depressive situation of the first-person narrator of Bouraoui's novel, she was able, at least, to *see* the aggression against her friend, the black woman from the desert who, in the Algerian household, took the place of otherness. For windows are transparent and beyond them the world opens up – inaccessible, but not inexistent, and visible. The narrator was also visible herself, to the man who came to marry her. Negotiation over her, over her body, took place even if she had no say in the matter. The idea of absolute boundaries, in other words, is a contradiction.

Equally close to home, so to speak, is the case discussed in the second chapter. The case is symmetrical: where the young girl locked up in an obsessive notion of fearful chastity could not go out, the letter-writer of the second chapter could not find refuge in the home. In the situation of civil war, another sense of boundaries comes into play, one where protection is vital, yet unattainable. Again, the young woman protagonist writes a depressed prose that betrays how the vitality of her needs is diminished by the state of all-encompassing violence. The combination of these two chapters brings out the ambivalence of the notion of boundary. Whereas absolute boundaries do not exist, some sense of distinction, clearly, serves a purpose. But the point is to conceive of that purpose in non-absolute terms.

A third case where "home" is the ground on which negotiation between self and other takes place, is that of the travelling European woman who is invited inside the home of the women she considers other, and whose strangeness she attempts to describe. Here, we saw the negotiation of what later became ethnographic writing, where the sense of hospitality, of being received as a guest, establishes a kind of modesty in the writer who is not at home, but not quite in the public domain either. Boundaries turn out to be a space where the encounter between self and other can take place, an encounter that can be written – inspiring writing in an intransitive sense, rather than writing "about". This, perhaps, is my non-expert definition of ethnographic writing.

The next three chapters developed this conception of boundaries in their more material appearance. The desert is such a crucial boundary space that it serves as such even within, for example, the North-African nations. For many of the narrators and characters who appear in this study, the Berber is always stranger, more other, than the Magrebhan for the European or the other way around. And where the European considers the desert a space to traverse, a space to map, for the inhabitants it is simply their space: the land that feeds them.

As in the first part, *The Function of Boundaries*, the second part, *Matter In and Out of Space*, opened with two cases that seem to be diametrically opposed. The fifth chapter staged an intercultural encounter on the basis of fashion, a fake encounter premised on imitation. Opposed to the harsh world of the desert, the smooth world of sex appeal is no better suited to accommodate otherness. We have seen that what seems an authentic "look" of hybrid cultural mixtures tends to return to haunt the capitalism that impelled it. This combination of desert and fashion, two spaces, or practices, of cultural negotiation, raises the issue of what underlies the fantasy, or construction if you like, of all those boundaries that plague us so today: of some sort of authenticity, to be defended, assaulted, conquered or bought.

If, in the end, authenticity turns out to be the most fake of all, a fiction of impossible reality of everything we desire and yet fear, then the fetishism of authenticity that regulates fashion and art, tourism and travel, is the key to my attempt in this book, at undermining the concept of boundaries that rules dichotomies, hostilities, and the overblown differences between people – and which makes the differences from which we can learn and which we can enjoy, near-invisible.

PART III

PLACING INGE E. BOER

SEVEN

Impressions Of Character: Hari Kunzru's *The Impressionist*

Murat Aydemir

Writing in *The New York Times*, critic Susannah Meadows reproaches British-Indian writer Hari Kunzru's *The Impressionist* (2002) for not offering convincing renditions of place and character. Partly set in colonial India, the novel fails to deliver the *couleur locale* Meadows demands from that exotic setting. "[A]s far as picturing India goes", she complains, "you're on your own". Additionally, the critic objects that the book is without a centripetal protagonist, deeming its main subject to be flimsy, blank, stunted, hollow, and paper-thin. For Meadows, then, the literary failure of the book hinges on its bland representations of character and place – or, more precisely, on the tenuous relationship holding between the two. For, if India were to be pictured more obligingly, presumably, then the book's subject could have come across as considerably less bland and paper-thin.

The terms of Meadows' critique suggest that realistic credibility or *vraisemblance* crucially depends on the maintenance of a measured relation between character and setting. Within that relation, the particularities of place should inform and substantiate the portrayal of character; yet, simultaneously, a character must stand out against that setting or background to move into focus. Since *The Impressionist* features a protagonist who travels from India to Britain to Africa, and whose identity changes to an extraordinary extent according to the demands of each setting he finds himself in, the novel questions our aesthetic ability (or willingness) to identify, and to identity with, a character who migrates and transforms.

As Meadows' review makes clear, the literary portrayal of characters who switch settings and change accordingly may at some point stretch beyond the limits of what readers can realistically recognize as a character. Such characters end up as flimsy and hollow non-characters.

In the case of Meadows' reading of *The Impressionist*, the "character effect", the reader's fleshing out of a character from words on paper, apparently misfires.[1] Yet, the book, if read less disparagingly, may offer the opportunity to counter the cultural prejudice that masks as aesthetic judgment. At the same time, the novel may contribute to Inge Boer's project of criticizing and nuancing the currency of the nomadic, migratory, exiled, or diasporic subject as a "jubilant metaphor" in contemporary Cultural Studies (Introduction). For, if it is true that meaning is organized "at the edges or boundaries between categories", as Boer, quoting art historian Linda Nead, maintains, then the crucial edge or boundary at stake for a possible "migratory aesthetics" of character entails the narrative border – simultaneously connecting and separating – between setting and character, or the visual one between background and human figuration.[2]

The novel suggests a specific aesthetic effect that comes into play when, through its elaboration of migration, the mutual dependency between the two comes under strain, either because character blends into setting too successfully, or because the border between place and character becomes blurry. That effect is already indicated in Meadows' review. For, the point of the parergonic sign of the cover photo of the American edition of the novel is not quite lost on the critic. Concluding her scathing review, she writes: "The cover, interestingly enough, is an out-of-focus black and white photo of a man. If there ever was a time to judge a book by its cover it is now, because you'll squint and squint at *The Impressionist*, but it'll never come into focus".

However ill-appreciated, this effect of repetitive squinting may help to suggest an aesthetics of character that does not lament but seizes on the out-of-focusness of a migrating character in its relation to changing settings.

---

[1] On narrative character as effect, see Bal (1985: 79).
[2] The phrase "migratory aesthetics" refers to a two-part workshop, organized by Mieke Bal and Griselda Pollock, held in January 2005 and 2006. The workshop investigated if and how aesthetic representations of migrancy are able to accommodate a new understanding of aesthetic categories as well as of the aesthetic itself.

Indeed, in her failed attempt to get the book in focus, Meadows repeats, hence performs, the squinting look that the book casts at its subject matter. In this essay, I will try to show that the novel's resistance to, or voidance of, the realistic *vraisemblance* of character representation in relation to migration, constitutes the novel's most intriguing contribution to the academic debate on inter- and crossculturality. And, as I will argue, this resistance *includes* available concepts of intercultural identity, such as hybridity, travesty, mimicry, and nomadism. Situated at the boundary between character and changing settings, as well as between character and various conceptualizations of transcultural identity, the novel's hero only momentarily achieves a recognizable and intelligible shape, to then lose it again and find another. To make sense of the book, the reader is forced to blink and squint between character, context, and concept. What *The Impressionist* thus offers is an epistemological aesthetic of a qualified perception of people and places, in which they intermittently move in and out of focus. In accordance with the book's title, that squinting aesthetic gets a familiar, if ambivalent, name: "impressionism".

Impressionism: Squinting and Blinking

> impressionist
> – a painter who endeavours to express the general impression produced by a scene or object, to the exclusion of minute details or elaborate finish; also, a writer who practices a similar method;
> – a comedian whose act consists of imitations or impersonations of well-known personalities.[3]

The book's title alludes to two uses of the word "impressionism" throughout the novel, the one performative, the other perceptual. In its first meaning, *The Impressionist* refers to the many-named title character who, according to the demands of the situation he finds himself in, performs nearly effortless impersonations of various ethnic, social, and sexual identities. These include Pran Nath Razdan, arrogant eldest son of a fiercely nationalistic Kashmiri family living in Agra; Rukshana, a *hijra* girl who is secluded in the *zenana*,

---

[3] Selected definitions from the online *Oxford English Dictionary* (1989). The definitions that follow are from the same source.

or harem, of the Mughal court of Fatehpur; Pretty Bobby, living in the outskirts of Bombay with the missionary family MacFarlane; and Jonathan Bridgeman, who, after attending public school at Chopham Hall in Norfolk, moves on to Oxford to join one professor Chapel as his research assistant on an ethnographic study of the Fotse tribe of West Africa. Each of these incarnations is as well defined as the next one.

Yet, these different place- and situation-bound impressions of personhood fail to coagulate into a formative character that travels from episode to episode, from setting to setting. The protagonist lacks all expectations that anticipate and motivate the next part; nor is he even remotely burdened with retroversions or flashbacks that take the reader back to previous episodes. The transitions from one incarnation to the next, moreover, are hardly elaborated upon. Hence, character in *The Impressionist* makes perfect sense *in situ* in each of its parts, while immediately blurring out of focus as soon as the reader attempts to connect these various appearances into a unified person.[4] Thus, the lack of focus with respect to *couleur locale* and character that Meadows decries does not so much emerge because both would be lacking in the book, but rather because the title character blends too perfectly into each environment, fits each identifying slot offered up within a particular situation too completely. As a paradoxical result, both setting and personhood lose the "character" that Meadows' demands of a bonafide literary novel.

The performative impressionism the book plays out reaches a self-reflexive highpoint when the protagonist visits a Paris cabaret, where a "nondescript little man" takes the stage (Kunzru 2002: 418). The man's performance exemplifies the method or procedure of the book as a whole: "Illuminated by a wobbly spotlight that casts a washed-out circle on the silver backdrop", the impressionist delivers credible renditions of various characters, each lasting "a few seconds, a minute. Each erases the last" (419). Against the silvery backdrop that serves as a makeshift setting, and illuminated by a mobile spotlight, each impersonation, convincing for the duration, only appears under the erasure of the next one. Yet, in-between the performer's sequential acts, the protagonist observes to his horror, "the

---

[4] In literary impressionism, Jack Stewart argues, character is "no longer conceived as a solid object to be grasped and presented; it is . . . destructured, pulverized into scintilla, to be assembled by the reader" (2002: 195).

impressionist is completely blank. There is nothing there at all" (419). The procedure of the impressionist's performance is remarkably similar to that of the history lessons which the protagonist, now in his capacity of Jonathan Bridgeman, receives at an English public school, even though these garner the exact opposite effect. While the man's act on the Paris stage conjures up arbitrarily changing identities from a fundamental blankness, the history lessons achieve the "eternal recurrence" of the same essential identity from the "blur" of the past (315). As the protagonist reflects:

> The boys are to trace the destiny of their island through a series of devotional tableaux, jewel-like moments which reveal essences, principles, axioms drawn out of race and blood . . . the past is depicted as a blur of large and uninteresting forces which only achieves clarity at certain points, when it instantaneously freezes into still compositions of shining faces and rich drapery (Kunzru 2002: 315-16).

Here, the impressionist's performances against the silvery backdrop are replaced by frozen tableaux of shiny faces and rich drapery. Yet, the jewel-like clarity and stillness of the scenes wholly depend on their momentary separation from the ongoing blur of history. The stability and recognizability of character thus established is only supported by the nationalistic frame that binds "essences, principles, axioms" to the singular setting of the island and its apparent "destiny". When such a frame is unavailable due to the blurring history that the alluring tableaux leave out, the result of the same procedure is blankness rather than clarity.

The play of the silver backdrop and the roving spotlight between which the impressionist conjures up his character impersonations from a fundamental blankness, also signals the second and perceptual usage of impressionism in the book. In *Downcast Eyes* (1993), Martin Jay traces the philosophical, art historical, and literary resonances of the term. In its name, the dominance of what Jay calls "Cartesian perspectivalism" came under attack from various angles from the second half of the nineteenth century onwards. Through impressionism, the accolade of the disembodied eye made way for incarnate vision; the emphasis on the observation of form was replaced by attention to the play of colour and light on irregular, textured surfaces; spatial vision was temporized; and geometric, "deep" perspective was substituted with flattened and foreshortened space (Jay 1993: 150-54).

A suggestive scene arrives when the main character, in his capacity as Pretty Bobby, retires to his room, which is adorned with a collage made up of portraits from magazines; it includes film stars, politicians, athletes, saints, as well as Indian gods and goddesses. Staring at this constellation, Pretty Bobby indulges in a game "in which he half closes his eyes, or opens and shuts them rapidly, smearing or flickering the faces together, making them into new ones, more fantastic, more interesting" (Kunzru 2002: 200). The temporality of the embodied glance, the blinking motions of the eyes, forge new and fantastic identities that exceed the contours of the individual portraits.

Whereas the sequential character impressions of the Paris performer are separated from each other by the blankness that also forms their ground, and while the recurring shiny tableaux of British identity are set-off from the blur of history that frames them, here the borders between the portraits on the walls become plastic and morphogenetic under a squinting and blinking eye. Rather than being erased or fixated, new characters emerge. "Smearing and flickering", the impressionistic glance makes productive the edges between the entertaining impersonations and the educational tableaux, seizing on the blankness and blurring that separate them. I wish to propose that the interplay and enduring tension between the performative and perceptual aspects of impressionism, compelling repetitive squinting, is what underlies the poetic of the book. The various renditions of identity *The Impressionist* delivers, each as crisp and credible as the next one, may at any moment washout into blankness as the wobbly spotlight catches the silvery backdrop.

The double impressionism of the book also enlists no less than four available concepts for conceiving of identity at, or across, borders: nomadism, hybridity, travesty, and mimicry. The novel stages incarnations of all four notions, identities that exemplify each aspect respectively. Hence, the realistic reading mode that requires a psychologically "round" main character, and that, as Meadows' review shows, cannot but fail, must make way for a way of reading the novel that is attuned to the concepts it draws on. Indeed, *The Impressionist* can be read as like a conceptual novel, even like a theory sampler. The focus the book lacks when read as a realistic novel may therefore sharpen as soon as this thoroughly conceptual nature is recognized. The different settings in which, or backdrops against which, the impressionist performs his acts of identity are not only historical, cultural, or social, but also include a series of concepts of interculturality.

However, the book conjures up such obviously theory-informed scenes that to recognize these concepts hardly seems a productive response. Clearly, *The Impressionist* does not offer itself up as "raw" or epistemologically dormant fiction to be illuminated by theory, as pure imagination awaiting reflection to bring out its significance. Each conceptual setting, staging the appearance of identity as informed by hybridity, travesty, mimicry, or nomadism, is as exemplary and illustrative as the next, yet failing to allow the reader to bring these together under a single heading. The simultaneous presence of several conceptualizations of intercultural identity in the narrative cannot but displace the hold of each over the discourse. In this way, the book pre-empts a merely descriptive or labelling use of concepts from the start. The novel resists both a realistic reading and a naively theoretical one, set-out to "apply" concepts of interculturality in order to determine its meaning. Or, to put this a different way, the performative force of the concepts, the boundary-crossing they enact rather than reflect upon, resituates their hold over the story. They do not so much cognitively capture an identity that traverses borders, but rather they themselves become part of the crossing they make intelligible.

In the course of the narrative, then, *The Impressionist*'s protagonist does not so much journey from event to event, but from setting to setting, from backdrop to backdrop, and from concept to concept. In this way, the narrative tries out, tries on, different conceptualizations of inter- or cross-cultural identity. The novel entrains, uses up, concepts. A conceptual approach to the book thus partakes of impressionism's perceptual aspect: hybridity, mimicry, travesty, and nomadism each allow for comparatively sharp looks at certain scenes or fragments of the novel. But these, too, are little more than temporary appearances that are staged under the erasure of the next one under a wobbly spotlight.

The impersonations of the main character, as well as the concepts of interculturality that inflect these impersonations, together forge an impressionistic rather than discrete understanding of the figuration of character in the novel in either realistic or conceptual terms. Between blinks of the eye, character in *The Impressionist* makes perfect sense, either realistically or conceptually. Yet, their simultaneity or unmotivated sequentiality provokes repetitive squinting. Like the successful impersonations of the impressionist, the intercultural concepts that the novel plays on are *performed*, that is to say, they are reiterated in fiction and enacted and visualized. In what follows, I will attend specifically to the conceptual impersonations that the book delivers within its double impressionistic frame.

Hybridity

> hybrid
> – offspring of a tame sow and a wild boar;
> – the offspring of two animals or plants or different species, or (less strictly) varieties; a half-breed, cross-breed, or mongrel;
> – anything derived from heterogeneous sources, or composed of different or incongruous elements.

The concept of hybridity is sandwiched uneasily between its racist past and its contemporary postcolonial usage. "'Hybrid' is the nineteenth-century's word", Robert Young argues in *Colonial Desire: Hybridity in Theory, Culture and Race*, "[b]ut it has become our own again" (1995: 6). In its critical return, Young continues, the term cannot but reiterate its assumption of distinct racial identities preceding their hybridization, its implicit "politics of heterosexuality", and its intimation of colonial desires, laced with abjection, which are ultimately complicit with colonialism itself (25; 3). The concept "changes as it repeats, but also repeats as it changes", Young concludes (27). Additionally, hybridity veers between a limiting usage, indicating specific identities and situations, and a generalizing one, in which, as Homi K. Bhabha has proposed, a "cultural hybridity that entertains difference without an assumed or imposed hierarchy" can become paradigmatic for the larger "colonial and post-colonial condition" (1994: 4; 9). Hence, the concept entangles the colonial past with the postcolonial present, as well as a narrow and a general usage.

In "Hybridity: A Slippery Trail", Isabel Hoving takes precisely "the nauseating, provocatively repulsive aspect" at the core of the notion, linked to the "unspeakable sexuality" of colonialism, as the vantage point for her re-evaluation of the concept (2000: 193). Rather than trying to clean up the term to accommodate its generalizing and celebratory usage in the vein of Bhabha,

Hoving proposes a conception of hybridity that remains wedded to "the anguished, paranoid discourse of the disturbed authority figure (the colonizer), and [to] those who have had to internalize that anxiety and loathing" (2000: 193). For Hoving, the term works to the extent it continues to specify the "ambivalent anxiety of the sex-obsessed colonial whose gaze fixes the peoples of colonized areas, as well as when s/he looks back at him/herself" (2000: 197).

In *The Impressionist*, hybridity is repeatedly elaborated through such an anguished and paranoid focalization by paternal authority figures. "[T]errified of pollution" and the "collapse of categories", the Kashmiri nationalist Pandit Amar Nath Razdan advocates policies that recommend the maintenance of strict demarcations between Indian communities and castes, which also inform laborious rules for personal hygiene, language use, etiquette, and dress sense (Kunzru 2002: 31; 33; 30). When his hometown Agra is struck by the influenza epidemic to which he will ultimately succumb, the Pandit suffers from nightmares in which both that setting and the various people living there indiscriminately merge:

> At night he dreams of the contagion. Bloated faces and the sound of coughing follow him through streets where the very houses and shops seem to melt into one another, losing their integrity, invaded by their own architectural disease. The dream people are horrific and indistinct. At a look or a touch, they blur into one another – woman into man, black into white, low into high. It seems the epidemic will obliterate all conceivable distinctions, hybridizing his whole world into one awful undifferentiated mass (Kunzru 2002: 35).

Setting and characters together melt into an "undifferentiated mass". At once the spiritual heart of the proud Razdan dynasty and a colonial city bustling with various communities and castes, Agra suffers an "architectural disease" analogous to influenza. Hence, Razdan's blurring focalization of the town and its inhabitants merely forms the flipside of his puristic politics.

Similarly, the colonial missionary Andrew MacFarlane stationed in Bombay, a man with "little capacity for vagueness", busies himself with the photographic and craniometrical classification of the subcontinent's races (Kunzru 2002: 226). However, malaria and climate work together to dissolve "Europe in heat and moisture, turning this man of God into a sensuous thing, a streaming body" (227). Eventually succumbing to his stubborn desires for the indigenous women he classifies as primitive, MacFarlane conceives a daughter, whom he describes as "a collapse. A blur" (230). Anxiously, the reverend imagines "his huge-headed yellow daughter, breeding a litter in the muck of the jungles, his own features distorting until the line petered out into a last hideous stillbirth" (232). The city of Bombay and the jungle form the suitably hot and moist settings that make the European character liquefy, blur, peter out.

In the perspectives of Razdan and MacFarlane, the book's protagonist can only appear as an abject hybrid. At his deathbed, the Pandit learns from a vindictive servant that his cherished son is actually the "bastard child of a casteless, filth-eating, left-and-right-hand confusing Englishman" (Kunzru 2002: 39). The reverend describes his adopted son as a "mongrel", a "hyphenate", speculating that his "form of hybridity might conceal all manner of antisocial tendencies" (198). A hybridizing focalization occurs, the novel suggests, when the impressionistic, fuzzy edges between classified identities are met with abjection. Thus, because the main character's hybridity remains consistently situated in, and focalized through, racist and puristic ideologies, personified by specific characters, the novel prevents the generalization and celebratory usage of the term in accordance with Hoving's re-evaluation of the concept. Hybridity, then, cannot fully account for the elusive character that is at the centre of the narrative. Indeed, the term cannot form the conceptual backdrop against which the impressionist will move into sharp focus.

Travesty

> travesty
> – dressed so as to be made ridiculous; burlesqued;
> – a literary composition which aims at exciting laughter by burlesque and ludicrous treatment of a serious work; literary composition of this kind; hence, a grotesque or debased imitation or likeness; a caricature;
> – an alteration of dress or appearance; a disguise; spec. (dressing in) the attire of the opposite sex.

Kicked out of the Razdan household after the disclosure of his dubious descent, the protagonist of the novel falls prey to a couple of brothel-keepers. Then, he is purchased to become part of the harem of the Nawab of Fatehpur, where the chief hijra informs him that "[w]e are all as mutable as the air! Release yourself, release your body and you can be myriad! Why try to stop a river? Why try to freeze a cloud?" (Kunzru 2002: 82). Dressed up as an Indian girl, the main character must now service the British Resident staying at the court, Major Privett-Clampe, who has a fondness for "beautiful boy-girls" (87).

However, the Major quickly tires of the boy's hijra outfit: "Look at that fancy dress they've put you in. You're supposed to be a chap, not a bleeding girl" (Kunzru 2002: 108). Subsequently, the boy-girl is dressed up by Privett-Clampe in his own school uniform to further facilitate their sexual encounters. Noticing he has "some white blood" in him, the Major also embarks on poetry and language lessons, which ultimately impart the boy with superb English diction (104). Gradually, Privett-Clampe's "sense of being a mentor" to the boy – initially a role-play merely adding a fetishistic charge to their meetings – takes over from his sexual desires. A sceptical courtier remarks, "The old hypocrite actually had the nerve to tell me he was interested in improving the boy's mind" (111).

In *Vested Interests* (1992), Marjorie Garber analyzes the figure of the transvestite as an index to what she calls "category crisis", a failure of definitional distinction. Always overdetermined, the transgression of gender ushers in a "mechanism of displacement from one blurred boundary to the other", also implicating class and race (Garber 1992: 16). The distinctions between categories, such as man and woman, black and white, colonizer and colonized, adult and child, are all interrelated to such an extent that to cross one, Garber argues, necessarily means to "slide along" the other (1992: 271; 274). Transgressing one boundary inevitably implies the transgression of others.

In *The Impressionist*, the protagonist's enforced transition from Kashmiri boy to a hijra girl offered up to the colonizer enables and prompts his next slide, switching from gender to ethnicity, to an English schoolboy "taught" by the Major, who relates to him as to a former self. On the one hand, the relation between hijra girl and colonial john can serve as the critical reminder of the colonial desire that the pedagogical situation, bent on "improving the boy's mind", at last erases. On the other, the Major's pedagogy maintains the hierarchy between adult and child, teacher and pupil, which also marks the

colonial project at large. As the narrator remarks of the British general
responsible for the massacre at Amritsar:

> the General thought of his bullets in pedagogical terms. Ethically, the dark-
> skinned races are like children, and the General was fulfilling the primary duty
> of the white man in Asia, which is to say that he was laying down a clear line.
> His bullets were reminders of the meaning of the law. Repeat after me (Kunzru
> 2002: 183).

As Boer reflects, the transgressions that cultural travesty makes possible
remain restricted to a tightly constrained limit imposed by the ideology that
views colonial subjects as children first, so that gender becomes secondary,
and hence optional (Chapter Five).

At the same time, the fetishized caricature of the English schoolboy that
the protagonist incarnates for the British Resident will also serve as his
effective disguise. A runaway from Fatehpur and on his way to Bombay, the
main character must pass a whipping post with men crawling and groveling
at the feet of British soldiers. He manages to pass indeed. Willing his pores to
close – "Skin to statue. White Marble. Impenetrable" – and holding "Privett-
Clampe's voice inside [his] mouth", he tells the soldiers, "I am very well. I
am going. Forthwith" (Kunzru 2002: 186). They let him go. In its oscillation
between (eroticized) caricature and disguise, then, the performance of
cultural travesty participates in the perceptual impressionism of the book: the
impressionist's character moves unpredictably in and out of focus,
hypervisible the one moment, practically invisible the next.

Mimicry

> mimicry
> – the action, practice, or art of mimicking or closely imitating, either in sport or
> otherwise, the manner, gesture, speech, or mode of action of persons, or the
> superficial characteristics of a thing;
> – a close external resemblance which a living creature bears to a different
> animal, or to some inanimate object. Also used of similar resemblances in
> plants.

In its slide from ostentation to disguise, travesty is similar to mimicry. In
Homi K. Bhabha's influential elaboration of the term, mimicry follows from

the fundamental ambivalence of colonialism as both a civilizing and an exploitative project, which thus interpellates colonized subjects to become more and less like "us" at the same time. According to Bhabha, the double bind translates into a precarious condition in which the colonized subject may at any time slip from registering as "almost the same but not quite" to "a difference that is almost total but not quite" (Bhabha 1994: 87; 90).

The vacillation condemns the colonial subject to what Bhabha describes as a "partial" presence, or a presence turned to "a part": firstly, in the sense of a performance, a role play that imitates the colonizer, in accordance with colonialism's civilizing mission; and, secondly, in the sense that only partial aspects of the colonizer's identity are ever made available for imitation, for instance dress or language (anything short of full equality), in order to continue to justify colonial exploitation (Bhabha 1994: 86; 91). Thus, the partial resemblances the colonized subject represents become disproportional, and hence farcical, in relation to the whole from which they are selected.

However, because the very ambivalence at the heart of mimicry cannot but continuously generate "its slippage, its excess, its difference", mimicry condenses at least three contradictory aspects or moments (Bhabha 1994: 86). As a colonial policy, it institutes what Bhabha calls a "flawed colonial mimesis, in which to be Anglicized is *emphatically* not to be English" (87). Additionally, through betraying "the ambivalence of colonial discourse", it also "disrupts its authority" (88). Finally, the colonial subject's acts of mimicry may rearticulate "the whole notion of identity and alienates it from its essence" (89).

The first aspect of mimicry describes the predicament of the members of the Agra Post and Telegraph Club in *The Impressionist*. Wearing hats at every occasion, frantically sipping tea, and endlessly discussing the Home Country they have never visited, they imitate partial objects of Englishness (Kunzru 2002: 46). As a result, they only manage to come across as *less* English: "One supposes it is sweet, in a way. But ultimately they are rather disgusting, those people" (46). The main character, however, consciously working to appropriate Englishness and passing successfully, takes mimicry to the next level. As Jonathan Bridgeman, the impressionist keeps a pocket book "with entries on Victoria Sponge, bumble bee, fair play and groundsman" (335). Yet, his mimicry far exceeds these partial objects.

Ultimately, the entries in his pocket book combine to suggest a complete "grammar of behaviour, a social language which might be written down and read off again" (335). Like travesty, then, mimicry combines both aspects of the impressionism the novel elaborates. Performatively, mimicry ranges from the farcical to the successful enactment of Englishness. Perceptually, mimicry makes porous and insecure the boundaries between imitation as a form of flattery, as ironic caricature, and as the alienation and appropriation of identity. The sincerest form of flattery, imitation can work to estrange the very thing to which it pays homage.

Nomadism

> nomad
> – a member of a people that travels from place to place to find fresh pasture for its animals, and has no permanent home. Also: an itinerant person; a wanderer.

The outer frame that the book's narrative traces from its beginning to its ending moves from trees to grass, and hence, from the arborescent to the rhizomatic, in terms supplied by Gilles Deleuze and Félix Guattari in their introduction to *A Thousand Plateaus* (1992 [1980]). Briefly, the arborescent indicates a way of thinking that takes the symbol and image of the tree as its organizing principle, whereas the rhizomatic is associated with fungi and grasses. The former is characterized by sedentariness, unity, hierarchy, and genealogy. The latter's values are nomadism, multiplicity, flatness, and anti-genealogy; in the rhizome, tree-like "lineages" are replaced with mobile and proliferating "lines" or "lineaments". The arborescent is tangentially related to the forests and fields of the West, the rhizomatic to the steppes and gardens, deserts and oases, of the East (Deleuze and Guattari 1992: 20). The two terms also oversee concomitant modes of political organization: the stable state versus a despotic rule constantly challenged by nomadic violence. Trees and grass respectively mark *The Impressionist*'s protagonist's birth at the beginning of the novel and his rebirth at its conclusion.

  The main character's British birth father Ronald Forrester is a colonial functionary labouring to fight dust, and hence, erosion and entropy, through a determined policy of tree maintenance in India. His underlings call him

"Forrester sahib", his friends, jokingly, "*Forrester the forester*" (Kunzru 2002: 3). At night, Forrester suffers from nightmares in which a multitude of uprooted trees perform frantic dances, forming a "musical comedy of trees" (4). Surprized on a lonely expedition by a tropical rainstorm that washes away the dusty soil to form mud streams, Forrester chances on the feisty Indian woman Amrita, who, under a duress comforted by the copious intake of opium pellets, travels with her retinue to her husband to be, Pandit Amar Nath Razdan. With the weather conditions causing unexpected opportunity, Ronald and Amrita make love in a cave, their sweat and the dust turning their skins "to an identical red-brown colour" (15). Their son grows up in the Pandit's household as Pran Nath Razdan, the impressionist's first incarnation; his whiteness is suitably mistaken as definitive proof for the purity of his Kashmiri lineage (20).

Towards the end of the book, the protagonist, now in his capacity of Jonathan Bridgeman, joins an ethnographic expedition studying the Fotse tribe of West Africa, a portion on the map the professor regards as inviting "blank white space" (Kunzru 2002: 370). The party of ethnographers experience some difficulty in getting to grips with the tribe's social organization, which is modelled on the rhizomatic needle grass that grows in the region: "The part of needle grass that is underground has no beginning and no end, a matt of fibres which lies hidden in the earth . . . Thus it is with the needle grass society, which has no head, no centre, which runs under the ground of Fotseland" (475). The ethnographers are all killed by the Fotse save for Jonathan, who is interred under the ground to rid him from the spirits that possess him. Lying drugged in a cave on a carpet of ancestor bones, Jonathan notices its dome covered with red handprints, moving in the lights of the torches (473).

Jonathan survives the ritual to take on his ultimate identity as a nomad living in the desert. He and his camel "trudge up the gentle windward slopes of the dunes, sliding down each leeward face in an ankle-deep cascade of sand . . . For now the journey is everything. He has no thoughts of arriving anywhere" (Kunzru 2002: 481). Hence, it would seem that, having completed the journey from trees to grass, from the arborescent to the rhizomatic, the impressionist finds his ultimate identity in the non-identity of the nomad, his ultimate setting in the non-place of the desert.

Deleuze and Guattari's conception of the nomad is criticized by Boer, who agrees with Christopher Miller's condemnation of the notion as partaking in a "violently representational, colonial ethnography" (Miller 1993: 13 quoted in Chapter Four). Representational, because Deleuze and Guattari's "nomadology" reiterates orientalist stereotypes that invoke an ideological image of the East. Colonial, because it confirms the view of the desert as empty, and hence readily inviting and legitimizing conquest. Indeed, "The Treatise on Nomadology" that is also part of *A Thousand Plateaux*, is littered with an assortment of orientalistic references to, for instance, roving bands, Genghiz Khan, Arab tribes, a Japanese fighter, the figure of the despot, and desert landscapes. So, as the authors themselves question, "What can be done to prevent the oriental pole from a fantasy that reactivates all the fascisms in a different way and also all the folklores, yoga, Zen, and karate?" (Deleuze and Guattari 1992: 418). That question remains to be answered.

However, the "empty space" of the desert that, for Miller, translates Deleuze and Guattari's notion of "smooth space", seems not entirely warranted. The desert is not so much empty because just nomads live there; rather, nomads actively produce smooth space as they blaze a violent trail through territories that are already ordered, metrically or otherwise, and organized politically by the power of states. This is why a roving fire supplies Deleuze and Guattari with a suitable metaphor for what nomads do to space: they negate and abolish its existing ordering, to then leave again (1992: 430).

Boer's scepticism towards the nomadic subject as a "jubilant metaphor" in contemporary Cultural Studies and feminism seems to me entirely warranted (Chapter One).[5] Indeed, Deleuze and Guattari themselves offer a series of arguments against such a usage. Firstly, they caution that the Oriental nomad is "not something to be imitated" (1992: 419). The nomad does not so much exist as an identity to take on, but merely to the extent that he creates smooth space.

Secondly, the alternative space the nomad creates only exists in relation to the state power, to which it forms a synthetic and necessary supplement

---

[5] Dasgupta points to an example of such a use of the term in Ranjit Hoskote's article "The Nomad Position" (2002). Hoskote writes: "as a figure or trope, the nomad signifies the transgressive and emancipatory gesture . . . it rejects borders, passports . . . the zones it occupies are transient" (quoted in Dasgupta 2005: 25-26).

(Deleuze and Guattari 1992: 464). Consequently, the sedentary state and the nomads who create smooth space are "equally present in all social fields, in all periods" (397). Political lobbies and multinationals are put forth as contemporary nomadic formations. And the distinction between nomad and state is characterized as a "tension-limit" (401), "a shifting borderline" (405), where the one is not necessarily better than the other, "just different" (410). Hence, even though their nomadology is associated with the East through its Orientalistic flavouring, the authors also concede they "are on the wrong track with all these geographical distributions . . . for there is no dualism, no ontological dualism between here and there" (22).

Finally, the nomad merely serves Deleuze and Guattari as a conceptual abstraction (1992: 463). The nomad cannot exist but for his intermixing with other non-sedentary figures, such as the migrant, who principally goes from one place to another (419); the artisan itinerant, who follows the material necessary for his craft, like iron (452); and the agricultural transhumant, who seasonally rotates between plots of land (452). At best, then, the nomadic can only be an aspect that necessarily relates to the sedentary subject framed by state power, and that can only exist in an impure intermingling with other instances of non-sedentary identity, who – unlike the nomad who, upon arrival, immediately leaves again – do impose an ordering on the spaces they inhabit. Simultaneously the radical opposite to the spatial order imposed by the state and its synthetic supplement, and simultaneously a discrete abstraction and a hybrid mingled with other non-sedentary characters, the nomad is necessarily a blurred and blurring category.

Thus, the nomadic non-identity that *The Impressionist* seems to recommend as the happy ending to the main character's series of impersonations is ultimately not available as the story's destiny. Perhaps we should have expected as much, since Deleuze and Guattari already warned in their introduction that the idea of a rebirth, of a new beginning, implies "a false conception of voyage and movement (a conception that is methodical, pedagogical, initiatory, symbolic)" (1992: 27). Much like state and nomad, the arborescent and the rhizome that mark the beginning and the ending of the book are, as Deleuze and Guattari write, "relative, always connected, caught up in one another" (11).

Therefore, the same rhizomatic frame or set-up for the novel's conclusion

– consisting of the Fotse needle grass society and the rituals that forge the protagonist's rebirth as nomad – also prevents that identity to function as the pedagogical and symbolic destiny of his quest. For, the rhizome, Deleuze and Guattari argue, "avoids any orientation towards a culmination point or external end" (1992: 24). The rhizomatic book they project laterally "flattens" its narrative and conceptual trajectories towards closure, laying out its ordered content made up of events, historical determinations, concepts, individuals, and social formations on a single and horizontal plane, a "single page, the same sheet" (10). Read in this way, the conclusion must be that the impressionist's becoming-nomad, which brings the book to closure, is his final and perhaps most persuasive conceptual impersonation. The desert, too, will not be his true home.

The Portrait Peels (Off)

The "characters" of migrants are easily reduced to either their original (culturalism) or their present setting (assimilationism). In its performances and perceptions of blurring, sliding, and mirroring characters, *The Impressionist* offers no realistic or conceptual narrative that can connect there and here, past and present. Yet, what is clear is that the notion of character the novel proposes is neither fully reducible to one or the other setting – as the protagonist jumps from setting to setting, from identity to identity, with remarkable ease – nor fully independent from the settings he inhabits, since each incarnation of the impressionist is decisively inflected by the constraints and possibilities of each situation. Thus, the novel refuses autonomous individualism as well as determinism.

The impressionistic view of the aesthetic category of the character that the book proposes instead consists of a series of interrelated steps. First, character is flattened against backdrop, immersed into setting, while the backdrops and settings are multiplied. Second, current concepts of intercultural identity are submerged into the narrative as well, levelled at its plane, so that they can only partially account for the character transformations that make up the novel. Hence, they are no longer available as external, meta-, or independent tools or "lenses". As in Deleuze and Guattari's rhizomatic book, character, setting, and concept are all resituated at the same plane or level. Third, the resulting imagery, with character, setting, and concept pressed together, becomes the object of the impressionistic glance, blinking and squinting, flickering and smearing. When the protagonist scrutinizes a picture of his birth father, he is not so much entranced by the identity it promises, but rather by the possibility of transformation it suggests as the light catches the silvering exposed at one of its corners:

> Pran handles the photograph as if it were a magical item, as if its power is in some way inherent in its substance, chemicals and paper laced with an energy of good and evil. He turns it over and over, examining every aspect, fascinated by the rip on one corner, by the way that at a particular angle the silvering catches the light and turns the image from a brown and yellow face to a featureless dazzle. An excess of light, a god, impossible to look on directly. For that one moment the silver is whiteness, all the blinding alien whiteness that his new father has poured into his once-comfortable life. He spends hours tilting the little picture to catch the light, repeating it again again again, feeling each time the thrill, the awe of transformation achieved by a tiny movement of his hands (Kunzru 1992: 64-5).

It appears that Meadows, in a way, may have been right after all: character in *The Impressionist*'s aesthetic of character is indeed paper-thin, perhaps even thinner. Yet, precisely this impressionistic "flattening" of character allows for the experiment with light and motion that can make a face, the exemplary carrier of identity, "dazzle" and suggest awesome possibilities for transformation. In this way, *The Impressionist* shows how even the rudimentary boundary between character and place, or between human figuration and backdrop, is not so much a two-dimensional or geometric entity, but, in Inge Boer's vein, a space in which things happen.

EIGHT

From Travelogue to Ethnography and Back Again? Hilma Granqvist's Writings and Photographs

Annelies Moors

Tracing the genealogies of ethnographic writing, one obvious category to look into is travelogues (Pratt 1992). In the nineteenth century such travelogues were not only produced by men who had travelled to far-away places, but women also took part in such endeavours and produced their own writings. In her third chapter, Inge Boer deals with travelogues of women travellers to the Orient as a particular form of ethnographic writing. For travel involves an "ethnographic impulse". Both travellers and anthropologists, sharing an interest in the everyday lives of Europe's others, produce knowledge by translating personal experiences into generalizations. In doing so they are faced with a similar problem, that is how to state the new and unknown in terms of the known in order to convey their experiences to the public "back home". Writing about their experiences with unfamiliar practices, they need to employ certain techniques to make their work legible to their intended audiences.

Boer is particularly intrigued by the techniques nineteenth century women travellers used to convey their experiences and perceptions. It is her analysis of the travel writings of Jane Dieulafoy, who accompanied her archaeologist husband to Iraq and Persia in the 1880s, that I take as the point of departure in this paper. Dieulafoy did not only write about the women she encountered, but also took photographs and had some of these images included in her publications. In analysing the text as well as the images, Boer draws on the work of Walter Benjamin to highlight that the photographs do not simply illustrate the text, but produce a narrative of their own:

> If the text represents an explicit desire for what Dieulafoy sees as the necessary emancipation of Persian women, the photographs at first glance appear to do the same. But, at another level, the photos add and feed into the fantasy of unveiling Oriental women. In this respect, the photographs act doubly: while maintaining and reproducing cultural and sexual "otherness", they simultaneously register the need for reform (Chapter Three).

In other words, while the written text points to women's oppression under Islam and expresses the need to improve their conditions, the photographs partake in another style of Orientalism. In staging their unveiling – hence expressing and producing a narrative of seduction ánd a desire to dominate women – this pictorial style ties in with conventional visual representations of Oriental women. While at first sight these two discourses may seem different, they converge in the ways in which they leave "the body of Oriental women indelibly marked by their difference" (Chapter Three).

As implied in the above, Boer points to one particular technique employed by Dieulafoy, namely a focus on the physical features and dressing styles of women. Similar to many other travelogues written by women, little information is provided about the conversations they had with the women they encountered on their travels. Instead, the book abounds in descriptions of dress and appearance, of the body and the face. Visuality is the privileged sense and dressing styles are seen as a form of expression and communication. Such descriptions may be seen as another attempt to locate the unknown within the known.

In this contribution I will analyse another instance of ethnographic writing, namely the early publications of Finnish scholar Hilma Granqvist. As one of the first women anthropologists, Granqvist engaged in long-term fieldwork in the Palestinian village of Artas, near Bethlehem, in the late 1920s. In the course of her fieldwork she took over 1.000 photographs, only thirty of which were published during her lifetime, all in her second book, *Marriage Conditions in a Palestinian Village II* (1935). Only much later did she start to work on a publication of her photographs, but she passed away before she could finish this project. Nine years after Granqvist's death, Karen Seger succeeded in publishing many of the pictures in *Portrait of a Palestinian Village: The Photographs of Hilma Granqvist* (1981).

In what follows, I will discuss some of the tensions between the "ethnographic impulse" in more popular writings versus those of academic anthropology of a certain time and place, taking into account written accounts as well as visual imagery. I set out by framing Granqvist's early work through a comparison with contemporary popular imaginings of women in Palestine, while simultaneously locating her at a particular moment in the development of anthropology as an academic discipline.[1] I then turn to Seger's publication and discuss how she translates Granqvist's work for a broader public at another historical moment, the 1980s. As it turns out, in spite of major differences, there are some interesting links between the techniques Seger employed in her "translation" of Granqvist's work and the ones Dieulafoy had employed a century earlier.

Out of History I: Palestine and Biblical Time

By far the most common topos in imaginings of Palestine in the earlier part of the twentieth century has been Palestine as the Holy Land.[2] Whereas such framing has a long history, nineteenth-century developments in scientific thinking brought about a novel style of representing Palestine as the Holy Land. Not only the geography of the land and its archaeological remains were seen as a direct link to Biblical times and as objective evidence of Biblical events, the inhabitants of Palestine were conceived of in a similar vein.

---

[1] Granqvist's early work refers to *Marriage Conditions in a Palestinian Village I*, published in 1931, and *Marriage Conditions in a Palestinian Village II*, published in 1935.

[2] For this framing I have made use of two archives of visual representation that enjoyed mass circulation at the time: picture postcards and the pictures and articles published in the *National Geographic Magazine* (for an analysis of these popular representations see Moors 1996). During the first decennia of the last century picture postcards, produced by commercial photographers for the tourist market, had become a highly popular means of disseminating visual images of Palestine, both in the European and American markets, and, with the development of international tourism, in Palestine itself. During roughly the same period, the *National Geographic Magazine*, based in Washington D.C., had become a major medium of visually representing the colonized world to a Western public. It was not only one of the first monthlies to make extensive use of photographs, but the ways in which it employed photographs greatly helped to establish it as both a popular and a scientific publication (see Lutz and Collins 1993).

Travel guides, such as the Baedekers recommended the Bible as the best source of information for visitors to the Holy Land. Moreover, in journals such as the *National Geographic* pictures and descriptions of the contemporary customs of the population of Palestine were employed to provide a didactic lesson about Biblical ways of living and to correct Western common-sense notions about Bible times.

The notion that the living image of figures and incidents from the Bible were to be found in everyday sites was built upon the assumption that the life of the present-day inhabitants of Palestine and their customs had not changed. In fact, the very inclusion of people in publications was based on the assumption that their appearance and way of living represented Biblical times. This was further reinforced by the use of captions and accompanying texts which employed terms as "primitive", "simple", "unchanged" and so on. The effect of such verbal and visual discourse, displacing the customs of the contemporary inhabitants of Palestine to a past of two millennia ago, was not only to erase historical change, but also to deny coevalness between the viewer and those depicted through the spatialisation of time (Fabian 1983). In other words, the Palestinian Arab population of Palestine on these postcards was depicted as living in an earlier historical epoch, which the viewers had long left behind.

Representations of Palestine's population were not only strongly influenced by the biblical discourse; other early nineteenth-century scientific discourses played their part as well. All of Palestine was to resemble the Holy Land, but some categories of the population were seen as more Biblical than others, with the practice of categorizing populations along lines of religion or habitat connected to evolutionist notions of hierarchical ranking, according to which different populations were regarded as relatively close or, inversely, at a remove from the pinnacle of civilization. Typologies based on such notions rapidly gained widespread currency amongst the public, and were to remain influential long after evolutionism had become discredited in academic circles. In travel books and guides, for instance, the division of Palestine's inhabitants into different categories is a constant theme, placing them in an internal hierarchy with regard to their propensity for change. Oftentimes the lifestyle of the Muslim villagers is assumed to approximate the biblical past most closely, and it is their customs that are presented to instruct the public about life in biblical times.

Whereas Granqvist worked with such Muslim villagers, photographs that evoke biblical connections are absent in her published work. Rather, she develops a strong critique of "biblical" framing. In her introduction, Granqvist describes how she set out in 1925 to travel to Jerusalem to study "the women of the Old Testament", convinced as she was that she would benefit greatly from observing life in the Holy Land (Granqvist 1931: 1).[3] Soon, however, realizing that archaeological courses and expeditions were insufficient to obtain new facts, she became involved in ethnographic fieldwork in the village of Artas.[4] As she herself put it: "I needed to live among the people, hear them talk about themselves, make records while they spoke of their life, customs and ways of looking at things" (Granqvist 1931: 2). Her fieldwork experiences stimulated her to develop a critical stance towards, as she called it, "the biblical danger". One of the central problems in the material about Palestine is, following Granqvist:

> There has been the temptation to identify without criticism customs and habits and views of life of the present day with those of the Bible, especially of the Old Testament . . . No one can get away from the fact that much is in agreement – the land and nature determine that. But in any case one must remember the whole time that it is Muhammadam Arabs, not Jews, whose traditions are being studied, and that there is a period of 2000 years and more between them – a gap which cannot be explained away merely by citing "the immovable East" (Granqvist 1931: 9).

Still, in the following chapters of her books, Granqvist regularly returns to such "biblical connections". The index of her two volumes on marriage conditions contains a long list of references to quotes from the Bible (Granqvist 1935: 340). In some cases these refer to a brief reference in a footnote, at other times biblical comparisons are included in the text itself. Granqvist's struggle with "the biblical danger" poignantly shows up in

---

[3] Granqvist (1891-1972) graduated at the faculty of arts at Helsinki University in 1921 in the subjects of pedagogy, history and philosophy. She then went on to write her doctoral thesis for Gunnar Landtman, professor of philosophy at the same university on the topic of "The Women of the Old Testament". After attending courses in Old Testament Studies at Berlin University, she left for Jerusalem in 1925 to take a course in Palestinian archaeology.

[4] One reason why she had chosen the village of Artas was that Louisa Baldensperger was willing to introduce and house her. Louisa Baldensperger was the daughter of an Alsatien missionary, whose father had settled in the village in the 1850s. She herself had been living there for over 30 years.

statements such as: "However much I tried to be on my guard against the danger of drawing strained biblical parallels, I had to admit that this was a modern example of the Old Testament story" (1935: 221).

If present-day readers may be struck by the tensions between Granqvist's critique of the "Biblical danger" and her own biblical comparisons and connections in her text, Granqvist herself saw her position as radically different from that of her predecessors and contemporaries. For that very reason she tries to preempt criticism of this particular aspect of her work:

> If in my work there are fewer quotations from the Bible than in most others, it has been from a perhaps exaggerated fear of uncritically mixing the old and the new. Just because there have been so many offences in this way it should be the object of a special inquiry to what extent the one or the other is connected with ancient times (Granqvist 1931: 10).

Out of History II: Between Evolutionism and a Synchronic Approach

In the popular imagery of publications such as the *National Geographic*, the centrality of the biblical discourse also meant that any traces of modernity were purposely left out (figure 14). For such photographs were of interest to a Western public, precisely because they provided an image of a different world, its inhabitants still living the life of Bible-times, or representing a romanticized Orientalist dream. Constructed as static, unchanging and traditional, they formed a vivid contrast with the increased popularity of the West as the agent select of change. After the British occupied Palestine in 1917, the British colonial administrators and their fellow Europeans were represented as a major force of change that was to positively affect Palestine and its inhabitants. With the growth of the Zionist movement, moreover, the new Jewish immigrants were presented as the epitome of modernity, embodied in the construct of the "pioneer".[5]

The ways in which Granqvist dealt with change in her work are complex. Whereas commercial photographers often consciously left out all traces of modernity, Granqvist did not. If the former usually show women carrying

---

[5] This did not preclude links with biblical times, but the activities of the new Jewish immigrants were not seen as simply reflecting events of the biblical past, but as consciously and actively creating these as part of a new culture. For an analysis of shifting representations of Palestinian women in the course of British mandatory rule over Palestine, see Moors (1996).

Figure 14. W. Robert Moore (December 1938). *Water, Jars, Ancient Symbols of Women's Toil.* In *National Geographic*, 718. Photo: W. Robert Moore/National Geographic Image Collection.

water in earthen jars, Granqvist also took pictures of women carrying water in large tin canisters, which, as she stated, were ousting the beautiful, hand-made water jars (figure 15; 1935: 22n; Seger 1981: 104). Other elements of change are visually present in her photographs as well, such as houses built from cinder blocks with corrugated iron roofing rather than the ancient stone-vaulted houses (Seger 1981: 106). In her writings she also mentions, for instance, men migrating to America, employment outside the village, and the introduction of cars. Still, it takes a close reading of her work to recognize such elements of change, for the impact of major political and economic changes is not seriously taken on. Also her large number of extensive footnotes, referring to an impressively wide array of sources in various languages, underline, perhaps unwittingly, the static nature of peasant life. For these footnotes are strongly comparative, employ a descriptive mode of writing without critical reflection, and produce an, at times overwhelming, feeling of decontextualization, with references to the ancient Hebrews or the ancient Arabs ("already amongst the ancient Arabs" [Granqvist 1935: 30]),

Figure 15. Hilma Granqvist (1935). *Drawing Water.* Plate 104. By permission of the Palestine Exploration Fund, London.

the Semites (1935: 98), and such varied locales as Morocco (Fez 400 years earlier 1935: 130), nineteenth-century Mecca and Armenia (1935: 98).

These apparent inconsistencies in Granqvist's dealings with change may be better understood if her positioning vis-à-vis the academic world and, more specifically, major shifts in contemporary anthropology are taken into consideration. Before completing her thesis Granqvist had taken a course in anthropology with professor Edward Westermarck at the London School of Economics, where she also met Malinowski. Her shift to ethnographic fieldwork brought Granqvist, however, into serious problems at her own university. In 1931 she was denied permission to defend *Marriage Conditions I* as her thesis at Helsinki University. Philosophy Professor Gunnar Landtman judged the basis of her thesis (a single village) too narrow for genuine scholarly research. Westermarck then supported her and in January 1932 she was able to publicly defend her thesis at Åbo Akademi University, where he also held a professorship.[6]

Granqvist worked at a historical moment when anthropology was in

---

[6] Amongst anthropologists her thesis was well received (see for instance the review of her work by Evans-Pritchard in *Man* 1937; Weir 1975). Still, she was never able to get a university position, and was also passed over for other positions, most likely because of gender considerations (Widén 1998).

transition from an older school – strongly influenced by evolutionist notions and employing a comparative method – to a more holistic, functionalist paradigm, arguing for the importance of long-term fieldwork in a particular locale (Stocking 1983). Convinced of the importance of in-depth research in a limited area, Granqvist stayed in the village of Artas for approximately twenty months. Besides pointing to the "biblical danger", she was also critical about existing research on Palestine as easy generalizations were made on the basis of particular local customs, collected from here and there, without clear acknowledgments (Granqvist 1931: 10). Pointing to the deficiencies in the sources used by those practicing the comparative method and arguing for the need to supplement these by purely monographic studies, she stated:

> But it is not surprising that they are deficient, seeing how casually they are often collected. To a great extent they are composed of opinions and statements of travellers and missionaries who have not had time or interest for an accurate study of the facts and have often confused their personal, sometimes extremely subjective, impressions and opinions or inserted them in place of the realities (Granqvist 1931: 5).

In her fieldwork, Granqvist was strongly influenced by the work of Rivers, in particular by the genealogical (or "concrete") method he had developed. So, she constructed genealogical trees and compiled marriage lists, going back four to five generations, as long as the inhabitants of Artas could remember. The genealogical method was, however, not simply a method to gather and organize kinship data, but functioned rather as a framework to connect various kinds of ethnographic information to individual persons, enabling the anthropologist to discover to what extent general rules were actually followed in practice. As Granqvist herself wrote:

> No longer is one content with general statements only of what custom requires or such indefinite expressions as that "polygynous men are numerous" . . . one insists on having *concrete facts*, details and figures. One draws up statistical tables, and genealogies, and all this brings into the science of ethnology a precision and solidity (Granqvist 1931: 6).

Granqvist's limited acknowledgement of the importance of processes of political and economic change are related, on the one hand, to elements from the older evolutionist and comparative method, and on the other hand, to those of the new functionalist paradigm. Whereas the main text of the book is based on her in-depth fieldwork in the village of Artas, the very extensive footnotes – unusual in monographs – link her work to an older, comparative paradigm, with little attention paid to the specificities of time and place. In reaction to the older evolutionist strands of thought, functionalism propagated a holistic, synchronic mode of analysis that focuses on the coherence of coexisting social forms and institutions rather than on their history.

Granqvist's lack of attention to economic and political change is perhaps further clarified by her focus on the single institution of marriage, rather than a holistic village study which, at least to some extent, would have brought in politics and economics.[7] The ways in which she employs the genealogical method also flattens the history of Artas. It is true that, at times, Granqvist is very careful in mentioning exact dates, especially with events she herself witnessed. Yet, she also tends to employ the ethnographic present, suddenly covering a time span of four to five generations.

On Dressing Styles and Women's Subordination

In the popular representation of women in Palestine two themes stand out. First, the overwhelming attention paid to styles of dress, but in a rather different way than in the case of Dieulafoy in Boer's contribution. The central theme of "unveiling", common elsewhere in the Orient, is not prominently present in representations of women in Palestine. In the Holy Land the exotic is not sexualized, but rather turned into the picturesque; it is not the odalisque, but the madonna that is central to the visual imagery of Palestine. As elsewhere in the colonized world, the various categories of the population of Palestine were represented as "types". Such a style of representation constructs an individual (or a small group of people) as an (anonymous) exemplar of a specific category, as spelled out in the accompanying captions and texts. Presented as essentialized abstraction, all references to time, place and other forms of contextualization were ideally

---

[7] In some ways her work was similar to that of Finnish anthropologist Edward Westermarck (1862-1939) who also did long term and in-depth fieldwork in Morocco and wrote monographs on particular aspects of rural Morocco. Theoretically, however, he remained close to the comparative method.

left out of the picture frame.

The ways in which such types were constructed differed according to time and place (Geary 1990; Edwards 1990). In Palestine they were firmly rooted in that strand of Orientalist discourse that produced highly romantic, mildly exotic and fabulous views, attractive to the public because of the particular combination of the familiar and the exotic. Particular forms of dress were employed as markers for particular types, be it "Bedouin types", "Mohammedan women", or "Bethlehem girls", while in pictures of landscapes and cityscapes beautifully dressed women were often employed to make the images more attractive and exotic. Similarly, work, such as carrying water jugs or produce on the head, was often described in terms of the picturesque, with the accompanying texts drawing attention to women's posture or to the beautiful clothing they wear. In this way, women were ornamentalized and their labour aestheticized.

The second theme is the trope of women's oppression, which was developed in a contrasting scheme to the gender equality that is a central element in constructing the modernity of Jewish immigrant women. Visually this was expressed through their dressing styles and the activities they engage in. Wearing shorts seems to be employed as a crucial metaphor for the modernity of the new Jewish immigrant women, who, as pioneers, build up the land together with their men. By contrast, photographs of Palestinian Arab women clad in long dresses, not only present them as picturesque, at times spectacular, and always mildly exotic, but were often accompanied by texts pointing to their gender subordination. Visually, one of the most persistent symbols of women's subordination is the carrying of materials on their heads. While also employed as an aestheticizing element within a discourse of the picturesque, these materials are at the same time proof of a life of drudgery, a notion firmly rooted in the discourse on the subordination of Oriental women.

In many ways Granqvist's photographs are different. They often express some sort of familiarity and closeness, rather than a feeling of distance between the photographer and those depicted, or a sense of objectification. Her photographs are obviously those of an amateur – the technical quality often leaves much to be desired – taking snapshots of loved ones. Also, in contrast to images of types, Granqvist took great care to name the people depicted, if not in the caption itself, then in the accompanying text.

Granqvist also dealt in a very different way with women's appearance and dressing styles. Whereas commercial photographers usually produced images of women in their most colourful, attractive and exotic costumes (not troubled by mixing elements from different clothing styles), Granqvist's photographs generally are not about women's dress. When the text of her books refers to women's dress, this is always linked to central issues discussed in the books, such as, for instance, when she elaborates on the wedding clothing worn by the bride (1935: 46; 66-67; 81; 111) and wedding guests (1935: 71). In those passages, precise information is provided and the meaning of the various clothing gifts is discussed, such as the political importance of the colours used. In addition, changes in dressing styles are also taken up, such as women wearing black sateen rather than blue cotton, and the introduction of stockings and shoes (1935: 45; 53; 60; 71). Women's clothing is not used to aestheticize photographs of work either. When women are depicted as engaged in work, Granqvist seems to attempt to present a detailed and exact record of certain tasks, such as spinning, weaving and making clay utensils. The focus is on the tasks at hand rather than on appearance (Seger 1981: 110-111; 124-125).

As previously mentioned, in commercial photographs of women the line between the discourse of the picturesque and that of Oriental women's subordination is a thin one. A poignant example is women carrying heavy goods on their heads. Granqvist's photographs do not invite such a focus on women's subordination. Whereas she does include pictures of women carrying food or firewood on their heads, she is careful to provide a text that foregrounds the women's point of view:

> The women are proud of being able to carry heavy burdens. They train themselves to be strong and competent. It makes them respected personally. They are conscious that everyone is watching them and expressing their opinions (Granqvist 1947: 158 quoted by Seger 1981: 106).

Granqvist is well aware of preconceived western notions of male dominance and women's subordination in the East. Intrigued by women's own views on polygyny, she argues that she will refrain from making statements about the women being happy or not, and takes issue with the ease with which judgments are made about "the position of Oriental women" (Granqvist 1931: 22).

In order to present a more nuanced view, she employs two lines of argumentation. On the one hand, she works at getting a view from within, making sure not simply to observe customs or ceremonies, but also to investigate local explanations, views and motives (1931: 19). In doing so, she explicitly acknowledges the advantage of having women as informants, as this gives her the opportunity to elaborate on women's strategies that have often gone unnoticed (1931: 22). When addressing "women's value", for instance, she points out that there are many strong women, and that their value depends a lot upon their personality (Granqvist 1935: 169). She writes extensively about women's important role in arranging marriages and the kind of strategies they follow, such as women preferring a bride from their own families (Granqvist 1931: 86). Further delving into marriage arrangements, she argues that not only women, but men are dependent as well upon their families to arrange a marriage (1931: 53; 57; 59). She mentions a host of particular cases in which women make their opinion heard, and points to cases of women owning land (1931: 28; 1935: 305) and other forms of property (1931: 45). Furthermore, Granqvist pays ample attention to the specific position of widows, underlining that a widow is economically much better off, more independent and has more freedom to act if she does not remarry (1935: 312). As she points out, after her husband's death a woman can have power, authority and freedom by remaining a widow (1935: 319).

On the other hand Granqvist critically investigates established Western notions – both popular and scientific – about women's subordination. This leads her to elaborate extensively on such vexed issues as marriage payments, polygyny and divorce. In an elaborate discussion Granqvist points out that the bride price cannot be considered as "the purchase of women" (1931: 132; 134; 143). Pointing out that polygyny in the case of barrenness of the first wife has only been seen from the male point of view, she points out that the wife may have her own reasons to encourage her husband to take another wife, such as securing her inheritance rights (1935: 211-12). She makes clear that what is known about divorce forms a highly incomplete picture, as in the

West usually men's formal rights and women's complete lack thereof are the only aspects considered. Underlining that her work is "based directly upon cases taken from real life" (1935: 257), Granqvist argues that it is of the greatest importance to collect comparative material on the numbers of divorces, its causes and effects, as this may result in important corrections of "our ideas of the powerful husband in the East" (1935: 284). For there are vast differences between the theoretical facility of divorce for a husband and the serious consequences he will face in practice (1935: 285). At the same time, under certain circumstances, women are actually very able to get a divorce, which also "disturbs belief in the husband's power in the Orient" (1935: 286).

Karen Seger: Popularizing Granqvist and Palestinian Rural Culture

Karen Seger's *Portrait of a Palestinian Village: The Photographs of Hilma Granqvist* (1981) is both an intervention in debates on Palestine in the 1980s and an ode to Granqvist's work. Whereas Seger refrains from taking an explicit political stance, by expressing the hope that the book will "stir interest in the rich and fascinating culture of the Palestinians" (1981: 15), she does introduce Granqvist's work as a counterimage to stereotypical images of Palestinians in Euro-American and Israeli discourse. The Seger volume is also a tribute to Hilma Granqvist and her work. In this large-size publication, Seger reproduced 226 of Granqvist's photographs, framing them by providing introductions and accompanying texts based on both Granqvist's published work and her unpublished notes. *Portrait of a Palestinian Village* presents a vivid visual image of rural Palestine in the early twentieth century, and has been instrumental in drawing attention to Hilma Granqvist's work amongst anthropologists.

A comparison of Granqvist's text, including her use of photographs in *Marriage Conditions II* (1935), and the ways in which Seger presents Granqvist's photographs, suggests some interesting contrasts. There is, of course, the obvious difference that Granqvist's two earliest volumes are about marriage conditions in Artas, while the Seger volume is about Granqvist and her photographs of a Palestinian village. It is no surprize then that the Seger volume includes a number of photographs of Granqvist herself, something Granqvist in her own book avoided. Granqvist's 1935 volume states on the title page "with 30 pictures by the author". These pictures are small black and white images, grouped two, or sometimes three on a page, with the three pictures at the beginning of the book clearly setting the stage. The first shot is of "The House in Artas where the Author lived", the second has as caption "Sitt Louisa [Miss Baldensperger], `Alya and Hamdiye", while the third reads "The East of the Village with the Gardens". Hence, whereas in the first volume Granqvist pointed to the importance of fieldwork in her introductory chapter on methodology, in the 1935 volume she establishes her presence as fieldworker by presenting pictures of her house (indicating that she lived in the village), her main contact and informants (Sitt Louisa), and of the two village women who were her main informants ('Alya and Hamdiya). The photograph of the Eastern part of the village completes the set of house, people and landscape, providing an overview of a major part of the village. The remaining twenty-seven photographs of marriage processions generally have very brief and general captions, but are referred to extensively in the text.

Let me also point out some less obvious differences. Seger leaves out some people's names and dates Granqvist had painstakingly provided. As a result, the presentation of the wedding ceremonies in Seger, for instance, gives the impression that this is one and the same wedding, while it is clear from Granqvist's book – providing the names and often also the dates – that these photographs were taken on three different occasions. Granqvist's work and its representation in the Seger volume is also divergent with respect to biblical time, dress and appearance, and women's subordination. While there are fewer references to biblical time in the Seger volume, some of the pictures, such as those of shepherds with lambs, can easily be linked to this theme. The fact that Granqvist had taken such photographs, but chose not to take them up in her publication, may be seen as an indication of her attempts to avoid the "biblical danger".

There is also a somewhat stronger focus on women's dressing styles in the Seger volume, not so much through the style of photography but rather in the information she provides in the texts accompanying the photographs. The main difference between Granqvist's work and the Seger volume is the less nuanced way in which Seger deals with "women's position". Seger foregrounds women's subordination through a variety of techniques. Some of the elements of women's strength Granqvist had mentioned cannot be found in the Seger volume. In the process of selecting a bride, for instance, no reference is made to the influence of female kin, a point underlined by Granqvist (1981: 75), while the potentially powerful position of widows is not mentioned at all (1981: 79). Also, Seger makes several general statements – such as stating that women are associated with the home and children and men with farming, politics, religion and the outside world – a mode of reasoning Granqvist had consciously avoided (1981: 102).

While these differences are to some extent one of historical moment, the different positions Granqvist and Seger take up, especially with respect to genre, intended audiences, and claims to authority, are more important.[8] Granqvist wrote her books while attempting to establish academic authority and credibility as an anthropologist, that is, as an anthropologist at a particular juncture in anthropological thought. As mentioned above, in the quotation about the deficiencies in the comparative method, Granqvist strongly underlined the differences between her own work and that of missionaries and travellers. The ways in which she dealt with photographs in her 1935 publication also needs to be seen within such a context. Up until 1910/20 photography had been part and parcel of a collective endeavour to collect anthropological material, to be used for comparative studies. This changed when the ideal method of anthropology became long-term research by an individual fieldworker in one particular place, often with a theoretical focus on social organization (Edwards 1992: 4; Poignant 1992: 64-65). Rather than collecting photographs for the sake of comparison, the inclusion of photographs in an ethnography started to function as an indication of presence of the anthropologist, without the need to depict that very anthropologist himself/herself (Pinney 1992: 78). The focus on social organization also discouraged the use of photography, as "social organization" is much harder to visualize than, for instance, material culture or ceremonies. Finally, the small number of photographs included may well have been the result of attempts to establish ethnographies as a genre

---

[8] One problem is that it is hard to say to what extent Granqvist's unpublished notes have given direction to the Seger volume. According to Shelagh Weir, one of the major criteria for Granqvist's specific use of photographs was their photographic quality. Granqvist was a rather inexperienced amateur photographer, and a considerable number of photographs were simply not suitable for publication (1975).

different from travel books (Poignant 1992: 64).

By contrast, Seger wrote a book that aimed at a larger, non-academic public. It was part of a trend in publications about Palestine and its history, a trend that that did not pay exclusive attention to formal politics, but also to Palestinian culture and everyday life. This attempt at popularizing ethnographic writing required an attractive publication, as exemplified by the large number of photographs and relatively simple accompanying texts. Seger had to diverge from Granqvist's work, as one of the latter's aims had been to establish academic authority, and in order to do so, to distance herself from more popular genres.

Hilma Granqvist's photographs and texts are quite different from those produced by more popular, commercial publishers. Even though for present-day readers biblical references stand out, compared to her contemporaries such references are not only small in number, but also framed by a critique of "the biblical danger". Women's dress styles are only considered where this is functional in light of the issues under investigation and her presentation of women's position is nuanced. Privileging the aural over the visual, Granqvist focuses on conversations and takes up the position of a listener, rather than a spectator. Weary of unwarranted generalizations, she deliberately produces an open text that allows for alternative interpretations:

> it appeared to me only right to present my material in the form in which I received it, so that in every case it would be known upon what I founded my conclusions. It is possible that others would read into it something different, and it must be valuable for those who have no opportunity of living among these people to see and form judgments on what the fellahin relate and how they relate . . . My material is thus a direct translation of the literal reports given by the women (Granqvist 1931: 21).

While the popular media employed imagery to attract the attention of a wider public, Granqvist took her photographs primarily a means of documentation for research purposes (as in series of pictures about how to make clay utensils), upon request of people she worked with, and as mementos of friends and acquaintances. The pictures she included in her early work are hence limited, with the selection clearly made within the boundaries set by anthropology as an academic discipline. Her motivation for taking pictures was in fact not publication, and it is exactly because she is not a highly skilled photographer that the imagery, through the indexical qualities of photography, presents us with interesting information. But it is only with the publication of the Seger book that her private pictures became public knowledge.

While Granqvist's produced a narrative that can be read as a strong critique of contemporary representations of women in Palestine (even if written for a limited academic audience), the Seger volume intended to use Granqvist's photographs to present an alternative view of the lives of Palestinian women in the rural areas some fifty years earlier, drawing attention to the "culture and history" of a people whose very existence had been denied.[9] Tensions and convergences between the texts and the photographs – as Boer discussed for Jane Dieulafoy's travelogue – are also present in the work of Granqvist and Seger. In an attempt to reach a broader public, Seger seems to move into the direction of some of the techniques Dieulafoy employed. While Seger's aim is to present Granqvist's photographs to a wider audience, her accompanying texts – in its greater emphasis on women's dress styles and their subordination – provide a particular framing that diverges to some extent from Granqvist's work. In other words, her attempts to connect with a more popular audience seem to have led to a perhaps inevitable flattening of Granqvist's more open and multifaceted work. Simultaneously, some of Granqvist's photographs in the Seger volume present elements of change and modernity that Granqvist mentions in her own work, in passing as it were, but does not really take on, because her work remains caught between a holistic, synchronic approach (in the main body of the text) and the older comparative/evolutionary perspective (in the footnotes). While in some cases she must have deliberately included traces of modernity such as metal containers, cinder blocks and corrugated iron roofs, the indexicality of the photographic, indiscriminately including everything in front of the lens, would also have made it difficult to avoid this. These photographs were, however, only published in the Seger volume, not in her own books.

Granqvist herself wrote her early books to position herself as a respectable

---

[9] Seger can also be read as a critique of authoritative Palestinian visual histories, a point made by Khalidi (1984), see Moors (2001).

academic, her intended audience consisting of her fellow-academics. Next to presenting an alternative view of Palestinian history, the Seger volume was also produced to draw attention to Hilma Granqvist's work as one of the earliest women anthropologists. It is ironic that in a sense Seger may have done her work too well. In his authoritative introduction to the anthropology of the Middle East, Dale Eickelman (1998) mentions both the work of Edward Westermarck and that of Hilma Granqvist, yet in a different way. Whereas both authors are referred to in the section on "further reading" at the end of the chapter on personal and family relationships, only Westermarck makes it into the chapter on "intellectual predecessors". More interesting, whereas Westermarck's work on marriage ceremonies in Morocco is mentioned with its exact reference provided as an example of older accounts of nineteenth- and early twentieth-century marriage practices in the Middle East, Granqvist's work only becomes visible through a reference to the Seger volume.[10] Directing present-day anthropologists to Seger's "translation" of Granqvist's work stands in a tense relation with Granqvist's attempts to position herself as a professional anthropologist.

---

[10] "Photographs of marriage practices in a small village near Bethlehem taken by the Finnish ethnographer Hilma Granqvist and a summary of her ethnographic work related to marriage appear in Karen Seger, ed., *Portrait of a Palestinian Village: The Photographs of Hilma Granqvist* (1981)" (Eickelman 1998: 172).

NINE

Between Hospitality and Hostility: Crossing Balkan Borders in Adela Peeva's *Whose is This Song?*

Maria Boletsi

In *Uncertain Territories* Inge Boer critically engages boundaries, by making them an object, and their theorization a task, for cultural analysis. Boundaries are more often than not perceived as anonymous, immobile, given entities that supersede the individual. Boer sets out to counter the naturalizing impulses that perpetuate this perception of boundaries. Furthermore, she counters the naivety inherent in the postmodern commonplace of a globalized world without boundaries. Visions that treat boundaries as mere obstacles that should be eradicated are for Boer not only utopian and deceptive but also dangerous, in that they bypass the crucial functions of boundaries and the power relations that are at play in processes of boundary construction. She is equally critical when it comes to celebratory theorizations of boundary-crossing and of metaphors of travel.

Boer recognizes boundaries as determining factors in the shaping of cultural spaces and in identity construction. She therefore wishes to make them visible as constructs and, consequently, contestable. Her aim in foregrounding boundaries in cultural analysis is first of all to expose their constructedness and arbitrary nature, which in turn makes them subject to modification or even radical change. In order to open the discussion, she poses questions as to the "how and why" of boundary construction and chooses a performative approach to boundaries as *functions*. Throughout the book, the common view of boundaries as dividing lines, which encourages a strictly oppositional relation between the two sides of the line, yields to an alternative, more productive approach: boundaries are theorized as (rhetorical or cultural) *spaces*, "where opposition yields to negotiation. In such a space, the multifaceted reality of intercultural relations takes on more prominence than the mere demarcation of a binary opposition would allow" (Introduction). In her close reading of literary works, visual objects and cultural phenomena, boundaries emerge as uncertain and at the same time productive spaces, in which contrasting visions meet each other, and where a fertile ground – so urgently needed in our times – is created for acts of negotiation and contestation to take place.

In this response I seek to bring Boer's theorization of boundaries to bear on another "uncertain territory": the Balkans. In order to stage this encounter, I will follow the journey of a popular song in the Balkans, as it unravels in the documentary film *Whose is This Song?* (2003) by Bulgarian filmmaker Adela Peeva. The film's journey across the borders of Balkan nations becomes an occasion to explore the complex function of geographical and ideological boundaries in the Balkans, as well as the violence and hostility that the trespassing of foreign territories and the unsettling of national narratives entails. The film foregrounds the inflexible and deeply rooted boundaries that delimit the national self. What is more, it underscores the thin line that separates hospitality from hostility, when a foreign object (the song) and its human carrier (here, the filmmaker) cross Balkan borders and turn up at the threshold of each nation.

In the beginning of her documentary, Adela Peeva explains in a voice-over how she commenced her journey for the making of *Whose is This Song?*:

> I was in Istanbul with friends from other Balkan countries – a Greek, a Macedonian, a Turk, a Serb and me, a Bulgarian. There I heard the song I want to tell you about. As soon as we heard the song, everyone claimed this song came from his own country. Then we started a fierce fight – whose is this song? I knew from my childhood the song was Bulgarian. I wanted to find out why the others also claimed the song was theirs.

The film starts with a warm and hospitable image: a group of friends from different Balkan countries sitting around a table in a tavern in Istanbul, eating, drinking, listening to live music and having fun. The scene seems to offer a celebratory microcosmic image of a multicultural community, where national boundaries dissolve and turn into a multicultural feast. This is how things go in the best-case scenario of globalization. Boer in her book warns against such idealized and celebratory imagery of a borderless world. In the film too, this image is soon to be disrupted, when the people around the table get into an argument regarding the origins of a song that the Turkish band is playing in the background. Seventy minutes later, the film ends with a dark image of fire and total chaos, as firemen and civilians from a Bulgarian village are struggling to put out a forest fire, initiated by fireworks and gunshots during a celebration of the Bulgarian struggle against Ottoman rule.

The process of this transformation of happy multiculturalism into a hostile image of violence and destruction is gradually laid out in the course of the film. The Apple of Eris is a haunting song, the ownership of which appears to be claimed by every Balkan country. Peeva therefore sets out on a journey with her camera across the Balkans, passing through Turkey, Greece, Albania, Macedonia, Bosnia, Serbia and, finally, Bulgaria, in search of the song's origins and its owner(s). She soon realizes that the song is sung everywhere in the Balkans and has fallen into different genres in every region: a love song, a song about the lower classes, a military march, a religious hymn, a gypsy song, and a patriotic anthem arousing the national spirit. In every one of its appropriations the song serves different purposes and ideologies.

In each country Peeva seeks out and visits people that can provide her with information about the song. Almost all the people she meets stubbornly claim the song as their own and devise elaborate stories to prove that the song's origins are indissolubly linked with their own nation. The filmmaker's encounter with her interviewees becomes an occasion for deep-rooted nationalism, strong feelings of superiority, and negative stereotyping of the neighbouring nations to manifest themselves. Contrary to the common saying that music unites people, contrary to the celebratory spirit of European unity and togetherness that is supposedly represented annually by the Eurovision song contest, and, not in the least, contrary to the filmmaker's own initial intentions, the documentary becomes an exploration of nationalism, hostility and ethnic conflicts that still impose rigid boundaries among the Balkan nations. As the film crosses Balkan borders following the song's journey, the questions that Boer asks in her introduction as to the how and why of boundary construction become more pertinent than the issue of the song's origins (Introduction). In a world of increasing globalization, migration and multiculturalism, people in the Balkans are fighting for the copyrights of cultural objects, with an unshaken belief in the myths about their origin. The documentary demonstrates the absurdity of any attempt at proving cultural purity. In so doing, it foregrounds the paradox of people who seem to have so much in common, and yet would be willing to fight to death for the authenticity and uniqueness of their culture, history, and heritage.

I see Peeva's documentary along the lines of migratory cultural commodities – a song, in this case. The viability of the notion "migratory" is questioned with regard to this song, since the application of the notion presupposes the acknowledgement of an object as a foreign entity, migrating into our space. Instead, the foreign identity of the song is here covered up, as the song is integrally incorporated in each country's national myth. The disruption, then, of notions of self and home when what is unmistakably "ours" escapes the national boundaries and proves to carry traces of foreignness, becomes one of the key-elements in the film and in my theoretical exploration. I will argue that the breaking up of certainties and local habits effectuated by the film turns certain boundaries into spaces of negotiation, in which the migratory object acquires agency over sovereign national narratives, here, of the Balkan nations. Filtered through the local, however, the overwhelming universality of the issues raised in the film becomes manifest as well.

Needless to say, migrating objects presuppose human agents who transfer them with their passage through places. At the boundaries of each country an encounter takes place between these migrants or travellers and their hosts, in which the issue of hospitality arises, in relation to people as well as to the cultural objects they carry with them. In the film, on a first level, hospitality is a significant notion in each nation's reception of the song. On a second level, the filmmaker is also a stranger and a guest in each country and in the home of each person she visits. Standing at the boundaries between nations, she faces the laws of hospitality and the thin thread that separates hospitality from hostility, or even violence. And yet again on a third level, a cultural object (the song) enters Peeva's film narrative and foregrounds the question of hospitality with regard to the filmmaker's reception of it. Can the hospitality of the filmmaker and, by extension, the author or the cultural analyst with regard to their objects be an unconditional act, or is it always regulated by certain laws set by the host? The complex and often antagonistic or authoritative relation of host to guest is acted out in the film on multiple levels and always on the borderline between hospitality and hostility or violence.

The Song's Impossible Truth

In *Whose is This Song?* the director chooses to be actively present in the documentary, as protagonist and narrator (with occasional voice-overs). She positions herself from the beginning as a Bulgarian filmmaker – in many ways an insider in the complex constellation of the Balkan nations – and explains her personal relationship to the song. Her position as an "insider" is, however, highly contestable. Despite her Bulgarian nationality, she is as much an outsider and a foreigner in the countries she visits, as she is an insider. Accordingly, her journey can also be viewed as an anthropological or ethnographic quest for the origins of a song, which would presuppose an outsider-observer's perspective. The ambiguity of her position raises the question of what it means to be an insider or outsider in the Balkans, and the answer is dependent on whether the Balkans can be treated as a homogeneous community.

Peeva's status as an insider would be supported by the assumption that the Balkans are an indivisible semantic space and a homogeneous cultural entity, widely defined by shared Byzantine, Ottoman and, more recently, communist legacies. According to this representational mode, quite prevalent in the West, not much difference is recognized among the Balkan countries (Iordanova 2001: 6-7).[1] In the writings of Samuel Huntington, for example, differences between the Muslim and Orthodox populations in the Balkans are

---

[1] The term "West" is of course highly relational. When employed in relation to the Balkans, it usually denotes Western Europe and the United States. In other contexts (in relation, for example, to the Orient) the term would possibly include the Balkan countries. Whether the Balkans are European or not is an object of academic and political debate (Todorova 1997: 7). The complex position of the Balkans in relation to Europe and their representation either as a bridge across cultures (the East and the West), or as the "other" in the margins of Europe, makes the use of the term "West" highly problematic in the discourse about the region.

bypassed, as all Balkan nations are culturally similar and united under one signifier, denoting the "other" of Europe and Western civilization (Huntington 1996: 158).[2] This oversimplified image, which gives no serious consideration to internal conflicts, tensions and contradictions within the Balkans, is quite dominant in Western popular and academic discourse and can sometimes be ascribed to the insufficient knowledge of Europeans and Americans with regard to the complexity of Balkan issues. When Balkan issues and conflicts seem difficult to grasp, they are often relegated to the Balkan's alleged irrationality. One of the documentary's reviewers writes: "The Balkans are a mystery to most Americans. Most of us probably know that they're in Europe, and that they used to be under the control of the Soviet Union. We might know about 'the former Yugoslavia', and we might know about Milosevic. The rest is confusing, something that hits the front page if American soldiers are killed, but that doesn't rate the first section of the paper under normal circumstances. In some ways, this film serves as a useful educational tool about the Balkans and their relationship to each other" (Phillips 2005).

This totalizing view is challenged in Peeva's film. As she delves into the Balkans in search of her song, she finds herself amidst a multiplicity of viewpoints and conflicting interpretative networks, which forecloses a unified metanarrative of the region's history (see also Iordanova 2001: 89). Paradoxically, the geographical and ideological boundaries of every Balkan nation are rigid and immobile within each nation's narrative, while at the same time they give the *impression* of being mobile, because they are highly contested and often collide with the boundaries of other neighbouring nations. But in their constant overlap and intermingling, these boundaries are not zones of negotiation: they remain thin lines, impossible to walk on, and triggering conflict whenever they intersect. As people in the film declare their nation's exclusive ownership over the song (with only two exceptions), the discussion about the song usually gives rise to a monologue from the interviewees about their nation.[3] In their statements, the geographic and

---

[2] According to Huntington (and others), the Balkans are not part of Europe and the West: "Europe ends where Western Christianity ends and Islam and Orthodoxy begin" (1996: 158).
[3] A Macedonian composer admits that the song cannot be Macedonian, as there is no such beat in his nation's folklore. Also, a Dervish in Macedonia says that the song came with the Turks a long time

discursive boundaries of each nation appear to be invested with a truth-value, which, according to Boer, "uses an inside perspective opposing us to whomever we find on the other side" (Introduction). Consequently, in their words the nation emerges as a superior entity, based for its singularity on exclusionary mechanisms and, primarily, on the "othering" and vilification of other Balkan nations.

A few examples: In Albania, a group of people in the street react strongly to Peeva's suggestion that the song might be Greek or Serbian. One of them says: "Serbs can never do a song like this. The Serbs have no traditions". Later on in the film, an accordion player in Bosnia states that the song is so beautiful that it can be nothing other than Bosnian. Upon hearing that the Serbs claim the song as well, an old Bosnian woman, who used to sing the song in her youth, exclaims: "My foot! It is ours!" In Macedonia, a Dervish man labels the Bosnian religious version of the song as a Jihad song used for Islamization in times of war, and then goes on to declare that the war in Bosnia was God's will, and can be partly ascribed to the mixed marriages in the region (between Muslims, Orthodox and Catholics). A Serbian priest objects to the song's assumed gypsy origins. He complains about the "gypsification" of every cultural element in Serbia, because he believes that gypsies have no traditions and identity of their own, but live parasitically on the traditions of others. In Bulgaria the song's lyrics celebrate the struggle against the Turks. When Peeva makes the mistake of telling a group of teenagers that their song might have originated with the Turks, their reaction is highly aggressive: "The Turks and Gypsies are the worst nations. I feel like crushing them only at the sight of them. If they are not Bulgarian they deserve a knife. We Bulgarians have to always support each other".

Obviously there are varied degrees in the hostility with which people react to the possibility of the song not being originally theirs. Variations in people's reactions depend on numerous factors, ranging from person-specific ones – such as individual disposition, profession, gender, age – to nation-specific parameters, such as the recent or less recent historical traumas and memories in each country. In addition, it is often in small rural villages and isolated regions closer to the borders of each country that Peeva faces the

---

ago. In the latter case, it is easier for him to assume the song's Turkish origin, because he shares with the Turks the same religious (Muslim) background.

most fierce fanaticism and intractable positions with regard to the song and
the nation in general. However, what is common in the reactions of the
people she interviews is their consistent wish to stay divided and not be
placed under a "Balkan umbrella". In the minds of most of them, the
boundaries that separate them from their neighbours are dividing lines, and it
is for this reason that every encounter with the other side is interpreted in
terms of conflict (Chapter Four).

Their overlapping and mutually exclusive national narratives, based on the
myth of the purity, homogeneity and continuity of the nation, make it
impossible to tell the history of the region – and that of the song's origins – in
a way acceptable to all its actors (Iordanova 2001: 89). The Western
construction of the Balkans as a unified signifier is debunked in the film, as
the (Western) viewer's stereotypical image of the Balkans is subjected to
what Boer calls "intercultural doubt" (Chapter Three). Consequently, Peeva's
initial desire to uncover the truth about the song's owners turns out to be
utopian. In the course of the film the question of the origins is obscured, as
the song assumes the role of a cultural commodity in the service of
nationalism.

Whose is This Song? leaves the viewer with quite a bleak image of Balkan
people. Their nationalism, stubbornness, parochialism, hostility or aggression
surface as dominant elements of their disposition. Even in many light-hearted
or comical scenes the viewer is tempted to laugh *at* and not *with* them, as the
comic elements are often related to the irrational that is supposed to typify
the Balkan character. While the film is deconstructing Balkan stereotypes, it
also seems to help confirm others.

The Balkans, according to Balkan historian Maria Todorova, have served
as a repository of negative features, upon which the self-congratulatory
image of the "European" has been constructed. Since the beginning of the
twentieth century, "Balkanization" denotes "a reversion to the tribal, the
backward, the primitive, the barbarian"; the Balkans are associated with
industrial backwardness, irrational and superstitious cultures, and lack of
advanced social relations (Todorova 1997: 3; 11). *Balkanism*, a term coined
in analogy to Orientalism to designate the Western representational mode and
discursive construction of the Balkans, is not only practiced by the Western
media and academia; it is also sustained by a number of Balkan intellectuals

and filmmakers, who reiterate existing stereotypes and further the othering of the Balkans by "perpetuating a trend of self-exoticism" (Iordanova 2001: 21).[4]

One could make the case that Peeva's documentary also contributes to the negative stereotyping of the Balkans. Balkan men in the film often appear quite crude and uncivilized. Their macho attitude and the patriarchal structures of their societies are exemplified in statements such as the following, made by a Bulgarian armourer: "what is a man with no knife? The same as a lady with no jewels".[5] Other people, such as a Turkish filmmaker in his sixties or an old Greek singer on the island of Lesbos are shown to be caught up in the past, irremediably nostalgic and thus refusing to live in the present. The latter attitude could also be seen as typical of a static Balkan (or more generally Eastern) universe, resistant to progress and unable to live up to the challenges of the present, let alone the future. In an article about the film in the *International Herald Tribune*, Peeva stated that her film "makes us laugh at ourselves" (Wood 2004). Self-mockery can surely be a sign of self-criticism and self-reflection, but it can also be seen as a self-indulgent act; and act, indeed, of self-exoticism.

However, I do not believe that the stereotypical elements in the film neutralize its explicitly critical and challenging stance. The film does not fall short of the complexity of the situation in the Balkans and preserves the contradictions and diversity of its material. It demystifies Balkan national narratives and the myths around the origins of cultural commodities. In so doing, it unsettles the certainties on which several stereotypes rest. In the end, the question of who the song belongs to, posed in the title, sounds at the same time naive, irrelevant and yet painfully pertinent. The possibility of the one truth about the song's origins has been replaced by multiple truths, like the layers of an onion with no core in the middle; nevertheless, the film is still all about ownership, mastery over the other and appropriation of the other's elements as indistinguishable parts of the self.

---

[4] Todorova (1997) recognizes the similarities between the two kinds of discourses (Orientalism and Balkanism), but refuses to see Balkanism as a subspecies of Orientalism and discusses the significant differences between the two terms. See, for example, her introduction.
[5] According to Todorova, balkanist discourse is singularly male (1997: 15).

Welcome to the Balkans: Exploring the Limits of Hospitality

The reception of the song by each host-country on its journey, but also the filmmaker's visits to different Balkan countries and her re-introduction of the song to the people in these countries as a foreign object, are worth examining as occasions of hospitality.

In *Of Hospitality*, Jacques Derrida makes a significant distinction between "absolute hospitality" and "conditional hospitality" – or what he calls the "pact of hospitality" (2000: 25). Absolute hospitality requires the opening of the host's home not only to a foreigner with a name and a definite status, but to "the absolute, unknown, anonymous other" (2000: 25; see also Chapter Four). It is hospitality *graciously* offered to the other, without any demand from the other or any imperative and sense of duty for the host (2000: 83). Conditional hospitality, on the other hand, requires a process of interrogating, identifying and naming the foreigner before welcoming him/her, and subjecting him/her to the laws of the host (2000: 27). In this latter case, the host maintains sovereignty over his home, and exercises it by filtering and choosing guests, thereby excluding, violating and doing violence (2000: 55). The guest has to obey the rules of hospitality, which are the rules the host has set. This kind of hospitality becomes a reaffirmation of the law of the same (Yeğenoğlu 2003: 8-9). The guest is welcome as long as s/he is subjected to the host's law. The two different kinds of hospitality are mutually exclusive:

> It is as though the laws (plural) of hospitality, in marking limits, powers, rights and duties, consisted in challenging and transgressing *the* law of hospitality, the one that would command that the "new arrival" be offered an unconditional welcome (Yeğenoğlu 2003: 77).

At some point in history, the song the film revolves around appears at the threshold of each country as a foreign guest, possibly carried by migrants entering the country or nationals returning from a foreign place. Its reception by the host nation, however, happens on a very specific condition: that the guest's identity be erased and reappropriated by the host. The guest-song becomes the sacrificial victim in an act of cannibalism, in which the guest is devoured by the host and lives on within the host's body, with all traces of its alterity disappearing. This act of violent assimilation implies that the host perceives the foreign guest as a threatening enemy.

According to Derrida, the foreigner can either be welcomed as a guest or as an enemy. This ambivalence indicates the thin line between hospitality and hostility, which is also inscribed in their common Latin derivation, *hostis*, (2000: 45). The invasion of foreign elements into one's national or cultural space often entails great anxiety and the feeling that one's identity is being threatened. The appropriation, then, of foreign, migratory elements to the extent that all traces of foreignness are swallowed up by the national narrative, is a way of dealing with the threat of the other. It is a mechanism not exclusive to the Balkans. Cultural commodities carried by migrants to Western European countries (and elsewhere) very often become an integral part of the host country, so that their foreign origin is either forgotten or deliberately suppressed.

The song's emergence in all the countries visited by Peeva is of course an unmistakable sign of intense processes of cultural exchange and commonality in the cultural identity of Balkan peoples. But it is a song everyone sings differently, with the different lyrics denoting the overlapping signifiers floating over the Balkan nations and fighting to write over the same cultural signified. Most people that appear in the documentary perceive cultural "exchange" as an unidirectional process. In this process, they deny having *received* from the other, and see themselves as the only agents *offering* elements to the other as generous gifts. According to this logic, neighbouring nations are seen as empty receptacles with a less solid history and tradition, capable only of passive reception. However, given the mutual nature of cultural influences, the hypocritical act of denying the possibility of the song's foreign origins as we see it in the film, becomes something like saying "no, thank you" to one's offerings and still grabbing the presents under the table.

Peeva's act of "knocking on people's doors" in the Balkans and *reintroducing* the song as a *foreign* guest after it has been appropriated by each host, generates confusion. The foreign song they hear *resembles* what they now assume as their own. It is subsequently received as an impostor or as their beautiful song's ugly and evil twin, who returns and threatens to overthrow the host's authority. The song's reappearance as foreign is perceived as an abuse or violation of the host's space, and therefore often results in hostile feelings not only towards the foreign version of the song but also towards the human agent who carries it into the nation's space. This agent is here the filmmaker, who often plays a tape with a foreign version of the song, or who constantly suggests with her comments and questions that the song might be foreign.

Peeva is not received as an insider in the countries she visits – as "one of us". She is seen as a guest, and thus a foreigner, but she is also not treated as an absolute and neutral outsider. With her status as a Bulgarian national, she induces two opposed attitudes in her hosts: in some cases she is welcomed as a "known" or "identifiable" foreigner. The hospitality she receives then is still far from being unconditional: the host welcomes her on the condition that she is aligned with his discourse and that she has earned (or will in the future repay) his hospitality. It is with such conditions in mind that a Bosnian musician greets and welcomes her: "My Bulgarian friend. You Bulgarians recognized Bosnia first when it was worst for us". On other occasions, however, she faces more suspicion and hostility than a filmmaker from a non-Balkan country would possibly face, because she is seen as a potential *spy* or *agent-provocateur* – a semi-outsider with inside knowledge and with unclear (political) intentions. As Boer remarks in her analysis of Claude Ollier's novel *La Mise en scène* (19982 [1958]), when the guest appears to interfere in the affairs of the host, s/he will be distrusted (Chapter Four). Peeva here does meddle in the affairs of her hosts: she provokes them with questions and tries to extract information and reactions from them. In so doing, she is constantly walking on a balancing rope between trust and distrust, hospitality and hostility.

On two occasions she is physically threatened for daring to suggest the song's foreign origins. One of these occasions erupts during a feast in a Serbian tavern, organized in her honour by a group of Serbs she met during the shooting of her film. Everyone seems to be having a great time. People are drinking, singing, telling jokes and everyone is laughing. However, the celebration takes a dramatic turn when Peeva decides to play the Bosnian religious version of the song on tape, in order to monitor their reactions. Upon hearing the song, everyone's expression changes. The filmmaker realizes that in the eyes of her hosts she has crossed a sacred boundary. The laws of hospitality they implicitly set for their "Bulgarian guest" are violated. At first they turn against the Bosnians and their version of the song: "The

Bosnians are fools. They have abused a beautiful love song and turned it into a war appeal". But soon afterwards their hostility is directed against Peeva. They wonder why she cares about the song so much and suspect her of political provocation. They stand up in anger and depart, leaving their honourable guest by herself, because they suddenly have doubts about her intentions. They believe they had wrongly identified this foreigner as a friend; their definition of "friend" presupposes that someone adheres to their law and narrative. "The curtain has fallen. We know who you are", they say to the whole film crew. But when Peeva poses the question again ("Who are we?"), it becomes evident in their answer that it is exactly their *ignorance* of their guests' real identity that has transformed their warm hospitality into fierce hostility: "I don't know who you are. Who actually are you? Do you have any ID? Any licence to shoot here at all?"

Conditional hospitality requires full identification of the stranger. When the stranger's identity in this case is suspected to be misleading and uncertain, her status as a guest falls through. The foreigner is seen as an intruder or trespasser, threatening the host's authority. Anyone who encroaches on the host's sovereignty is regarded as an "undesirable foreigner, and virtually as an enemy" (Derrida 2000: 54-55). The series of questions about her identity is part of the interrogatory process for the identification of the foreigner, which Derrida describes as part of the pact of hospitality. Her rights as a guest are withdrawn and yield to prohibitions (they question her licence to shoot there), while official identification is now demanded as proof (an ID). The hostility of the hosts almost turns into physical violence when a man threatens to knock her down on the floor.

The filmmaker stands at the significatory boundaries of the Balkan cultures, which is where, according to Homi Bhabha, the problem of cultural interaction emerges and where "meanings and values are (mis-)read or signs are misappropriated" (1994: 50). The filmmaker's presence generates tension in the unifying operations of each discursive community and endangers the stability of its boundaries, because it forces upon it the encumbrance of alterity. The different lyrics attached to each version of the song change the aesthetics of the song, its genre, the way it is perceived, and the feelings it evokes. These aesthetic alterations often cause indignant reactions, as when the people in Serbia realize that the Bosnians "have turned a beautiful love song into a call for war".

But whenever Peeva plays the song to people as it is performed in another Balkan country, the dissonant sound of the other's song is disquieting and almost perceived as a cacophony, *precisely because it sounds strangely familiar*. The recognition of similarity with the other endangers the superior identity of the national self, which is based upon difference and opposition. Ultimately, the film gives rise to the paradox that what keeps Balkan peoples divided is the very fact that they have things in common. In each national text these similarities are (mis)read as differences or, where they cannot be circumvented, as elements of the self, which have been stolen and abused by others as well. "Why Turkish and not Albanian?" an old man in an Albanian music school protests; "Maybe the Turks took it from us. We are one of the most ancient peoples". A little later in the film, the men in the Serbian tavern who have just listened to the Bosnian version of their song, cry out: "This is theft, simple abuse. Outrageous!"

Towards an Ethics of Hospitality

Towards the end, the filmmaker finds herself in Bulgaria, attending the celebrations for the Bulgarian struggle against the Ottomans, during which the song is also being sung. After mentioning to the Bulgarian people attending that the song is claimed to be Turkish, she is told (by her own people this time) that she runs the risk of being stoned. An old man cries out: "I'll hang the one who says the song was Turkish on that oak tree". In all the other countries she had visited she had been a foreigner/guest, and in some cases she had experienced the transformation from guest to enemy. Now she is "at home", in Bulgaria, and yet she still finds herself in the position of the foreigner or, even worse, the insider who, by questioning the national truths, turns into a hated foreigner and runs the risk of being expelled from the community. In the end, Peeva poses as a foreigner among the people of her nation, because her journey outside the boundaries of her national community has exposed her to the impossibility of one national truth in the Balkans. She becomes aware of the arbitrariness and artificiality of the boundaries of national narratives, which are often constructed to conceal similarity among Balkan peoples. At the same time, she is also made painfully aware of the multiple functions of boundaries in Balkan space, which make it extremely difficult to denaturalize and challenge them.

Nevertheless, a boundary shift does take place within the film and in the filmmaker/protagonist herself: setting off from a secure position within the safety of her national boundaries, she eventually loses the ground beneath her feet. This feeling of displacement, as Boer argues, becomes "the moment of insight and healing" (Chapter Two).[6] She, as well as the (Balkan) viewers of the film, is invited to a self-reflection, which requires a distancing from oneself, a viewing of oneself as other (a stranger). Her challenge to the "truth" of the song's origins and to its secure place within her national narrative entails the questioning of her own identity, which has been (at least partly) shaped within this narrative. The song that Peeva in the beginning often referred to as "hers", has escaped her and can no longer be in her possession – not in anyone's possession.

The cinematic narrative starts out like a fairy tale, with Peeva's voice-over promising to tell us about the journey of a song, in the hope of untangling the truth about its owners. In the very final shots of the documentary the camera is recording a raging forest fire, the function of which is evidently symbolic as well as painfully real.[7] The director's voice-over returns here for the last time, announcing the unexpected outcome of her fairy-tale and her disillusionment at the subversive turn her story took:

> My song changed beyond recognition. I was standing alone in the crowds waiting for the celebration to be over. When I first started searching for the song I hoped it will unite us. I had never believed that the sparkles of hatred can be lit so easily.

The use of voice-over is often examined as an authoritative device of imposing coherence upon a film narrative. Likewise, Peeva's voice-over can be seen as an attempt of the "host" to retain mastery over her narrative and her object-guest (the song). But in its final appearance in the end, her voice-over is also present to concede defeat. Her attempts to lead her object in the

---

[6] Boer makes this point with regard to Asma's feeling of displacement in Hanan al-Shaykh's novel *Poste restante Beyrouth* (1995).
[7] As I mentioned in the beginning of this paper, the forest fire is lit as a result of the fireworks, gunshots and canon firing during the Bulgarian celebration of the struggle against the Ottomans.

direction she initially aimed for – a song that unites – have failed. The foreignness of the song invades the director's narrative and shifts its initial intentions. To be sure, consciously or not, the director also plays a role in the film's change of direction. For example, although she sets out to let the song operate as a unifying factor, in her role as an interviewer, she often seeks and provokes hostile reactions by suggesting the song's foreign origins to her interviewees. In the end, the documentary still tells a story; and just like every good story, this one needs the element of *peripeteia*, a sudden reversal of fortune, without which it would probably be much less gripping. The end of Peeva's journey may disappoint her, but it also entails "the excitement of discovering that what we see differs from what we thought we knew", a feeling that in Boer's view helps us deal with cultural difference (2004b: 195).

I would also argue that in her attitude towards her object the director performs her own act of hospitality. Her hospitality may not be "absolute" or totally unconditional, but it has a distinctively less authoritative and intrusive character than conditional hospitality, as Derrida describes it. The director comes to accept the guest/object of her film without proof of its origins and without wishing to own it. She welcomes the other together with the challenge of its difference – an act which always entails a certain risk, as there is no guarantee about the outcome of this encounter.[8] She thereby allows her guest to *take place in the place that she offers it* (Derrida 2000: 25). This opening up of one's space for the other to happen is for Derrida an aspect of absolute hospitality. According to Boer, hospitality in this case becomes "the meeting place" for different subjectivities, "the site where encounter becomes possible" (Chapter Four). The threshold of the host is no longer a boundary line that can be trespassed or not, but, in Boer's vein, it becomes an uncertain territory where host and stranger can stand, together (Introduction).

As a result, her guest/object brings about a slight shift in the host's initial plans, and a displacement and repositioning of the host. Sometimes it is the guest that "becomes the one who invites the one who invites" – "the host's

---

[8] See also Derek Attridge's discussion of the act of opening oneself to the other and its implications (1999: 27-29). For Attridge, this act always involves a risk – "Since by definition there can be no certainty in opening oneself to the other, every such opening is a gamble" – but a risk worth taking.

host". The master then enters the home *through* the guest and by the grace of the guest (Derrida 2000: 124-25). In the film, Peeva and the Balkan viewer become for a while foreigners in their own "home", be it Bulgaria, another Balkan country, or the Balkans in general. In the end, the song invites this viewer to re-enter the Balkan space without her previous certainties and sense of mastery, but as a guest in her own home, a home which is being critically re-examined under the impact of the song's foreignness.

In all the above aspects, the film becomes a challenging testing ground for Boer's theory of boundaries. The hostility and violence triggered by the film's multiple boundary-crossing stresses the urgency of Boer's theoretical views. At the same time, it also adds to her insights the realization that, when put from theory to practice, the view upon boundaries as functional spaces of negotiation is not a theoretical tool that can effortlessly be endorsed at will. In a region such as the Balkans, where every nation's being is based on boundaries that exclude foreignness and differentiate self from other, the theoretical rendering of boundaries as Boer develops it comes at a cost. However, and for that very reason, it is all the more significant when a widening of boundary lines takes place in an act of hospitality such as that of this film. This widening in Peeva's film does not develop smoothly and does not lead to any resolution of conflict; on the contrary, it ignites confrontational scenes and hostility. As Boer argues, the encounters that take place at the space of boundaries should not be idealized, because "they are not likely to be peaceful" (Chapter Two). But it is only in such uncertain and contested territories, such spaces of negotiation, where productive criticism can be performed and "newness may occur" (Chapter Two). The unsettling feeling with which the viewer leaves the film is already a sign of a small widening of the secure boundaries we live by.

It is in this unstable boundary space, I believe, that an ethics of hospitality can be developed in relation to migratory aesthetics. The aesthetics of migration often require a small remoulding of the aesthetic space of the self: of elements in our everyday life, of the things we love around us, of the songs we sing. Migratory objects invite a reconfiguration of the same, so that it can "host" the aesthetics of the foreign object, without fully absorbing its traces of otherness. In the case of this song, the rules of the host (each Balkan nation) demanded the appropriation of the object, so that the authority of the national myth would be reinstated. The integration or assimilation of migrants in Balkan but also in Western European countries and elsewhere, comes down to a similar strategy. However, the success of such strategies is never definitive or permanent, because migrating people as well as objects have a palimpsestic existence: they keep carrying traces of foreignness from their previous journeys, traces which can resurface through various critical interventions.

The Past in the Present

In the palimpsest, Boer's favourite conceptual metaphor in *Disorienting Vision*, "even when the writing is completely erased, it is still visible in the traces it leaves behind in the parchment" (Boer 2004b: 19). For Boer the palimpsest is not located in the object itself, but in "readings that partially overlap as the process of interpretation is traced" (2004b: 19). In the case of the song, the object itself was reinvented by every nation, so as to conceal its palimpsestic traces from other places, nations and periods. In *Whose is This Song?*, then, the act of "rereading" that Boer recommends is performed in the revisiting of the song through its diverse Balkan hosts. Her filmic "rereading" deconstructs what the object "wants to show itself to be" in the hands of each host, and denaturalizes each version of the song as an authentic national product (2004b: 19). It therefore foregrounds the song's protean qualities and reveals the palette of cultural translations that have taken place in its appropriation by each nation. In addition, Peeva's "rereading" critically unfolds the song's plural text, without bypassing what Boer calls "the epistemological predicament" of the filmmaker's own position and involvement in her narrative (Boer 2004b: 19).[9] The film involves a reflection on the shifting relation between herself and her object. Consequently, the filmmaker's disappropriation of the song in the end is not an act of objective distancing or stepping out of her narrative, but an inevitable outcome of this reflective involvement.

Furthermore, the song in the film highlights what the palimpsest always

---

[9] For Boer, the acknowledgement of this "epistemological predicament" in every act of interpretation is constitutive of what she calls a "palimpsestic rereading" (2004b: 19).

implies: the continuous presence of the past in the present (Boer 2004b: 195). The song's shifting lyrics in each nation, as well as people's charged reactions to its foreign versions, indicate that the song is immersed in history. As a carrier of different versions of historical memory, the song in the film rekindles historical traumas and triggers hostility. Historical memories are inscribed in the song's lyrics, as well as in all the places the filmmaker visits. Various shots in the film make this suggestion: images of military parades celebrating the siege of Constantinople by the Turks, Enver Hoxha's bunkers in Albania, bombed buildings in Sarajevo, ruined or deserted orthodox churches in Macedonia, celebrations of the struggle against the Ottoman Empire in Bulgaria. Such shots remind us that heated discussions about the song and its origins are situated in a heavily charged historical context. The event of the song in the film changes the dominant perception of the region's history as a singular narrative, by exposing the plural, conflictual histories in the Balkans through the different, foreign versions of the song. The song's palimpsest thus reveals sharp-edged chips of history that keep haunting the present through the song's melody.

The film's foregrounding of the violent and contradictory faces of this history through the song, points towards the need to work through the past, without erasing or leaving it behind. The film's suggested strategy for this process of working through involves creating awareness of history's multiple versions, conflicting narratives and non-unified, unresolved character. On a most basic level, it is the awareness that the same song is sung in many different ways. This is the face of the past that the song-as-palimpsest brings forth. And this is, I believe, where the film's main critical intervention lies.

The traces of the past are still there in the present of every place, affecting its life in more or less evident ways. It is the same with the imprints that people leave in their passage through places. Just like the erased characters leave their traces on the page, "the human characters inhabiting this land at a certain moment in time leave traces even though their existence is short and volatile in comparison to the eternal or even to the geographical *longue durée*", Boer writes in *Disorienting Vision*. "The passing through and fading away of peoples can, however, be read by means of the signs that remain"

(Boer 2004b: 157).[10] The "passing through" of Inge Boer, my teacher, has left such traces that stubbornly remain in the rereadings of her texts and in the writings of her students, colleagues, and people inspired by her thought, like myself. They also reside in the memory of the people who knew her, or – to borrow Toni Morrison's stronger word in *Beloved* for a memory that is alive – in their *rememory*.[11]

In *Beloved* Toni Morrison writes about the life of the past in the present in people's rememories, in a passage where the protagonist, Sethe, is talking to her daughter, Denver. I almost compulsively wish to cite these lines here, in the knowledge that I am misusing them and tearing them out of their context:

> "I mean, even if I don't think it, even if I die, the picture of what I did, or knew, or saw is still out there. Right in the place where it happened".
> "Can other people see it?" asked Denver.
> "Oh, yes. Oh, yes, yes, yes. Someday you will be walking down the road and you hear something or see something going on. So clear. And you think it's you thinking it up. A thought picture. But no. It's when you bump into a rememory that belongs to somebody else. Where I was before I came here, that place is real. It's never going away . . ."
> Denver picked at her fingernails. "If it's still there, waiting, that must mean that nothing ever dies".
> Sethe looked right in Denver's face. "Nothing ever does", she said (Morrison 1987: 36).

---

[10] Boer makes this point in her discussion of Madame De Gasparin's travel narrative.
[11] Toni Morrison uses in *Beloved* the word "rememory" to underscore that the past is alive in the present.

TEN

Borders of the Art World, Boundaries of the Artwork: On "Contemporary Art from the Islamic World"

Begüm Özden Fırat

Uncertain Territories is an attempt to return social, cultural and geographical implications and manifestations of borders and boundaries to contemporary theory, particularly in the practice of cultural analysis. Inge Boer's concerns are particularly relevant in our times, when uncritical discussions of globalization, multi-culturalism and cosmopolitanism and metaphorical overuse of concepts like travel, migration, or nomadism, as well as naive debates on exile and diaspora, prevail not only within the humanities but in other intellectual communities as well, ranging from media analysts to governmental advisors. Boer's critical stance towards the use of concepts cherishing unrestricted mobility and permanent border-crossings is an effort to mark the boundaries in their cultural manifestations, not in the form of strict lines and dots, but as spaces of negotiation and, most importantly, of contestation.

Throughout her work, Boer works against "naturalizing impulses", impulses that erase the human activity involved in constructing boundaries, or that, by contrast, render them stable and immobile, yet invisible. However, instead of trying to make boundaries visible by strictly defining them as attempts to answer what and where they are, Boer suggests to theorize them in terms of a function. In *Uncertain Territories*, borders are taken as spaces of negotiation not only in terms of mapping them as functions of imprisoning, transgressing and translating, but also as tools for continuous questioning of the dynamics of cross-cultural representation.

In this book, the boundary as a function works in two interconnected ways. First, it is taken as a critical concept in the close analysis of texts ranging from novels to contemporary fashion advertisements in bearing on the texts themselves as well as on the theories and concepts that we work with in cultural analysis. Secondly, it becomes a self-reflective tool for a constant scrutiny of the work of the analyst and her conceptual boundaries in meaning-making processes and interpretative strategies. By employing this tool, Boer constantly brings the geopolitics of knowledge and the borders of knowledge construction under scrutiny. In this sense, Boer's suggestion of conceptualizing the border as a space of negotiation and contestation not only opens the possibility of putting the concepts and the texts "we" work with under erasure but also firmly situates the cultural critic in this contested space, both individually and institutionally. In Boer's works not only the object of analysis but also the subject doing the analysis is being challenged and changed in the process. She writes: "In the process of a theorizing that includes such self-reflection, one indeed leaves home, to return to the same location, but not quite as the same person" (Chapter Two).

This self-reflective journeying was also at stake in Boer's previous book, *Disorienting Vision* (2004b), which deals with nineteenth-century French Orientalist texts and images by means of a pluralist palimpsestic rereading process that analyzes them beyond stereotypical oppositions. As the title suggests the book is devoted to disorienting the investigating eye of the critic; not in order to return to a safe and stable "home", but in order to complicate the analysis and dislocate the subject. Simultaneously, she sought to "re-orient one's relationship to 'the Orient'" as an "imaginative geography" through shrewd analyses of historical cross-cultural representations in which contemporary debates on politics and culture are constantly taken as "retrospective source, rather than an evolutionary outcome, of what we consider now to be a formative period of ongoing discursive models" (Bal in Boer 2004b: xiv; Boer 2004b: 9). Keeping the present and the past in constant contact, Boer strived for an alternative theorization of cross-cultural representation, a commitment that she carries on in this book.

Inspired by Boer's work, this article concentrates on the functioning of borders within the institutionalized Western art world. I focus on the function of borders used in the promotion of non-Western art, and of contemporary art practices from the Islamic territories in particular. Intrigued by the recent Western fascination with works of artists either living in Islamic geographies or as migrants in the West, I will first discuss the employment of the term "contemporary Islamic art" as a new visual category in the consumption of global cosmopolitan culture. Subsequently, I will concentrate on the *Veil* exhibition that was held in different art galleries in the UK in 2003 as an illustrative case of the functioning of the concept. In the last part I will analyze a work by the artist *Ghazel*, displayed in the *Veil* exhibition. In this discussion, I will focus on cross-cultural viewing processes, by engaging the concepts that Boer introduced and problematized in her quest for another way of theorizing the dynamic processes of cross-cultural representation.

"Contemporary Art From the Islamic World"[1]

The *Veil* exhibition and Ghazel's "Me" series can be considered as a part of the contemporary phenomenon of "art from the Islamic world". The debut of the term occurred in 1989 when the Barbican Centre in London organized the exhibition titled *Contemporary Art From the Islamic World*, which was presented as the "first exhibition of contemporary Islamic art" by artist and art historian Wijdan Ali (quoted in Abdallah 2005). During the nineties, names like Shirin Neshat and Mona Hatoum made their way as international artists with an "Islamic background" living and working in the West, who became salient figures representing contemporary Islamic art. In the past five years, many other "artists from the Islamic world" have been introduced to the Western art world, thanks to the hype of exhibitions displaying works of the "Muslim artists" either living in the so-called Islamic territories or in the

---

[1] Even tough the use of "contemporary art from the Islamic world" as an artistic category is quite common, I believe the term is usually associated with an online journal with the same title published on the website *Universes in the Universe: Worlds of Art*. Issues of *Contemporary Art From the Islamic World* consist of articles, information, and pictures concerning "contemporary visual arts with essential sources or references in the Islamic world". In the editorial, the editors are cautious with this term by stressing that Islamic world "meant here in its cultural sense" which actually aims to show "the diversity of artistic expressions and individual positions of artists who live in Islam-influenced countries or regions, or consider their cultural home to be in such places but live elsewhere" <http://www.universes-in-universe.de/english.htm>.

Figure 16. Ghazel. *Venus* (1997). Copyright: Ghazel and ADAGP.

West, accompanied by relevant publications and critiques in art magazines.[2] This ever-increasing interest in the artistic practices from the previously neglected Muslim cultures can partially be explained by the prevailing discourse of new internationalism within the art world, which presents the adjective "contemporary" as a common visual language that equalizes and harmonizes Western and non-Western art alike. In such an artistic discourse, the traditional "arts of the Islam" is replaced with the vague term contemporary art which suggests cultural openness by its multiple techniques and forms – from photography to multi-media installations – and through its institutional structuring that encompasses the art gallery, the exhibition space, the biennales within metropoles carried by internationally renowned curators and art critics. In the web-like, poly-centred structure of the art world, Sharjah in United Arab Emirates can be an artistic centre as much as New York or Berlin and a Lebanese artist has the same chance as a young British artist of being discovered by curators travelling the globe.[3]

While disregarding geographic, national, racial and ethnic boundaries, the art world simultaneously reinforces them. This reification occurs when the knowledge and experience of the other is "integrated" in the centre by providing a separate space for the previously marginalized art practices and artists on the basis of their difference from the centre.[4] Indicative in this sense is the recent use of artistic categories such as contemporary "Latin American", "Asian", or "African" art with references to vast geographical areas that separate them from the art of the centre. Here, the geographical border between the centre and the periphery is discursively reconstructed, but, by means of what Boer calls naturalizing impulses, it is made invisible because the art of the margin is spatially incorporated within the centre –

---

[2] To list but a few of these exhibitions: *Far Near Distance: Contemporary Positions of Iranian Artists*, (March – May 2004), House of World Cultures, Berlin, Germany; *Poetics of Proximity*, (February – March 2004), Guggenheim Gallery, Chapman University Orange, CA, USA; *DisORIENTation: Contemporary Arab Artists From the Middle East,* (March – May 2003), Haus der Kulturen der Welt, Berlin, Germany; *Harem Fantasies and New Scheherazades*, (19 February – 18 May 2003), Centre de Cultura Contemporània de Barcelona, Barcelona, Spain.
[3] For unrestricted mobility of curators or "the selective curator tourism" and the failing task of the curator as a cultural translator, see Rossi (2002).
[4] For the persistence of the Western art world as the center, the failure of the new internationalism and strategies for the art from/of "the peripheries", see the collection of essays in *Global Visions: Towards a New Internationalism in the Visual Arts*, edited by Fisher (1999), most notably Gerardo Mosquera's contribution (1999: 133-39).

think of, for example, Documenta 11 – and fixed within the Occidental imagination.

In such a structure of the art world, the "artist from the Islamic world" becomes an ethnographer who represents and translates the cultural or ethnic other for the Western viewer. In his article "The Artist as Ethnographer?" Hal Foster argues that in the Western art world, artistic transformation as the site for political transformation has always been located elsewhere, in the field of the other – the cultural, oppressed postcolonial, subaltern other – and that this outside field of the other is the point of subversion of the dominant culture. Consequently, Foster asserts that the culturally othered artist has automatic access to this transformative alterity (1999). However, this artistic/political transformation brought about by the artist by means of her privilege of *being* the cultural other, takes place in the centre, within the Western art world, which dislocates the transformative potential of the boundary space.

Through her work, the culturally othered artist as the ethnographer brings the knowledge and the experience of the cultural other to the other side of the border in a similar manner as Boer discusses for the nineteenth-century travelogues of Madame de Gasparin and Jane Dieulafoy. The cross-cultural encounter in the ethnographic field suggested by Boer's analysis comprises a boundary space where cultural negotiation takes place. However, in the case of the contemporary art world such space is replaced by the borderless cultural discourse of cosmopolitanism in which "the unique expression of the non-Western is Western reflexively and automatically" (Brennan 2001: 675). Ultimately, within the institutionalized art world, the artist as ethnographer translates the experience of the other for the centre. The intercultural movement takes place, not within the boundary space, but within the borderless discourse of cosmopolitanism, which actually operates within clear material boundaries.

Contemporary Islamic Art: Why Now?

What – other than cherishing liberal cosmopolitan ideals – motivates this current interest in contemporary Islamic artistic practices of the art world? Is art from the Islamic territories simply a new colour added to the panoramic view of the Western metropoles, following the previous enthrallment with art from Latin America, Africa and, most recently, China? Following art critic and curator Gilane Tawadros, director of the Institute of International Visual Arts (InIVA), I would argue that this recent artistic curiosity should be contemplated within a historical and political context in the absence, in most cases, of a meaningful historical context or critical self-reflection on the part of curators, critics, and artists. Tawadros appropriately asks:

> Is it a coincidence then that the military re-occupation of the Middle East by the new imperial power, America and its allies, has been accompanied by a renewed interest in the culture of the Middle East? Just as Napoleon arrived in 1798 with his army of academics, scholars, and artists to map out Egypt and its culture, so 200 years later, planes bring an army of curators to Teheran, Beirut, and Cairo to "discover" contemporary art in the Middle East and "make it totally accessible" to European audiences (Tawadros 2004).

It is an intriguing question and the comparison of cultural implications between Napoleon's and G.W. Bush's international policies is provocative. Tawadros raises the problem of the appropriation of politics within the cultural sphere and the complicity of institutional art with power structures.

However, within 200 years, it seems the discourse of Orientalism changed to a certain extent, at least the "artistic practice" of it. Whereas in the nineteenth century, Western artists and men and women of letters would travel to the Islamic lands with the desire to make the East totally accessible to the European audience, the art world of the twenty-first century, ironically, lets the "Muslim other" represent herself. Yet, the criteria for this representation are set by the Western art institution materialized by its curators and critics. As Dina Ramadan (2004) notes, the local artists have to deal with issues such as religion, gender and repression of the state that are deemed important by the international community, and these issues must be addressed in an appropriately ideological manner. In a very similar way to Napoleon's project of the "visual mapping of the Orient" by visual artists, aiming to make it "totally accessible to European scrutiny" in a visual language that could be legible, today's art world makes the Islamic world culturally available to the Western viewer on Western terms.

As the cultural heritage kept in the museums in Iraq has already found its way to the Western art market following the US invasion, many new artists from the Islamic world have been discovered and have exhibited their works for the Western audience in international exhibitions, biennales and art galleries. In this sense, it is not coincidental that in 2003, in the wake and aftermath of the invasion of Iraq by the US army and its allies, the number of exhibitions on contemporary art from the region has increased so as to establish "a real dialogue between the cultures". *Veil* was one among many other exhibitions focusing on the issues concerning the cultural difference of the Islamic cultures and their possible representations in the western art world.

Veil – The Exhibition

Veil was a touring exhibition organized in 2003-2004 by the Institute of International Visual Arts (InIVA) curated by artists Zineb Sedira and Jananne Al-Ani and two other curators, David A. Bailey and Gilane Tawadros.[5] *Veil* included works by over a dozen contemporary artists. In contrast to similar exhibitions elsewhere, *Veil* had a "historical section" which consisted of Gillo Pontecorvo's infamous film "The Battle of Algiers" (1965), photographs by the psychiatrist and photographer Gaëtan de Clérambault, and Marc Garanger's series of women forced to unveil for French identity photographs, taken whilst he was a soldier during the Algerian War of Independence (1954-62).

As the press release puts it, *Veil* examines:

> one of the most powerful symbols in contemporary culture . . . this is the first major exhibition and publication to explore the position of the veil in today's complex global order, endlessly repositioned by changing world events . . . The exhibition disrupts contemporary notions of the veil but ultimately the project intends to become a starting point for a new international dialogue across cultures within the visual arts arena.[6]

Indeed, *Veil* is one of the most well-researched and informed exhibitions organized under the banner of art from the contemporary Islamic world. The publication accompanying the exhibition serves as a key work on the issue of

---

[5] Touring dates and localities of the exhibition were: The New Art Gallery Walsall, (February – April 2003); Bluecoat Gallery & Open Eye Gallery, Liverpool, (July – August 2003); Modern Art Oxford (November 2003 – January 2004) and Kulturhuset Stockholm (Feb – May 2004). It is important to note that in the exhibition catalogue it is stressed that the project was conceived well before the events of September 11, 2001, researched and developed by Zineb Sedira and Jananne Al-Ani over a period of four years, see Bailey and Tawadros (2003: 18-39).
[6] See <http://www.iniva.org/press/press018>.

veiling from a visual art perspective. It includes the essays written for the exhibition as well as important theoretical essays by authors ranging from Leila Ahmed to Frantz Fanon. The exhibition also stands out in the sense that it is a thematic one, focusing on the symbolic significance of the veil and veiling in contemporary culture. In so doing, it extends the debates on representation and the veil in a complex and provocative way. Moreover, the inclusion of the historical part next to the contemporary works uniquely frames the issue within a historical colonial context.

It is, however, unsettling to realize that the contemporary part of the exhibition consists of works by artists from the so-called Islamic region – mostly from North Africa and Middle East, living in Europe, with the exception of Elin Strand and the AES art group – whereas the historical part includes solely the works by western "artists". As such, this discrepancy comments on the historical shift in terms of the "expository agency" representing the orient.[7] Within the exhibition space, the displays of Pontecorvo's documentary works and Garanger's photographic images, alongside the mixed-media drawings of Emily Jacir and Ghazel's video monographs, not only problematize the colonial gaze cast by the West on Islamic cultures, but also bring forth the dynamics of neo-Orientalism in the art world in which the "Islamic other within" is *given* the privilege and the authority to visualize the othered culture.

As I argued above, the employment of contemporary art from the Islamic world as an artistic category undermines the authoritative voice of the Western subject as the expository agent by replacing it with the *authentic authority* of the non-Western artist. Ironically, the promotion of Muslim artists in such exhibitions as possessing "an intimate knowledge of both Western and Eastern cultures", as curator Jananne Al-Ani puts it, reasserts values like authenticity, originality, singularity, as well as the notion of the artist as the creator, so banished under poststructuralism and postmodernism.

The name of the artist – mostly with a hint to her non-Western origin – not only refers to a genuine link of the artist to her community, which gives her

---

[7] I borrow the term "expository agency" from Mieke Bal's *Double Exposures: The Subject of Cultural Analysis* (1996). In this book, the term stands for the subject of semiotic behavior in which the constative use of signs prevails, which includes practices like visual pointing – display in the narrow sense – on the basis of a narrative. It is bound to subjects and embedded in power structures, hence, only those who are invested with cultural authority can be expository agents (Bal, 1996: 8).

an authentic insight to the site, but also authorizes her works as representing the "real orient". Here, the emphasized presence of the artist's name works not unlike the way the absence of wall captions, titles and names in the *Insel Hombroich* museum that Boer analyzes in Chapter Six. In her analysis, Boer illustrates how such absences foster the discourse of authenticity to the level of fetishism, which straddles the aesthetic-anthropological divide. Similarly, the presence of the non-western artist's name works as a indexical sign bridging the gap between aesthetics and politics.

The authority of the artist from the Islamic territories residing in the West – as in the case of most artists in the exhibition – is intensified by her ability to transgress cultural and geographical boundaries. Her cultural in-betweennes gives her "an intimate knowledge of both Western and Eastern cultures", which makes her not only an insider but also a "privileged outsider" to both cultures. Such promotion of the artist as a privileged outsider frames her as yet another nomadic subject who has relinquished "all idea, desire, or nostalgia for fixity", in favour of a nomadic consciousness, with "an acute awareness of the nonfixity of boundaries" and "the desire to go on trespassing, transgressing" (Braidotti 1994: 36). Hence, the artist residing in spaces in-between perpetually transgresses material and metaphorical boundaries, which gives her a "peripheral consciousness" representing the alleged reality of the itinerant-worker, the illegal alien, the cross-border sex-worker, and various brands of displacement, diasporas and hybridity which Braidotti calls alternative figurations of post-humanist subjectivity (Braidotti n.d.).

It is this "easy travel between metaphor and the life conditions of groups of people" that Boer rejects more or less in the same manner as Sara Ahmed, who argues that the representation of nomadism in terms of thought implies that it can be separated from the material social relations in which "thought" itself is idealized as the rational capacity of well-educated subjects (Ahmed 1999: 335). As Boer counters in her analysis of *La Voyeuse interdite*, "only from the perspective of the inside would it be possible to postulate the freedom of the nomad, intellectual or otherwise" and the movement of the nomads are "inspired by outside conditions that impose restrictions upon them" (Chapter One).

It is worth noting that in Boer's analyses the inside and the outside coincide on the border. This may also be the reason why most of the artists in the *Veil* exhibition, in one way or another, wear the veil on their bodies, like Shirin Neshat's veiled self-portraits *Women of Allah*, Zineb Sedira's photographic triptych *Self-portraits* or *the Virgin Mary* and Ghazel's veiled video triptych *Me* series. All three works attempt to dis-orient vision and envision images where "cultural otherness can find a space other than its stereotypical manifestation" (Chapter Five).

Boundaries Of the Veil, Veil As the Border: Ghazel's *Me* Series

Picture a woman carrying out the ordinary daily activities, eating, smoking, riding a motorbike, cutting the grass, dancing, driving or exercising. Or, imagine her performing perhaps a bit unusual actions, such as mountain climbing, playing squash or diving. Now, dress her up with a black veil while undertaking the pursuits of all these various activities. Will it be a commendable image or perhaps a visual oxymoron? If it is an oxymoron, then, according to the Oxford English Dictionary, the image should express a situation that should be "in its superficial or literal meaning self-contradictory or absurd" but it should also "involve a point". Fortunately, a certain artist who has a point that actually acts upon the nature of this visual oxymoron has thought of such images.

The work of Ghazel, entitled *Me*, is a video triptych consisting of forty planned films collectively lasting almost eight hours.[8] Each short film in the series contains some ten autonomous scenes presenting the artist engaged with some activity. The installation of the Me series consists of the videos running simultaneously on three different monitors situated next to each other, so that the random interaction of the images is the installation.

These images can be seen as moving self-portraits of Ghazel, each presenting a single shot of the artist herself engaged in some sort of activity, including swimming, eating, smoking, exercising, biking, dancing or boxing, which she performs with a tightly worn black chador. These "veiled video-diaries" are accompanied by qualifying texts in English or French, or both; these intertitles do not translate but rather comment on the images. The texts

---

[8] Me series is an ongoing project. At the time of writing, there were 620 scenes lasting almost 17 hours – each ten scenes make a film, so they are called "me 1", "me 2", and so on until "me 62".

Figure 17. Ghazel. *Soccer* (1997). Copyright: Ghazel and ADAGP.

are mostly uttered in the "I" pronoun, usually referring to the images in an ironical manner. Both the use of the first person pronoun and the irony suggested in the texts create an intimate relationship with the viewer involving a comedy of visual/textual daily confession of the artist.

Like most artists in the exhibition, Ghazel was born and grew up in a Middle Eastern country and then moved to Europe for educational reasons. As her story goes, seven years after the Islamic Revolution Ghazel left Iran at the age of nineteen, moving to France where she now lives and works. She made her artistic debut in 1997, when the French Immigration Office denied her a residence permit and forced her to leave the country. As a counter-reaction, Ghazel printed posters where, beside the photographs of herself, the following text was printed: "URGENT, Woman, 30, artist of Middle Eastern origin and WP (without permit) seeks a husband, from EU, preferably France, contact e-mail . . .", and distributed it in public spaces.[9] After starting off her artistic career with such a provocative work, Ghazel exhibited the Me series for the first time in 2000. Between 1997 and 2000, she exhibited completely different works in Iran that have never been displayed in the West. After the debut of the Me series, she extensively exhibited in the West, including at the Venice Biennale, but also in Havana, Tokyo, Zagreb and Sarajevo. Yet, it is plausible to argue that Ghazel is a diasporic artist producing in and for the West and, putting it bluntly, her works deal with the representation of diasporic identity. Her constant touch with Iran frames and promotes Ghazel as an authentic artist with a poetic insight into both her country of origin and her own diasporic experience.[10]

Almost all the critical texts I have read about Ghazel's work point to an

---

[9] The Wanted project is a work in progress. Ghazel finally got her residence permit in 2003 and since then she is offering marriage to an illegal man. For the online images of Wanted (Urgent), see <http://artefact.mi2.hr/_a01/artists/ghazel/WANTED4/urgent.html>.

[10] It is worth noting that independent curator Rose Issa, who is a specialist on visual arts from the Middle East and North Africa, presents Ghazel as one of the much-celebrated Iranian artists who regularly travels between Iran and France for "inspiration" (2004). However, this particular introduction of the artist disregards her professional works and long/short term projects in which she has been involved in Iran. These include The Correction Center for delinquent juveniles (girls): art therapy workshops/Khaneyeh Sabz (House for street children): art therapy workshops, Tehran in 2000; Street Children Project, a 4 month project, written and realized by the artist; in Tehran, in 1999 and The Correction Center for delinquent juveniles (boys); art therapy workshops, Tehran between 1997 and 1999. I would like to thank Ghazel for directing my attention to these hardly mentioned works of her and providing me with the details of the projects.

"evident visual paradox" incorporated in her Me videos. The absurdity of a woman wrapped in fabrics who insists on conducting activities that require the body to move freely. Obviously, this paradox does not emerge from any body or any fabric. The tension takes place between the body of the artist, and the veil that has become one of the most contested cross-cultural symbols representing the submissive Muslim women in the West. However, in the films, the veiled body is far from being a passive one. On the contrary, she is physically assertive and seems to be actively participating in the everyday life, not only in the sacred private sphere but also in the public one, by means of her sheer presence.

Thus, in the Me series, the stereotypical solemn Muslim woman image is replaced by a vigorous woman who transgresses boundaries quite easily. With the ever-present chador, the woman climbs mountains, wins the big cup in ice-skating, scuba dives, takes ballet classes or goes to the gym, all signs of being a modern Western woman, which is hardly in harmony with the stereotypical image of a Muslim woman in veil. As such, she trespasses the invisible border between the West and the East, modern and traditional, hence the boundary between "us" and "them". Like Mrs. Bennis' continuous travel back and forth from one culture to the other in *The Forbidden Roof-Terrace*, which Boer analysed in Chapter One, the woman in the Me series crosses the border between cultures, codes and languages. If these simple border-crossings, achieved in a world where boundaries are said to be blurring, create the visual paradox inherent in the films, then the question arises, "whose paradox is this?" My answer would be that the paradox literally lies in the eye of the beholder, who is ultimately the Western viewer encountering the work in the art galleries or exhibition halls in different Western metropolises.

By the mere incorporation of the veil, it is possible to interpret these videos, momentarily interrupted by still texts, as the artist's negotiation with her cultural past within the present. In fact, without the veil, the woman would have seemed like any woman carrying on ordinary acts not worth filming. Following Meyda Yeğenoğlu's (1998: 119) argument that the veil should be seen as a fundamental piece conjoined with the embodied subjectivity of Muslim women, Ghazel's act of wearing the veil works on two levels: firstly, with the veil, she embodies an anonymous Muslim woman taken out of space and time, and in so doing she becomes a representative of "the Muslim woman" as such. Secondly, as an "emancipated" artist living in the West, she performs her "former self" in Iran where she should have been wearing the veil in her everyday life. It is only by means of the veil that the artist can visually perform the "former self" to the Western audience so that she remains the authentic artist who is expected to have experienced wearing the veil.

But the figure is hardly "authentic". The artist performs her veiled self over and over in the theatricality of the videos, exemplified by the stage-like setting – which can be anywhere and everywhere – and the exaggerated gestures of the artist which turns the veil into a mere costume. At this point, the act of veiling can be seen as a "parody of the self" in which the artist enacts the former veiled self, which, in turn questions the originality of the authentic artist imposed by the Western viewer. Besides mocking the idea of originality, the self-parody ridicules the Western obsession with the veil as the site of oppression and the marker of cultural difference. The work invites the viewer to laugh at the absurdity of the veiled woman as she sunbathes or ballet-dances, which is an inverted critique of what actually amuses the viewer: cultural difference understood through the employment of cultural stereotypes.

However, contrary to my reading, most of the art critics argue that by performing these eccentric veiled activities the artist "reflects on her multiple imperfect identities and her foreignness both at home and abroad" (Issa 2004: n.p.). Here we are back at the naturalization of cultural difference in dichotomies, such as unveiled/veiled; active/passive; visible/invisible, oppressed/emancipated. Therefore, as the critics' insistence indicates, no matter how subversive a parody of the self can be in terms of questioning authenticity, it is through these dichotomies that the non-Western artist and her work are being framed. Similar to Timothy Brennan's argument that the phenomenology of "third-world literature" not only affects the reception, but in part dictates the outcome which frames the hybrid artist in terms of "being rather than doing" (1997: 203-04), it seems that contemporary art criticism embraces and promotes the works of non-Western artists in terms of a witnessing that allegedly reveals their paradoxical experiences. Provided with such a frame, the viewer can safely laugh at the parody of the veiled woman performing the possible instances of the modern daily life of any Western woman.

Yet, the familiarity of these activities also encourages the viewer to identify with the woman on these three monitors; just like the viewer, the veiled woman enjoys swimming and takes care of her physical appearance. Simultaneously, the viewer is forced to disidentify by means of the ever-present veil as the marker of otherness. In the viewer's visual encounter with the veiled other, the daily life, despite of all its familiarity, becomes uncanny, through the other's reappropriation of the everyday. The woman acts like anybody else, she walks freely in public spaces, drives her car confidently, even plays the guitar on the pavement, yet she is always "with" the veil. As Jananne Al-Ani suggests, the appearance of the veil in every episode actually "reduces its significance; it becomes banal and everyday as it does in any society in which it is omnipresent" rather than making it an exclusive textual marker of cultural difference (2003: 103). It is hence from the other side of the border – i.e. in West – that this everyday banality is seen as paradoxical and troubled.

Ironically, rather than marking her authentic Islamic identity, the artist's act of veiling herself can also be interpreted as a different form of what Boer calls cultural cross-dressing. In Ghazel's work, as well as Neshat's and Sedira's that I mentioned above, the veil works in a similar manner with contemporary fashion ads and eighteenth-century *turquerie* paintings, discussed by Boer as instances of making use of hybridity (Chapter Six). In contrast to the cases analysed by Boer, the subject performing the "as if" in the works in the *Veil* exhibition is presented as already "culturally other". However, it is plausible to argue that a similar "act of dressing up as if" can be traced in these works, not in the sense of a desire to be an oriental woman but as restaging of a collective experience. Yet, in Ghazel's act of cross-dressing, the desirable upper-class oriental woman is replaced by an ordinary, anonymous Muslim woman, be it far away in Afghanistan or in the cosmopolitan Western metropolises. As such, the artist's act of veiling works as a reminder of Boer's critique of images of otherness "presented with such frequency and self-evidence that they receive an authenticity that completely lacks any awareness of the political implications of the fundamentally contradictory character of cultural cross-dressing" (Chapter Six).

With Boer's critique in mind, Ghazel's "act of dressing up as if" also evokes the image of the "migrant Muslim woman within". In the videos the background serves as a generic stage.[11] One can get a glimpse of the cityscape or the countryside yet will never manage to recognize it as a specific "place".[12] Consequently, this indistinct stage can be anywhere and everywhere. She can be in distant Iran or in any of the Muslim countries to which she belongs, but she could also be just around the corner as soon as the viewer leaves the safe doors of the art gallery. In the second interpretation, the cosmopolitan urban space turns into a site where the veiled other can expose the practice of "Islamic everyday life", however defined. Disguised by the veil that turns the Muslim women into anonymous multiple "Aishes", Ghazel then also performs the migrant other within the everyday of the West. And through this everyday suggested by the videos, the Western viewer is being asked whether she would accept the "other within" when she walks out of the door, in spite of her difference.

As such, Ghazel's veiled monographs bring the "real nomad" back on stage, right in the middle of the cosmopolitan everyday life in which the Muslim other has become more and more visible and more threatening. At this point, one has to question the transformative potential of artworks such as Ghazel's Me series. These works problematize cultural difference by challenging the viewer's complicity and embedded stereotypes, when alleged cultural dialogue seems to be replaced by propaganda and violence. If we accept that the modes of appropriation of cultural products change depending on cultural-social spaces in which they are produced, circulated and received, where can we locate a critical viewer when multicultural everyday has

---

[11] In the "Introduction" to the exhibition catalogue, it is stated that the films were shot in Iran, Paris, Montpellier and New York – note that Iran is used as a generic term almost referring to a non-place in contrast to the mentioned cities.

[12] Here I use the term "place" in contrast to those of "location" and "space"" as discussed by Boer in *Disorienting Vision* (2004b). She argues that the orient as "location" signifies the Western desire to know and actually see and experience the orient whereas the term "space" reflects how the orient functions as a reservoir for fears and fantasies in the West. She casts these two terms against "place" as the inhabited point in space, since neither of them, in contrast to the term place, "engages with the felt, experienced place where so-called Orientals live their lives" (Boer, 2004b: 25). This inability to mark the scenes within particular place is closely related to Boer's discussion of the desert in Chapter Four, which for the Western eyes is empty – hence, non-place – and flavored with Orientalist connotations. For the viewer, the non-place of the videos, then, invokes a metaphorical desert standing for the distant Islamic territories that in turn reconstructs the "Orient" as a "space" and a "location".

become a site of conflict pushing cultural dialogue to the margins? If we acknowledge the culturally and socially framed boundaries of the viewer's meaning-making process, as well as her complicity with the disseminated neo-orientalist discourse, then how can cultural otherness find a space outside of stereotypical articulation?

These questions bring me to Homi Bhabha's concept of the "third space" emerging in the interstices between different cultures, which is characterized by the cultural hybridity of its inhabitants (1994). In this liminal space the old concepts of nation, ethnicity, gender, class or history no longer hold. Instead they are replaced by permanent cultural negotiations, flows and movements breaking up the constructed oppositions that empower the weak who are subjected to the contemporary conditions of displacement and diasporic experience.

But who negotiates, who translates in this space? Can these processes be mutual, especially if we think about the modes of appropriation I mentioned above? Particularly if one considers Bhabha's comments on Fanon's analysis of the Algerian struggle for independence, where he writes that the free Algerian people can negotiate and translate their cultural identities in a discontinuous intertextual temporality of cultural difference. Here, the freedom is formulated in the following sentence: "they can construct their culture from the national text translated into modern Western forms of information technology, language, dress" (Bhabha 1994: 38). Following Bhabha's suggestion, it is the cultural other who has to do the translation and negotiation, whereas the terms of this translation are already maintained by the modern Western forms. What is at stake here is the telos of the imperial project when the third-world subject becomes able to "deconstruct the epistemic violence of colonialism . . . by way of Continental theory" as Brennan argues (2002: 675).

Ghazel's Me series could serve as a perfect instance of the functioning of the liminal space and in-between designations of identities in a process of symbolic interaction that prevents identities from settling into primordial polarities. Ghazel, the nomadic artist cum displaced subject, translates the Western form of technology, video, Western languages with their imperfect grammar, and the practices of dressing and everyday life. However, in such formulation, it seems as if the process of cultural negotiation is already accomplished in the work. The migrant artist performs the translation of norms and codes, since she has a "double vision" (Bhabha 1994: 85-92), while the space left to the viewer is to appreciate the artist's translation in comparison with her own stereotypes. But why would the viewer of the work negotiate if she actually created the diasporic situation and set the agenda and conditions for the acts of translation? The viewer's vision is hardly likely to be doubled if it is complicitous with a media-prompted neo-Orientalism that re-assimilates difference and the notion of hybridity.

As a site of privileged, textual, discursive space accessible only to the creative subjects with epistemological privilege, the intervention of the third space thus neglects the material conditions of the everyday life as it is experienced by "the other within" in cosmopolitan urban spaces. As such, it neglects the negotiations and *negations* against the coercive and perhaps violent nature of "the outside of the third space" that actually has strict boundaries. No doubt, Bhabha's liminal concepts have enormous appeal both within academia and in other intellectual communities. After all, we all want to believe that the cosmopolitan location is one where binary oppositions have become irrelevant, that the new playing field is one of performative contestation rather than of ethnic, national or gender separation and rivalry. However, if we neglect the persistence of the binary constructions and structures "outside of the liminal space" – an outside riddled with clear boundaries – "we", cultural critics, risk becoming complicitous with the ethics of a new material reality of globalization which finds its reflection in the idea of cosmopolitanism (Brennan 2002: 662-63). As those who think of ourselves as being involved in a theoretical enterprise that is cultural – one that deals with images, arts, everyday practices, and forms of entertainment – we "have to be very cautious . . . [of] positing anything like a 'diasporic public sphere' the hopeful vision of non-white, non-western exiles in metropolitan enclaves making good while making do" (Brennan 2002: 686).

Inge Boer's *Uncertain Territories* provides us such a cautious and critical theoretical intervention and shows us how the practice of cultural analysis can be politically resonant. She points at the persistence of the clash between the oppressor and oppressed, male and female, master and victim in such a way that undoes the binaries by the unstable and negotiated functioning of the borders and boundaries. In such theorizing, borders not only materialize in a world where they are said to be disappearing, they also become a contested component of identity construction and cultural production. By focusing on how borders host cross-cultural encounters, Boer's mode of analysis furthermore aims to reveal the unequal power relations in the processes of boundary construction. Moreover, her critical stance against the naive use of border-crossing metaphors – which reduce experience into simple formulation of "what happens to people" – reminds us how borders work otherwise: as spaces of exclusion hence, of negation. In this respect, Boer's work offers an understanding of our times: one not directed to a hopeful vision of the "beyond" of borders, as Bhabha has it, but a way of border thinking where the border itself becomes a productive space.

In a similar manner, works like Ghazel's Me series suggest us a way of rethinking the concepts and theories we, cultural critics, have at hand. Me series subtly resist the naive use of concepts such as liminality and hybridity. It works towards its *outside*, drawing on and towards the encounter of the viewer with the work. The boundary between the viewer and the work emerges as a space of negotiation where the viewer is invited to think alongside the work and reconsider her own paradox and stereotypes. Moreover, as I mentioned above, the boundary between the art gallery and its exterior "everyday life" converges in this space of encounter in which the viewer is encouraged to consider the experience of the other in the cosmopolitan urban-scape that has clear borders. Contemporary Islamic art resides within this cosmopolitan urban-scape and it is the interlacing of Boer's "border theory" with the objects discussed in this chapter that brings out what might otherwise be invisible: the functioning of borders and boundaries within the global art world and cultural criticism.

ELEVEN

Giving Life: Inge Boer's Postcolonial Theory

Isabel Hoving

One morning, over coffee, Inge Boer asked me, bright-eyed and eager: "Who has been the main source of inspiration then, for your academic work?" For her, there was no doubt: it had always been Edward Said. He had inspired her in many aspects, especially in her desire to produce academic work that would also be socially and politically relevant. But her question betrayed another characteristic of her work: the fact that she took it for self-evident that our scholarly work would be fuelled by inspiration, passion and curiosity.

Remarkably, she assumed that not just her close colleagues and friends, with whom she shared a comparable theoretical drive, but all her colleagues, and even the writers, painters and travellers she studied, were motivated by desires and interests as ardent and complex as her own. In contrast to many of her fellow postcolonial scholars, instead of primarily criticizing the greed and desire for power in the projects of exploration and colonialism, she liked to emphasize the *curiosity* that drove travellers toward remote regions – "travel . . . is propelled by a curiosity about other cultures similar to the professional interest that inspires ethnographers" (Chapter Three). If this curiosity leads to efforts to master cultural otherness by capturing it in familiar categories, it will also produce layered texts and images that exceed and subvert their own categories.

This ambivalence opens up a space for self-reflection, and for the possibility of another, innovative and liberating look. Granted: curiosity, a far from innocent drive – archaically it was "a *blameable* tendency or desire to inquire into or seek knowledge" (Webster; my emphasis) – may easily lead to exoticization and/or appropriation, but its dynamic and everyday nature may urge us to look again, to look in a different way, to be dissatisfied with one's own strategies of knowing. This is what Boer has always been after: instead of the look that tries to master, empty out and kill what it sees (Chapter Three), she probed for a life-giving way of reading "against the grain", or, in the words of Kaja Silverman: the productive look, generating the process of "learning to see differently, but only after having recognized the necessary struggle with dominant elements of the screen" (Boer 2004b: 14). This is the look that restores life to the spaces eradicated by the colonial gaze (Chapter Four).

The Fight Over Said's Legacy, and the Problem of "The Political"

Where does this scholarly attitude leave Boer's work, in the large field of postcolonial studies? What does her work teach us about the tensions and conflicts within postcolonial studies, and what can we learn from the way it relates to those?[1]

As a passionate student of Edward Said, she may in the first place be situated in relation to the debates that have been, and are still raging about Said's work – work that is often defined as the originating moment of postcolonial theory. A good example of the debate is Robert Young's belligerent attack on Edward Said's use of Foucault's concept of discourse. Young takes his point of departure in the widely expressed critique that Said's notion of colonial discourse is reductive because, among other things, it "produces a textualized version of history", thus short-circuiting the "labyrinthine questions of representation and its relation to the real", and because it refuses to take into account "the particularity of historical and geographical difference" (Young 2001: 408). Young argues that these and

---

[1] With the term "postcolonial studies" I refer to studies addressing the cultural practices that work through the legacies of colonialism. I want it to include both postcolonial theory (by Said, Bhabha, Spivak and all those who offer self-conscious forms of "high" theorizing) and postcolonial criticism (as the broad variety of literary approaches that draw on other sources). The distinction is by Bart Moore-Gilbert (1997). Most of Boer's work would count as postcolonial theory.

other objections could easily be answered by returning to Foucault's concept of discourse, as "none of these would apply to Foucault's original model" (408).

Young's surprisingly stark criticism strikes me primarily as an impatient move to overtake Said and leave him behind, opening up a newly configured field of postcolonial criticism, governed by new stars, and unmuddled by the intricate complexities of "travelling theory". British postcolonial scholar John McLeod answers this move with grace and cool; after pointing out that Said wants to do something *different* from Foucault – that is, he wishes to relate discursive systems to individual texts, in meticulous close-readings – McLeod states:

> Advocates of context-sensitive criticism must beware blinding themselves to the creative potential of "travelling theory" which, as Anglophone postcolonialism vividly demonstrates, can be enormously and urgently creative in breaking and making intellectual paradigms (McLeod 2003: 200).

More elegantly still, Boer takes her distance from Young's fight with Said over the map of postcolonial studies. In her Introduction to *After Orientalism* (Boer 2004c), she does not run to Said's rescue by explicitly defending his approach. Instead, in an independent argument about both the drawbacks and weaknesses of Said's work, she demonstrates her feminist position by relating to Young's critical essay in an oblique, independent way. She quotes one particular argument from Young's larger study that she, as a feminist, considers relevant (about post-colonialism's unfinished task of inquiring into gender), and some passages of the essay in which Young admits the productivity of Said's concept of discourse – and she leaves it at that.

Not the desire for power, but that for knowledge is what fuels Boer's work. Instead of redrawing the map of postcolonial studies, and thus claiming a new authority, she prefers to search the existing map for its promising sites, and tries to find a productive trajectory from there. In contrast to Young, she *does* observe the productivity of travelling concepts; this shouldn't come as a surprise, as Boer's work is generally marked by a firm belief in the promise of movement and interaction. For that reason her work cannot be said to directly *oppose* the critique of travelling theory and the problematic search for origins in Young's essay. Not opposition, but resonance is the key operation guiding Boer's movements through this field of inquiry (Chapter One). Instead of opposing Young, then, she evades the power game, refuses to claim or attack authority, and searches for those elements in Young's work with which she can interact.

This might already count as an answer to the question to what extent Boer's writing can be seen as following up on Said's project. Its interest lies not in criticizing it, but in extending his project (the critique of colonial discourse), through a series of detailed analyses of texts, images and cultural practices. Rather than to focus on the text under scrutiny itself, or to trace the workings of colonial discourse, as Said did, Boer looks above all at the intricate interactions between the text, its readers (herself included) and its authors. In her eyes, it is in these interactions that meaning is produced, a meaning that responds to (neo-)colonial discourse in ambivalent ways. If Said's work was sometimes accused of ignoring the importance of agency in the workings of texts referring to (neo-)colonial discourse (Chapter Five), Boer's succeeds in avoiding that criticism by adding to Said's insights a focus on the interaction between readers and text that is implied in cultural analysis. Nor can Boer's work be said to neglect work by artists outside the Western cultural canon, as the critics of Said accuse him of doing. But, again, that does not mean that Boer's work can be understood as opposed to Said's. Rather, it is travelling *with* Said's work, responding to its most promising and enthusing aspects, and elaborating on them.

Boer's elaboration of Said's project has resulted in a series of close readings of varied texts, images, and practices such as fashion and art collecting and exhibiting, with the aim "to achieve another way of theorizing about dynamic processes of cross-cultural representation" (Introduction). This emphasis on representation seems to come close to those postcolonial theoretical practices that have been criticized for their emphasis on the textual to the detriment of the political, and the cultural to the detriment of the material, especially when drawing from so-called "high theory". Theorists like Homi Bhabha have been especially targeted. On the one hand, these critiques can often be rebutted by pointing out their own theoretical debts, their naive understanding of "reality" and their reduction of what Young called the "labyrinthine questions of representation and its relation to the real" (see Moore-Gilbert 1997 for an effective, serious response to these critiques). On the other hand, their criticism that some postcolonial theories downplay the importance of the political should not be so easily dismissed. The political has always been at the heart of postcolonial theorizing. Postcolonial studies came into being when the relation between representation and the political (notably colonial rule) was put on the agenda of literary studies, most famously by Edward Said's *Orientalism* (1978). Remarkably, it is Said who is now criticized for not taking seriously enough the project he started himself: bringing the political into the field of Commonwealth literary studies. The many practitioners in the field have often been driven by the same critical, emancipatory and liberatory zeal as Said: by analysing and criticizing colonial discourse, postcolonial studies might help undo (neo-)colonial discursive structures, open up opportunities for the emancipation of voices from the South and East, and perhaps even contribute to the shaping of new geopolitical relations.

The fact that these desires have been analysed and heavily criticized in their own right, does not mean that they should be dismissed as irrelevant or too politically correct. Gayatri Spivak is often quoted for her highly intelligent criticism of the urge to move outside the dominant institutions and discourses, but she is surely well acquainted with the same desires herself. If Spivak, referring to the postcolonial, talks about the condition of inhabiting "a space that one cannot not want to inhabit and yet must criticize" (1993: 64), that does not mean that critical postcolonial subjects, such as postcolonial scholars, should simply begin *wanting* to inhabit that dominant space.

The question about the relations between the textual and political, the cultural and material, is therefore still relevant, though far from unequivocal. It is even at the heart of the present-day crisis in postcolonial studies. This crisis was articulated by Moore-Gilbert in 1997, here by paraphrasing Stuart Hall:

> the impasse which now besets the field derives from the failure of its practitioners to be sufficiently interdisciplinary, to move out from a focus on essentially literary concerns to engage with disciplines like economics and sociology, in particular, which are addressing the material operations and cultural consequences of globalization, in a quite different manner to what is habitual in the arena of postcolonial studies (Moore-Gilbert 1997: 186).

What was habitual in the arena of postcolonial studies was the recourse to the concept of discourse – which has been extensively problematized – and the routine references to the workings of race, class and gender. The response to the impasse has been varied. Whereas some scholars chose to move away from interdisciplinarity towards a renewed focus on close readings of literary texts, others, such as Young, began to concentrate on the political contexts of postcolonial writing (2001), for example by situating Derrida's fascination for difference within the context of his Algerian youth. The book you are holding now is remarkable because it shows a wide variety of possible responses to this desire to relate to "the political".

Reading "The Political" as "The Economic"

I will begin my sketch of the variety of these responses with Chapter Five of this study, on cultural cross-dressing. This chapter offers a highly explicit focus on the political and material dimensions of cultural practices, by addressing economic power structures. More conventional analyses of orientalist discourse, or of the widespread tendencies to exoticize cultural otherness, would restrict themselves to a critical analysis of the imagery in orientalist fashion ads, theorizing, perhaps, the concept of identity implied in these masquerades. But this chapter doesn't stop there.

Self-consciously, it constructs a genuinely interdisciplinary frame to reflect on the implications of the use of the concepts of cultural cross-dressing and hybridity. By including the global fashion industry in this frame, it becomes possible to articulate a well-founded critique of the naive celebration of the transgression of boundaries and of hybridity: "Globalized capitalism . . . has a stake in cultural mixing" (Chapter Five), as Boer states dryly. In her eyes, the freedom "to transgress the boundaries the . . . culture of capital has erected and maintains for its benefits" is less a subversive movement than a commodity that can be *bought*. In her attention to global capitalism as the necessary context for considering the productivity of theoretical concepts, Boer shows herself to be a perceptive reader of Spivak's work. Moreover, she contributes to the debate on the question how not just literature, but also literary theory is implicated in (neo)colonialism.

One early insight that sprang forth from the analysis of colonial discourse was the statement that the European "civilizing mission" could be seen as the cultural dimension of the project of colonisation, which is primarily economic and political. Though it would not do to keep differentiating the cultural from the economic and political as if these levels could be analysed as ideological superstructure and economic base, it is still worthwhile to think about the relation between cultural practices and the economic and political project of globalisation. Yes, the task to analyse the workings of (political) power has been defined in much more sophisticated ways; the nuances brought by Gramsci's concept of hegemony, or the immense productivity of Foucault's concept of discourse were not lost on postcolonial scholars. But, as Benita Parry and others argue, this does not mean that the older notions of power, such as physical oppression, intimidation or capitalist exploitation, have become obsolete. They may still do very well to analyse the harsher conditions of all those who are not part of the (postcolonial) elite. In the same vein, academic practice itself may well be analysed in its relation to the global knowledge industry. To what extent has research become implicated in this economic structure? If the traditional departments of English studies were (also) aiming at educating and training the elite from British colonies, what kind of intellectuals are produced by the literary departments of our day?

These questions are relevant, and Marxist traditions of thought could help answer them. Boer's systematic references to global capitalism and the market in Chapters Five and Six testify to the productivity of Marxist insights within the field of postcolonial studies. However, Boer is not a Marxist. There are instances in Boer's writing where one would expect an interpretation according to lines of class, but finds a reading that partly evades, partly exceeds that focus. In Chapter Four, for example, Boer discusses the imagination of the desert in connection with the genre of the still life. Leaving aside John Berger's Marxist analysis of the still life in the early seventies, when he read the genre in its function of reinforcing the wealthy owner's sense of class superiority by celebrating his riches, she takes Norman Bryson's analysis of still life as being about hospitality as her guide.[2] Far from being about lifeless objects, he argues, still life is about

---

[2] Rather than an alternative, this reading could be an elaboration of Berger's statement. If Berger is highlighting the issues of commodification, he is also pointing at the human relationships that motivate this presentation. Still life, then, is indeed about interaction rather than about lifeless objects.

human relationships. Thus, Boer is able to construct a frame of interpretation by means of the notions of death and life, absence and presence.

If it is possible to understand a painting of the desert as a still life in the traditional sense by emphasizing the absence of human beings and the signs of death, it is also possible to read it contrapuntally, as Said would say following Bryson, by highlighting the signs of human presence that shaped the desert, and brought it to life. Indeed, only in this way does it become possible to articulate a critique of a variety of manners of appropriation, including those that were not motivated by class interests. This frame allows Boer to criticize (1) the colonialist discursive strategies that empty out landscapes of human life, and present them as lifeless objects to be appropriated (à la Pratt 1992); but it also allows her to criticize (2) the ethnographic desire in postmodern theory (Deleuze and Guattari 1992 [1980]); Braidotti 1994); (3) to point at the anxiety in western practices of understanding space as objective abstraction (e.g. mapping); (4) to present an alternative Algerian imagination of the desert, where the desert appears to be a lived space, shaped by human history – and, ultimately, (5) to reflect upon the limitations of a culturally specific interest in boundaries as "lines" rather than as "negotiated spaces", an attitude that forms an obstacle to postcolonial theorizing. A Marxist approach alone could never have accomplished.

This is a good example of a postcolonial analysis that highlights the workings of the political in cultural practices by understanding objectivation in a broader sense than as merely the effect of the market. Boer extends this analysis into a critique of "the politics of quotation". She treats this critique more extensively in Chapters Four and Five, where a sobering critique of the celebration of the figuration of the nomad is offered. Her intervention in a scholarly debate makes clear what happens if one denies the specific political and economic experience of a historic group of people on which one models one's theoretical concepts (the nomad, nomadism). The remedy offered is this: historicize the landscape, historicize the condition of its inhabitants. Another example of an analysis that enhances the productivity of Marxist concepts by taking them out of the context of a Marxist political or economic debate is Boer's enlightening focus on class, in addition to gender, race and ethnicity, in the analysis of cultural cross-dressing, a practice that seems perhaps primarily gendered and racialized. This example shows that the focus on class does not have to be a hackneyed routine; it can produce unexpected insight into the social and political effects of a cultural practice. It testifies to the consistent need, in cultural analysis, to acknowledge the capitalist organisation of Western societies, even if it does not seem relevant to the debate.

Reading "The Political" as Text

What can be gathered from these examples is that postcolonial scholars have other concerns than those central to the disciplines of sociology or political science. Their aim is not just, or not necessarily, the unmasking of the economic and political interests of dominant discourses. Postcolonial theory is not party politics; Boer's serious criticism of both the discourse of globalization *and* that of anti-globalism (Introduction) speaks to that. What postcolonial theory sets out to do, is, on the one hand, to work from an awareness of the social and political effects of all cultural practices, including all knowledge practices, while, on the other hand, also insisting on the semiotic, or, more specifically, linguistic nature of the workings of the political – and therefore also on the individual efforts to come to terms with the political.

The second chapter is an example of the productivity of the latter work. The analysis of two novels by a Lebanese and an Algerian author brings to the fore the transgression of protective boundaries caused by civil war, the situation under which these novels were written. Boer refers to postcolonial theorist Homi Bhabha's observation of the violent and irretrievable intrusion of the public into the private sphere as a condition of postcoloniality, which can be defined as "unhomeliness" (Chapter Two), but she takes his argument in another direction by insisting on the need to analyse the context and history of such intrusions, rather than to merely posit this unhomeliness. It is therefore necessary to analyse the (violated) boundaries as *sites of negotiation*. More to the point, however, it is also necessary to recognize the possibly "linguistic nature of this negotiation" (Introduction). Writing can be a life-saving instrument to negotiate the threat and anxiety of these politically motivated transgressions.

Such close readings help to unravel the opposition between "text" and "context". Boer shows that cultural practices intervene in concrete political processes, and that political processes are actualized by interventions in both the sphere of political and social activism, and the sphere of media, publicity, literature and theory. This observation is elaborated by taking up Derrida's discussion on text and frame (as an alternative to "context"), and Jonathan Culler's extension of his argument. The notion of "context" then appears not to signify the material conditions that would shape a "text": "context is not given but produced . . . contexts are just as much in need of elucidation as events" (Culler 1988: ix quoted in Chapter Six). We are led to conclude that it is not helpful to assume a fundamental difference between text and context.

However, the insight in the discursive nature of both literary writing and political "contexts" does not imply that postcolonial scholars should be satisfied by merely referring to the critical or subversive potential of certain textual strategies. As Boer's work shows, if we want to understand the "dynamic processes of cross-cultural representation" (Introduction), we must inquire into the political effects of certain forms of writing and theorizing, and consider the question how certain strategies of dressing, writing and theorizing relate to the logic of the global market. Postcolonial studies move between the extremes of that scale: the specific analysis of the relation between discursive practices and economic structures on the one hand (Chapter Five); and the analysis of language as a site of political negotiation on the other (Chapter Two). Boer's work explores both extreme and intermediate positions, without ever losing sight of the indispensability of the extreme ends. Such a flexible approach is a sound remedy against tendencies to reduce history, or the material, to "text" – or to reduce the textual to a mere vehicle of fancy, which would somehow exist outside reality.

What Postcolonial Theory is About

Above, I have tried to situate Boer's work within the field of postcolonial studies by showing how it relates to one of the defining debates in the practice. But Boer's work is postcolonial in an even more fundamental way. One of the main issues in postcolonial studies is that of place, for, as Boer explains elsewhere, "the imaginative geography informing intercultural contacts remains a formidable obstacle" (2004c: 10). The greatest relevance of Said's work lies, for her, not in its critique of Orientalism, but in its critical aftermath – of which her work is a part. While Boer's statement about the effects of the western imaginative geography is an observation that would be relevant to the study of globalization as well, the way in which she follows up on the issue leads to a new understanding of what postcolonial theory is really about.

In Chapter Three, she articulates the effect of a way of reading that obeys the logic of colonial discourse: "All is dead: this, it seems, is the result of viewing the world beyond 'our' boundary from hither" (Chapter Three). For Boer, postcolonial theory should try to counter the destructive gesture in (neo)colonial and ethnographic discourses: the emptying out of landscapes, the erasing of human presence, imposing absence, death and emptiness. In response to Deleuze's vision of landscape, she teases out of seemingly lifeless locations the different agencies responsible for their appearance. Instead of seeing boundaries as fixed, natural lines, they are now imagined as being shaped by intense negotiations. Instead of theorizing space as abstract structure, as map, Boer evokes space as *thirdspace* (Soja 1996), or lived space. This lived space must necessarily be a historical site, which is shaped, seen and experienced by the people who inhabit and traverse it: because of the interconnection with a personality, the desert can be understood "as a multiple, inhabited, palimpsestic geographical and metaphorical place" (Chapter Four). Suddenly, then, the seemingly dead desert is recognizable as a moment in a vivid string of events and encounters. In other words, if the colonial gesture is killing, then Boer's approach is life-giving.

This life-giving gesture is repeated in the analysis of orientalist paintings and pictures: seemingly passive women on the canvas or in pictures are brought to life, to transgress boundaries, to reveal how they evoke desires that counter the accompanying text that is meant to frame them in other ways; thus, the complex interaction with its onlookers is brought the fore (Chapter Three). Likewise, fashion is not only shown to be a semiotic system, but also a part of an economic exchange (Chapter Three). Instead of merely discussing representations, then, this book conjures up the living effects of seemingly lifeless images on people, and the passionate struggles and clashes of interests that lie behind seemingly straightforward images. Life is restored to the stereotypical scenes that colonial discourse had dispossessed of life and agency.

Life, agency, interaction, effect, transformation, these are the key-concepts in Boer's life-giving work. However, her love of interaction and mobility does not lead to the sort of fascination one sometimes finds in those following the old masters of postcolonial thought, who try to capture the dynamics of globalisation. Highly influential Caribbean writers, poets, and theorists, such as Edouard Glissant, Antonio Benitez-Rojo, and Wilson Harris began, in the course of their careers, to take recourse to a highly seductive rhetoric that imagines the energies of globalisation, as if they were autonomous forces, creating turbulence and chaos independent of the material world they act upon. Their imaginary is seductive, and its poetry is often wonderful, but, as Glissant points out, it concerns a poetics rather than a theory.

If postcolonial scholars, following the poets, begin to take speed itself, the flight, the lines and relations themselves as their object of study, adopting the poet's metaphors as theoretical concepts, postcolonial studies threatens to lose its explanatory force. As Peter Hallward argues, the poetic celebration of singularity should not be mistaken for a postcolonial aesthetics (2001). Boer's work takes its distance from these confusions, taking specificity instead of singularity as her guiding concept. Instead of explaining the condition of the postcolonial world as being caused by an unfettered, chaotic turbulence, she scrutinizes the specific histories of the interactions and conflicts that are continuously shaping the world. Not the lines, but the peopled spaces have her attention. She has, I think, in line with Hallward, performed and shown a path to more productive ways to theorize postcoloniality and globalization.

Who is our source of inspiration, in our academic work? In all the aspects I have outlined above – the respect for the complexity of other people's desires, the scholarly generosity and refusal of power games, the flexibility in relating the cultural to the material, the political to the textual, and vice versa, but especially the desire to bring to life what dominant discourses and practices such as (neo)colonialism have emptied out – Inge Boer's project is a continuous, joyful life-giving inspiration to scholars who are as much moved by the spirit of the resistance to (neo)colonialism as by the life-giving confusions of art.

Bibliography

Abdallah, Monia. 2005. "Analyse topique d'une caractérisation artistique: Etude des lieux communs dans l'art contemporain islamique". *Image revues: Histoire, anthropologie et théorie de l'art.* <http://www.imagesrevues.org/archives/Articles/ArticleAbdallah.htm> (April 2006).

Accad, Evelyne. 1990. *Sexuality and War: Literary Masks of the Middle East.* New York: New York University Press.

Ahmed, Leila. 1992. *Women and Gender in Islam: Historical Roots of a Modern Debate.* New Haven, CT: Yale University Press.

Ahmed, Sara. 1999. "Home and Away: Narratives of Migration and Estrangement". *International Journal of Cultural Studies* 2.3, 329-47.

Al-Ani, Jannane. 2003. "Acting Out", in D. A. Bailey and G. Tawadros (eds.). *Veil: Veiling, Representation and Contemporary Art.* London: inIVA, 90-119.

Al-Shaykh, Hanan. 1986. *The Story of Zahra.* Translated by P. Ford. London: Quartet.

———. 1995. *Beirut Blues: A Novel.* Translated by C. Cobham. New York: Anchor Books.

———. 1995. *Poste restante Beyrouth.* Translated by M. Burési and J. Chehayed. Arles: Actes Sud.

Alloula, Malek. 1986. *The Colonial Harem.* Minneapolis: University of Minnesota Press.

Alphen, Ernst van. 1988. *Bij wijze van lezen. Verleiding en verzet van Willem Brakmans lezer.* Muiderberg: Coutinho.

———. 1997. *Caught by History: Holocaust Effects in Contemporary Art, Literature, and Theory.* Stanford: Stanford University Press.

———. 1999. "Symptoms of Discursivity: Experience, Memory, Trauma", in M. Bal, J. V. Crewe and L. Spitzer (eds.). *Acts of Memory: Cultural Recall in the Present.* Hanover, NH: University Press of New England, 24-38.

Apter, Emily S. 1999. *Continental Drift: From National Characters to Virtual Subjects.* Chicago: University of Chicago Press.

Art in America. 1989 (July).

Attridge, Derek. 1999. "Innovation, Literature, Ethics: Relating to the Other". *PMLA* 114.1, 20-31.

Augé, Marc. 1995. *Non-places: Introduction to an Anthropology of Supermodernity.* Translated by J. Howe. London/New York: Verso.

Bachelard, Gaston. 1994. *The Poetics of Space.* Translated by M. Jolas. Boston: Beacon Press.

Bailey, David A., and Gilane Tawadros (eds.). 2003. *Veil: Veiling, Representation, and Contemporary Art.* Cambridge, MA/London: MIT Press and inIVA.

Bair, Deirdre. 1990. *Samuel Beckett: A Biography.* New York: Summit Books.

Bakhtin, Mikhail. 1981. *The Dialogic Imagination.* Translated by C. Emerson and M. Holquist. Edited by M. Holquist. Austin, TX: University of Texas Press.

Bal, Mieke. 1985. *Narratology: Introduction to the Theory of Narrative.* Translated by C. van Boheemen. Toronto: University of Toronto Press.

————. 1991. *Reading "Rembrandt": Beyond the Word-Image Opposition.* New York: Cambridge University Press.

————. 1994. "Telling Objects: A Narrative Perspective on Collecting", in J. Elsner and R. Cardinal (eds.). *The Cultures of Collecting.* Cambridge, MA: Harvard University Press, 97-115.

————. 1996. *Double Exposures: The Subject of Cultural Analysis.* New York: Routledge.

————. 1997. *The Mottled Screen: Reading Proust Visually.* Translated by A.-L. Milne. Stanford: Stanford University Press.

————. 2003a. "Her Majesty's Masters", in M. Zimmerman (ed.). *The Art Historian: National Traditions and Institutional Practices.* Williamstown, MA: Clark Art Institute, 81-109.

————. 2003b. "Visual Essentialism and the Object of Visual Culture". *Journal of Visual Culture* 2.1, 5-32.

————. 2006. "Narrativity and Voice", in K. Brown (ed.). *Encyclopedia of Language and Linguistics.* 2nd ed. Oxford: Elsevier.

Bal, Mieke, and Norman Bryson. 1991. "Semiotics and Art History". *Art Bulletin* 73.2, 174-208.

Ballestero, Catherine. 1996. *Un Cabinet d'amateur ou le "testament artistique" de Georges Perec.* Paris: Éditions du Seuil.

Barthes, Roland. 1967. *Système de la mode.* Paris: Éditions du Seuil.

————. 1981. *Camera Lucida: Reflections on Photography.* Translated by R. Howard. New York: Hill and Wang.

————. 1986. "The Reality Effect", in *The Rustle of Language.* Translated by R. Howard. New York: Hill and Wang, 141-54.

Beckett, Samuel. 1953. *L'Innommable.* Paris: Éditions de Minuit.

Béguin, François. 1991. "Stratégies frontalières dans les Pyrénées a la fin de l'ancien régime", in C. Descamps (ed.). *Frontières et limites.* Paris: Editions du Centre Pompidou, 49-69.

Benjamin, Walter. 1968a. "The Task of the Translator", in *Illuminations.* Translated by H. Zohn. New York: Schocken, 69-82.

————. 1968b. "The Work of Art in the Age of Mechanical Reproduction", in *Illuminations*. Translated by H. Zohn. New York: Schocken, 217-52.

Benrabah, Mohamed. 1998. "La Langue perdue", in M. Benrabah et al (eds.). *Les Violences en Algérie*. Paris: Jacob, 61-87.

————. 1999. *Langue et pouvoir en Algérie: Histoire d'un traumatisme linguistique*. Paris: Séguier.

Benrabah, Mohamed et al (eds.). 1998. *Les Violences en Algérie*. Paris: Jacob.

Bhabha, Homi K. 1994. *The Location of Culture*. London: Routledge.

Birkett, Dea. 1989. *Spinsters Abroad: Victorian Lady Explorers*. Oxford/New York: Blackwell Publishers.

Boer, Inge E. 1994. "This is Not the Orient: Theory and Postcolonial Practice", in M. Bal and I. E. Boer (eds.). *The Point of Theory: Practices of Cultural Analysis*. Amsterdam: Amsterdam University Press, 211-20.

————. 1995-1996. "Despotism from Under the Veil: Masculine and Feminine Readings of the Despot and the Harem". *Cultural Critique* 32, 43-73.

————, (ed.). 2004a. *After Orientalism: Critical Entanglements, Productive Looks*. Amsterdam/New York: Rodopi.

————. 2004b. *Disorienting Vision: Rereading Stereotypes in French Orientalist Texts and Images*. Amsterdam/New York: Rodopi.

————. 2004c. "Introduction: Imaginative Geographies and the Discourse of Orientalism", in I. E. Boer (ed.). *After Orientalism: Critical Entanglements, Productive Looks*. Amsterdam/New York: Rodopi, 9-21.

Bouraoui, Nina. 1991. *La Voyeuse interdite*. Paris: Gallimard.

Bourdieu, Pierre. 1989. *Distinction: A Social Critique of the Judgment of Taste*. Translated by R. Nice. London: Routledge.

Braidotti, Rosi. 1994. *Nomadic Subjects: Embodiment and Sexual Difference in Contemporary Feminist Theory*. New York: Columbia University Press.

————. n.d. "Difference, Diversity and Nomadic Subjectivity" <http://www.let.uu.nl/~Rosi.Braidotti/personal/rosilecture.html> (April 2006).

Brennan, Timothy. 1997. *At Home in the World: Cosmopolitanism Now*. Cambridge, MA: Harvard University Press.

————. 2002. Cosmo-Theory. *The South Atlantic Quarterly* 100.3, 659-91.

Breukink-Peeze, Margaret. 1989. "Een fraaie kleding, van den turkschen dragt ontleent. Turkse kleding en mode à la turque in Nederland", in H. Theunissen, A. Abelman and W. Meulenkamp (eds.). *Topkapi and Turkomanie: Turks-Nederlandse ontmoetingen sinds 1600*. Amsterdam: De Bataafse Leeuw, 130-40.

Brown, Peter R. L.. 1981. *The Cult of the Saints: Its Rise and Function in Latin Christianity*. Chicago: University of Chicago Press.

Bryson, Norman. 1990. *Looking at the Overlooked: Four Essays on Still Life Painting*. Cambridge, MA: Harvard University Press.

—. 1994. "Art in Context", in M. Bal and I. E. Boer (eds.). *The Point of Theory: Practices of Cultural Analysis*. Amsterdam: Amsterdam University Press, 66-78.

Burgelin, Claude. 1988. *Georges Perec*. Paris: Éditions du Seuil.

Burgin, Victor. 1996. *In/Different Spaces: Place and Memory in Visual Culture*. Berkeley: University of California Press.

Butler, Judith. 1990. *Gender Trouble: Feminism and the Subversion of Identity*. New York: Routledge.

—. 1993. *Bodies that Matter: On the Discursive Limits of "Sex"*. New York: Routledge.

Calhoun, Craig J. 1992. *Habermas and the Public Sphere*. Cambridge, MA: MIT Press.

Calkins, N. A. 1880. "Object-Teaching: Its Purpose and Provenance". *Education* 1, 165-72.

Cardinal, Roger. 1994. "Collecting and Collage-Making: The Case of Kurt Schwitters", in J. Elsner and R. Cardinal (eds.). *The Cultures of Collecting*. Cambridge, MA: Harvard University Press, 68-96.

Castle, Terry. 1986. *Masquerade and Civilization: The Carnivalesque in Eighteenth-Century English Culture and Fiction*. Stanford: Stanford University Press.

Chaussinand-Nogaret, Guy. 1990. *La Vie quotidienne des femmes du roi: D'Agnès Sorel à Marie-Antoinette*. Paris: Hachette.

Clifford, James. 1988. *The Predicament of Culture: Twentieth-Century Ethnography, Literature, and Art*. Cambridge, MA: Harvard University Press.

—. 1989. "Notes on Theory and Travel". *Inscriptions* 5, 177-88.

—. 1991. "Four Northwest Coast Museums: Travel Reflections", in I. Karp and S. D. Lavine (eds.). *Exhibiting Cultures: The Poetics and Politics of Museum Display*. Washington/London: Smithsonian Institution Press, 212-54.

Conley, Tom. 1998. "Algeria Off-Map". *Parallax* 7, 99-112.

Cooke, Miriam. 1992. "Arab Women Writers", in M. M. Badawi (ed.). *Modern Arabic Literature*. Cambridge: Cambridge University Press, 443-62.

—. 2001. *Women Claim Islam: Creating Islamic Feminism Through Literature*. New York: Routledge.

Coombes, Annie E. 1994. *Reinventing Africa: Museums, Material Culture, and Popular Imagination in Late Victorian and Edwardian England.* New Haven: Yale University Press.

Cresswell, Tim. 1997. "Imagining the Nomad: Mobility and the Postmodern Primitive", in G. Benko and U. Strohmayer (eds.). *Space and Social Theory: Geographical Interpretations of Post-Modernity.* Oxford: Blackwell Publishers, 360-82.

Culler, Jonathan. 1981. "Apostrophe", in *The Pursuit of Signs: Semiotics, Literature, Deconstruction.* Ithaca: Cornell University Press, 135-54.

———. 1988. *Framing the Sign: Criticism and Its Institutions.* Norman/ London: University of Oklahoma Press.

Damisch, Hubert. 1994. *The Origin of Perspective.* Cambridge, MA: MIT Press.

Dasgupta, Sudeep. 2005. "The Memory of Hope: Migratory Aesthetics in the Politics of *Before Night Falls*". In *Migratory Aesthetics*, conference reader. Amsterdam/Leeds: ASCA/CentreCath.

Dekker, Rudolf, and Lotte van de Pol. 1989. *The Tradition of Female Transvestism in Early Modern Europe.* New York: St. Martin's Press.

Deleuze, Gilles, and Félix Guattari. 1980. *Mille plateaux.* Paris: Éditions de minuit.

———. 1992. *A Thousand Plateaus.* Translated by B. Massumi. London: Athlone Press.

Depardon, Raymond, and Titouan Lamazou. 2000. *Rêve de déserts.* Paris: Gallimard.

Derrida, Jacques. 1967. *L'Écriture et la différence.* Paris: Éditions du Seuil.

———. 1987. *The Truth in Painting.* Translated by G. Bennington and I. McLeod. Chicago: University of Chicago Press.

Derrida, Jacques, and Anne Dufourmantelle. 2000. *Of Hospitality.* Translated by R. Bowlby. Stanford: Stanford University Press.

Diderot, Denis, Jean d'Alembert, and Pierre Mouchon. 1751. *Encyclopédie; Ou Dictionnaire raisonné des sciences, des arts et des métiers.* Paris: Briasson etc.

Didi-Hubermann, Georges. 1985. *La Peinture incarnée.* Paris: Éditions de minuit.

Dieulafoy, Jane. 1887. *La Perse, la Chaldée et la Susiane.* Paris: Hachette.

———. 1989. *Une Amazone en Orient: Du Caucase à Persépolis, 1881-1882.* Paris: Phébus.

———. 1990a. *En Mission chez les immortels: Journal des fouilles de Suse, 1884-1886.* Paris: Phébus.

———. 1990b. *L'Orient sous le voile: De Chiraz à Bagdad, 1881-1882.* Paris: Phébus.

Djaout, Tahar. 1987. *L'Invention du désert.* Paris: Éditions du Seuil.

Djebar, Assia. 1957. *La Soif.* Paris: R. Julliard.
——. 1995. *Le Blanc de l'Algérie.* Paris: A. Michel.
——. 1999. *Ces Voix qui m'assiègent: En Marge de ma francophonie.* Paris: A. Michel.
Duncan, Carol. 1995. *Civilizing Rituals: Inside Public Art Museums.* London: Routledge.
Edwards, Elizabeth. 1990. "Photographic 'Types': The Pursuit of Method". *Visual Anthropology* 3.2-3, 235-59.
——. 1992. *Anthropology and Photography 1860-1920.* New Haven, CT: Yale University Press.
Eickelman, Dale F. 1998. *The Middle East and Central Asia: An Anthropological Approach.* Upper Saddle River, NJ: Prentice Hall.
Elsner, John, and Roger Cardinal (eds.). 1994. *The Cultures of Collecting.* Cambridge, MA: Harvard University Press.
Entwistle, Joanne. 2000. *The Fashioned Body: Fashion, Dress, and Modern Social Theory.* Cambridge: Polity Press.
Fabian, Johannes. 1983. *Time and the Other: How Anthropology Makes its Object.* New York: Columbia University Press.
Fisher, Jean, (ed.). 1994. *Global Visions: Towards a New Internationalism in the Visual Arts.* London: Kala Press in association with inIVA.
Fisk, Robert. 1990. *Pity the Nation: The Abduction of Lebanon.* New York: Atheneum.
Flaubert, Gustave, and Francis Steegmuller. 1987. *Flaubert in Egypt: a Sensibility On Tour.* Chicago, IL: Academy Chicago Limited.
Foster, Hal. 1994. "The Artist as Ethnographer", in J. Fisher (ed.). *Global Visions: Towards a New Internationalism in the Visual Arts.* London: Kala Press in association with inIVA, 12-19.
Foucher, Michel. 1991. *Fronts et frontières: Un Tour du monde géopolitique.* Paris: Fayard.
Garber, Marjorie. 1992. *Vested Interests: Cross-Dressing and Cultural Anxiety.* New York: Routledge.
De Gasparin, Valérie 1867. *À Constantinople.* Paris: M. Lévy.
Gast, Marceau. 1983. "Mutations sahariennes", in E. Lambert and A. Laurent (eds.). *Désert: Nomades, guerriers, chercheurs d'absolu.* Paris: Éditions Autrement, 65-80.
Gautier, Théophile. 1847. *Le Salon de 1847.* Paris: M. Lévy.
——. 1855. *Les Beaux-Arts en Europe 1855.* Paris: M. Lévy.
Geary, Christraud. 1990. "Impressions of the African Past: Interpreting Ethnographic Photographs from Cameroon". *Visual Anthropology* 3.2-3, 289-315.
Ghoussoub, Mai. 1998. *Leaving Beirut: Women and the Wars Within.* London: Saqi Books.

Gibson-Graham, J. K. 1996. *The End of Capitalism (As We Knew It): A Feminist Critique of Political Economy*. Cambridge, MA: Blackwell Publishers.

Goldman, Lucien. 1964. *The Hidden God: A Study of Tragic Vision in the "Pensées" of Pascal and the Tragedies of Racine*. Translated by P. Thody. London: Routledge.

Gracki, Katherine. 1996. "Writing Violence and the Violence of Writing in Assia Djebar's Algerian Quartet". *World Literature Today* 70.4, 835-43.

Granqvist, Hilma. 1931. *Marriage Conditions in a Palestinian Village I*. Helsingfors: Akademische Buchhandlung.

———. 1935. *Marriage Conditions in a Palestinian Village II*. Helsingfors: Akademische Buchhandlung.

Grootenboer, Hanneke. 2005. *The Rhetoric of Perspective: Realism and Illusionism in Seventeenth-Century Dutch Still-Life Painting*. Chicago: University of Chicago Press.

Grosrichard, Alain. 1979. *Structure du sérail: La Fiction du despotisme asiatique dans l'Occident classique*. Paris: Éditions du Seuil.

Gupta, Akhil, and James Ferguson (eds.). 1997a. *Anthropological Locations: Boundaries and Grounds of a Field Science*. Berkeley: University of California Press.

———. 1997b. "Beyond 'Culture': Space, Identity, and the Politics of Difference", in A. Gupta and J. Ferguson (eds.). *Culture, Power, Place: Explorations in Critical Anthropology*. Durham, NC: Duke University Press, 34-51.

Haak, Bregtje van der. 1996. "Ik ben hard voor mezelf en ook voor anderen" (I am Demanding towards Myself and Others). *Elle*, 14.

Hales, Peter B. 1995. "Surveying the Field: Artists Make Art History". *Art Journal* 54.3, 35-41.

Hallward, Peter. 2001. *Absolutely Postcolonial: Writing Between the Singular and the Specific*. Manchester: Manchester University Press.

Hamon, Philippe. 1981. *Introduction à l'analyse du descriptif*. Paris: Hachett.

———. 1984. *Texte et idéologie*. Paris: Presses Universitaires de France.

Hannoyer, Jean, (ed.). 1999. *Guerres Civiles: Economies de la violence, dimensions de la civilité*. Paris: Karthala.

Haraway, Donna. 1991. "Situated Knowledges: The Science Question in Feminism and the Privilege of Partial Perspective", in *Simians, Cyborgs, and Women*. New York: Routledge, 183-201.

Hart, Lynn M. 1995. "Three Walls: Regional Aesthetics and the International Art World", in G. Marcus and F. Meyers (eds.). *The Traffic in Culture: Refiguring Art and Anthropology*. Berkeley: University of California Press, 127-50.

Hélie-Lucas, Marie-Aimée. 1993. "Women's Struggles and Strategies in the Rise of Fundamentalism in the Muslim World: From Entryism to Internationalism", in H. Afshar (ed.). *Women in the Middle East.* New York: St. Martin's Press, 206-41.

Henry, Jean-Robert. 1983. "Le Désert nécessaire", in E. Lambert and A. Laurent (eds.). *Désert: Nomades, guerriers, chercheurs d'absolu.* Paris: Éditions Autrement, 17-34.

Hooper-Greenhill, Eilean. 2000. *Museums and the Interpretation of Visual Culture.* London/New York: Routledge.

Hourani, Albert H. 1992. *A History of the Arab Peoples.* New York: Warner Books.

Hoving, Isabel. 2000. "Hybridity: A Slippery Trail", in J. Goggin and S. Neef (eds.). *Travelling Concepts I: Text, Hybridity, Subjectivity.* Amsterdam: ASCA Press, 185-200.

Hull, Gloria T., Patricia Bell-Scott, and Barbara Smith (eds.). 1982. *All The Women are White, All the Blacks Are Men, But Some of Us Are Brave: Black Women's Studies.* Old Westbury, NY: Feminist Press.

Humbert, Jean-Charles. 1996. *La Découverte du Sahara en 1900.* Paris: L'Harmattan.

Huntington, Samuel P. 1996. *The Clash of Civilizations and the Remaking of World Order.* New York: Simon and Schuster.

Iordanova, Dina. 2001. *Cinema of Flames: Balkan Film, Culture and the Media.* London: British Film Institute.

Jay, Martin. 1994. *Downcast Eyes: The Denigration of Vision in Twentieth-Century French Thought.* Berkeley: University of California Press.

Johnson, Barbara. 1987. "Apostrophe, Animation, and Abortion", in *A World of Difference.* Baltimore: Johns Hopkins University Press, 184-200.

Jullian, Philippe. 1977. *The Orientalists: European Painters of Eastern Scenes.* Translated by H. Harrison and D. Harrison. Oxford: Phaidon.

Kabbani, Rana. 1986. *Europe's Myths of Orient.* Bloomington: Indiana University Press.

Kaplan, Caren. 1996. *Questions of Travel: Postmodern Discourses of Displacement.* Durham, NC: Duke University Press.

Karp, Ivan, and Steven D. Lavine (eds.). 1991. *Exhibiting Cultures: The Poetics and Politics of Museum Display.* Washington and London: Smithsonian Institution Press.

Kastner, Joachim P. 1992. "Heerich in Hombroich", in *Die Bauten der Insel Hombroich.* Neuss: Insel Hombroich.

Khalidi, Walid, and Institute for Palestine Studies. 1984. *Before Their Diaspora: A Photographic History of the Palestinians, 1876-1948.* Washington, DC: Institute for Palestine Studies.

Khemir, Mounira. 2000. "The Infinite Image of the Desert and its Representations", in R. Depardon, T. Lamazou and P. Virilio (eds.). *The Desert*. Paris: Fondation Cartier pour l'art contemporain/ Thames and Hudson, 51-62.

Klein, Melanie, and Juliet Mitchell. 1987. *The Selected Melanie Klein*. New York: Free Press.

Klein, Naomi. 2000. *No Logo: Taking Aim at the Brand Bullies*. New York: Picador.

Klinkenberg, Rob. 1989. "Insel Hombroich: Het museum waar kunst mag vergaan". *Avenue*, 67-71.

Kristeva, Julia. 1980. *Desire in Language: A Semiotic Approach to Literature and Art*. Translated by T. Gora, A. Jardine and L. S. Roudiez. New York: Columbia University Press.

Kunzru, Hari. 2002. *The Impressionist*. London: Hamish Hamilton.

Lane, Edward W. 1978 [1836]. *An Account of the Manners and Customs of the Modern Egyptians Written in Egypt During the Years 1833-1835*. London: East-West Publications.

Lazreg, Marnia. 1990. "Feminism and Difference: The Perils of Writing as a Woman on Women in Algeria", in M. Hirsch and E. Fox Keller (eds.). *Conflicts in Feminism*. New York: Routledge, 326-349.

―――. 1994. *The Eloquence of Silence: Algerian Women in Question*. New York: Routledge.

Lefebvre, Henri. 1991. *The Production of Space*. Translated by D. Nicholson-Smith. Oxford/Cambridge, MA: Blackwell Publishers.

Lévi-Strauss, Claude. 1964. *Le Cru et le cuit*. Paris: Plon.

Lorde, Audre. 1984. "The Master's Tools Will Never Dismantle the Master's House", in *Sister Outsider: Essays and Speeches*. Trumansburg, NY: Crossing Press, 110-113.

Lukács, György. 1971 [1917-18]. *History and Class Consciousness: Studies in Marxist Dialectics*. Translated by R. Livingstone. Cambridge, MA: MIT Press.

Lutz, Catherine, and Jane L. Collins. 1993. *Reading National Geographic*. Chicago: University of Chicago Press.

Magné, Bernard. 1989. *Perecollages 1981-1988*. Toulouse-le-Mirail: Presses universitaires du Mirail.

Makdisi, Jean Said. 1990. *Beirut Fragments: A War Memoir*. New York: Persea Books.

Martin, Jean-Hubert et al. 1989. *Magiciens de la terre*. Paris: Éditions du Centre Pompidou.

Martinez, Luis. 1998. *La Guerre civile en Algérie*. Karthala: Paris.

Martino, Pierre. 1906. *L'Orient dans la littérature française au XVIIe et au XVIIIe siècle*. Paris: Hachette.

Marx-Scouras, Danielle. 1993. "Muffled Screams/Stifled Voices". *Yale French Studies* 82, 172-82.

Massey, Doreen B. 1994. *Space, Place, and Gender.* Minneapolis: University of Minnesota Press.

McLeod, John. 2003. "Contesting Contexts: Francophone Thought and Anglophone Postcolonialism", in C. Forsdick and D. Murphy (eds.). *Francophone Postcolonial Studies: A Critical Introduction.* London: Arnold, 192-201.

Memmi, Albert. 1977. *Le Désert: Ou, la Vie et les aventures de Jubaïr Ouali El-Mammi.* Paris: Gallimard.

Mernissi, Fatima. 1987. *Le Harem politique: Le Prophète et les femmes.* Paris: A. Michel.

———. 1988. "Women in Muslim History: Traditional Perspectives and New Strategies", in S. J. Kleinberg (ed.). *Retrieving Women's History: Changing Perceptions of the Role of Women in Politics and Society.* New York: Berg, 338-55.

———. 1990. *Sultanes oubliées: Femmes chefs d'Etat en Islam.* Casablanca: Éditions Le Fennec.

———. 1994a. *Dreams of Trespass: Tales of a Harem Girlhood.* Reading, MA: Addison-Wesley Publishing Corporation.

———. 1994b. *Het Verboden Dakterras.* Translated by R. van Hengel. Breda: De Geus.

Miller, Christopher L. 1993. "The Postidentitarian Predicament in the Footnotes of *A Thousand Plateaus*: Nomadology, Anthropology, and Authority". *Diacritics* 23.3, 6-35.

Miller, Nancy K. 1988. *Subject to Change: Reading Feminist Writing.* New York: Columbia University Press.

Mitchell, Timothy. 1988. *Colonizing Egypt.* Berkeley: University of California Press.

Mitchell, W.J.T. 1984. *Iconology: Image, Text, Ideology.* Chicago: University of Chicago Press.

Mohanty, Chandra Talpade. 1988. "Under Western Eyes: Feminist Scholarship and Colonial Discourse". *Feminist Review* 30, 65-88.

———. 1991. "Introduction. Cartographies of Struggle: Third World Women and the Politics of Feminism", in C. T. Mohanty, A. Russo and L. Torres (eds.). *Third World Women and the Politics of Feminism.* Bloomington: Indiana University Press, 1-48.

Mondzain, Marie-José. 2004. *Image, Icon, Economy: The Byzantine Origins of the Contemporary Imaginary.* Translated by R. Franses. Stanford: Stanford University Press.

Montesquieu, Charles-Louis de Secondat, avec des notes de Voltaire, de Crevier, de Mably, de la Harpe, etc. 1927 [1748]. *De l'Esprit des lois.* Paris: Librairie Garnier Frères.

Montfrans, Manet van. 1999. "D'un Cabinet d'amateur à l'autre", in *Georges Perec: La Contrainte du réel.* Amsterdam/Atlanta: Rodopi, 287-373.

Moore-Gilbert, Bart. 1997. *Postcolonial Theory: Contexts, Practices, Politics.* London: Verso.

Moors, Annelies. 1996. "On Appearance and Disappearance. Representing Women in Palestine under the British Mandate". *Thamyris* 3.2, 279-310.

———. 2001. "Presenting Palestine's Population: Premonitions of the Nakba". *MIT Electronic Journal For Middle East Studies* 1.1, 14-26. <http://web.mit.edu/cis/www/mitejmes> (April 2006).

Morrison, Toni. 1987. *Beloved: A Novel.* New York: Plume.

Mosquera, Gerardo. 1994. "Some Problems in Transcultural Curating", in J. Fisher (ed.). *Global Visions: Towards a New Internationalism in the Visual Arts.* London: Kala Press in association with inIVA, 133-39.

Motte, Warren F. 1984. *The Poetics of Experiment: A Study of the Work of Georges Perec.* Lexington, KY: French Forum.

Nead, Lynda. 1992. *The Female Nude: Art, Obscenity, and Sexuality.* New York: Routledge.

Noble, Richard. 2002. "Mona Hatoum: A Living Between". *Parachute Contemporary Art Magazine* 108 (October), 178-92.

Nochlin, Linda. 1983. "The Imaginary Orient". *Art in America* (May-June), 46-59.

Ockman, Carol. 1995. *Ingres's Eroticized Bodies: Retracing the Serpentine Line.* New Haven, CT: Yale University Press.

Ollier, Claude. 1982 [1958]. *La Mise en scène.* Paris: Flammarion.

Pacteau, Francette. 1994. *The Symptom of Beauty.* Cambridge, MA: Harvard University Press.

Pape, Marie Elisabeth. 1989. "Turquerie im 18. Jahrhundert und des 'Receuil Ferriol'", in G. Sievernich and H. Budde (eds.). *Europa und der Orient 800-1900.* Gütersloh/München: Bertelsmann Lexicon Verlag, 305-24.

Peirce, Leslie Penn. 1993. *The Imperial Harem: Women and Sovereignty in the Ottoman Empire.* New York: Oxford University Press.

Peltre, Christine. 1997. *Les Orientalistes.* Paris: Éditions Hazan.

Perec, Georges. 1979. *Un Cabinet d'amateur: Histoire d'un tableau.* Paris: Balland.

Phillips Jr., Michael. 2005. Review of *Whose is This Song?* <http://goatdog.com/moviePage.php?movieID=579> (November 2005).

Pietz, William. 1985. "The Problem of the Fetish, I". *Res* 9, 5-17.

————. 1993. "Fetishism and Materialism: The Limits of Theory in Marx", in E. S. Apter and W. Pietz (eds.). *Fetishism as Cultural Discourse*. Ithaca, NY: Cornell University Press, 119-51.

Pinney, Christopher. 1990. "Classification and Fantasy in the Photographic Construction of Caste and Tribe". *Visual Anthropology* 3.2-3, 259-89.

————. 1992. "The Parallel Histories of Anthropology and Photography", in E. Edwards (ed.). *Anthropology and Photography 1860-1920*. New Haven, CT: Yale University Press, 74-97.

Poignant, Roslyn. 1992. "Surveying the Field of View: The Making of the RAI Photographic Collection", in E. Edwards (ed.). *Anthropology and Photography 1860-1920*. New Haven CT/London: Yale University Press, 42-74.

Pollock, Griselda. 1999. *Differencing the Canon: Feminist Desire and the Writing of Art's Histories*. London: Routledge.

Pomian, Krzysztof. 1987. *Collectionneurs, amateurs et curieux: Paris, Venise, XVIe-XVIIIe siècle*. Paris: Gallimard.

Pratt, Mary Louise. 1992. *Imperial Eyes: Travel Writing and Transculturation*. London/New York: Routledge.

Price, Sally. 1989. *Primitive Art in Civilized Places*. Chicago: University of Chicago Press.

Proust, Marcel. 1981. *Remembrance of Things Past*. 3 vols. Translated by C. K. Scott-Moncrieff and T. Kilmartin. London: Penguin Books.

Ramadan, Dina. 2004. "Regional Emissaries: Geographical Platforms and the Challenges of Marginalization in Contemporary Egyptian Art". <http://www.apexart.org/conference/ramadan.htm> (July 2005).

Ribeiro, Aileen. 1984. *The Dress Worn at Masquerades in England, 1730 to 1790, and its Relation to Fancy Dress in Portraiture*. New York: Garland Publishers.

Robbe-Grillet, Alain. 1953. *Les Gommes*. Paris: Éditions de minuit.

————. 1955. *Le Voyeur*. Paris: Éditions de minuit.

Roche, Daniel. 1989. *La Culture des apparences: Une Histoire du vêtement (XVIIe-XVIIIe siècle)*. Paris: Fayard.

Roider, Karl A. 1982. *Austria's Eastern Question, 1700-1790*. Princeton, NJ: Princeton University Press.

Rose, Issa. 2004. "The Fabric of Life and Art". <http://archiv.hkw.de/en/dossiers/iran_dossierroseissa/kapitel1.html> (August 2005).

Rosenberg, Pierre, and Marie C. Sahut. 1977. *Carle Vanloo: Premier peintre du roi (Nice, 1705 – Paris, 1765)*. Nice: Musée Chéret.

Ross, Andrew. 1998. *Real Love: In Pursuit of Cultural Justice*. New York: New York University Press.

Rossi, Leena-Maija. 2002. "On the Edge of the Field or Inside the Plane: Airplanes and Artworld Revisited". *Invisible Culture: An Electronic*

Journal for Visual Culture.<http://www.rochester.edu/in_visible_culture/
Issue4-IVC/Rossi.html> (April 2006).

Rössler, Beate. 2004. "Privacies: An Overview", in B. Rössler (ed.).
Privacies: Philosophical Evaluations. Stanford: Stanford University
Press, 1-18.

Russo, Mary. 1986. "Female Grotesques: Carnival and Theory", in T. de
Lauretis (ed.). *Feminist Studies. Critical Studies*. Bloomington: Indiana
University Press, 213-29.

———. 1995. *The Female Grotesque: Risk, Excess, and Modernity*. New
York: Routledge.

El-Saadawi, Nawal. 1980. *The Hidden Face of Eve: Women in the Arab
World*. Translated by S. Hetata. London: Zed Press.

Sahlins, Peter. 1989. *Boundaries: The Making of France and Spain in the
Pyrenees*. Berkeley: University of California Press.

Said, Edward W. 1978. *Orientalism*. New York: Pantheon Books.

———. 1983. "Traveling Theory", in *The World, the Text, and the Critic*.
Cambridge, MA: Harvard University Press, 226-47.

———. 1993. *Culture and Imperialism*. New York: Knopf.

———. 2001. "Orientalism Reconsidered", in *Reflections on Exile and Other
Essays*. Cambridge, MA: Harvard University Press, 198-215.

Sarraute, Nathalie. 1939. *Tropismes*. Paris: Éditions de Minuit.

Sarup, Medan. 1994. "Home and Identity", in G. Robertson (ed.). *Travellers'
Tales: Narratives of Home and Displacement*. London: Routledge, 93-
105.

Scarry, Elaine. 1985. *The Body in Pain: The Making and Unmaking of the
World*. Oxford: Oxford University Press.

Schwartz, Ineke. 1995. "Een oud eiland vol verrassingen tussen het groen".
De Volkskrant, August, 8, 1995, 8.

Seger, Karen (ed.). 1981. *Portrait of a Palestinian Village. The Photographs
of Hilma Granqvist*. London: Third World Centre for Research and
Publishing.

Ségur, Louis-Philippe, comte de. 1859. "Mémoires, souvenirs, et anecdotes,
par le comte de Ségur", in M. F. Barriere (ed.). *Bibliothèque des
mémoires: Relatif à l'histoire de France pendent le 18e siècle*. Paris:
Librairie de Firmni Didot Frères.

Shaw, Stanford J. 1976. *History of the Ottoman Empire and Modern Turkey*.
2 vols. Cambridge: Cambridge University Press.

Silverman, Kaja. 2000. *World Spectators*. Stanford: Stanford University
Press.

Smith, Bonnie G. 1981. *Ladies of the Leisure Class: The Bourgeoises of
Northern France in the Nineteenth Century*. Princeton, NJ: Princeton
University Press.

Soja, Edward. 1996. *Thirdspace: Journeys to Los Angeles and Other Real-and-Imagined Places.* Cambridge, MA: Blackwell Publishers.
———. 1999. "Thirdspace: Expanding the Scope of the Geographical Imagination", in D. B. Massey (ed.). *Human Geography Today.* Cambridge: Polity Press, 260-79.
Spivak, Gayatri C. 1993. *Outside in the Teaching Machine.* New York: Routledge.
———. 1996. "Woman As 'Woman'", paper presented at the conference *Modern European Images of the "Other".* University of Bergen (Norway).
———. 1999. *A Critique of Postcolonial Reason: Toward a History of the Vanishing Present.* Cambridge, MA: Harvard University Press.
Spyer, Patricia. 1998. *Border Fetishisms: Material Objects in Unstable Spaces.* New York: Routledge.
———. 2000. *The Memory of Trade: Modernity's Entanglements on an Eastern Indonesian Island.* Durham, NC: Duke University Press.
Stagl, Justin. 1990. "The Methodizing of Travel in the 16th Century. A Tale of Three Cities". *History and Anthropology* 4, 303-38.
Stewart, Jack. 2003. "Impressionism", in P. Poplawski (ed.). *Encyclopedia of Literary Modernism.* Westport, CT: Greenwood Press, 193-96.
Stocking, George. 1983. "The Ethnographer's Magic: Fieldwork in British Anthropology from Tylor to Malinowsky", in *Observers Observed. Essays on Ethnographic Fieldwork.* Madison: The University of Wisconsin Press, 70-121.
Stoler, Ann L. 2002. *Carnal Knowledge and Imperial Power: Race and the Intimate in Colonial Rule.* Berkeley: University of California Press.
Suolinna, Kirsti. 2000. "Hilma Granqvist: A Scholar of the Westermarck School in Decline". *Acta Sociologica* 43.4, 317-23.
Tawadros, Gilane. 2004. "Curating the Middle East. From Napoleon to the Present Day". *Contemporary Art from the Islamic World*, 4. <http://www.universes-in-universe.de/islam/eng/2004/01/tawadros/index.html> (June 2005).
Todorova, Maria. 1997. *Imagining the Balkans.* New York: Oxford University Press.
Tsing, Anna. 2000. "Inside the Economy of Appearances". *Public Culture* 12.1, 115-44.
Vadée, Michel. 1973. *L'Idéologie.* Paris: Presses Universitaires de France.
Venuti, Lawrence. 1998. *The Scandals of Translation: Towards an Ethics of Difference.* London/New York: Routledge.
Weir, Shelagh. 1975. "Hilma Granqvist and Her Contribution to Palestine Studies". *British Society for Middle Eastern Studies* 2.1, 6-13.

Widén, Solveig. 1998. "Alma Söderhjelm and Hilma Granqvist". *Gender and History* 10.1, 133-42.

Williams, Raymond. 1980. *Problems in Materialism and Culture: Selected Essays*. London: Verso.

Wills, Claire. 1993. *Improprieties: Politics and Sexuality in Northern Irish Poetry*. New York: Clarendon Press.

Wolff, Janet. 1990. "The Invisible Flâneuse: Women and the Literature of Modernity", in *Feminine Sentences: Essays on Women and Culture*. Cambridge: Polity Press, 34-50.

———. 1993. "On the Road Again: Metaphors of Travel in Cultural Criticism". *Cultural Studies* 7.2, 224-39.

Wolff, Larry. 1994. *Inventing Eastern Europe: The Map of Civilization on the Mind of the Enlightenment*. Stanford: Stanford University Press.

Wood, Nicholas. 2004. "The Strains of a Balkan Ballad". *International Herald Tribune*, 16.11.2004, 12.

Ybarra-Frausto, Tomas. 1991. "The Chicano Movement/The Movement of Chicano Art", in I. Karp and S. D. Lavine (eds.). *Exhibiting Cultures: The Poetics and Politics of Museum Display*. Washington/ London: Smithsonian Institution Press, 128-50.

Yeğenoğlu, Meyda. 1998. *Colonial Fantasies: Towards a Feminist Reading of Orientalism*. Cambridge: Cambridge University Press.

———. 2003. "Liberal Multiculturalism and the Ethics of Hospitality in the Age of Globalization". *Postmodern Culture*, 2.13. <http://www3.iath. virginia.edu/pmc/issue.103/13.2yegenoglu.html> (April 2006).

Young, Robert. 1995. *Colonial Desire: Hybridity in Theory, Culture, and Race*. London/New York: Routledge.

———. 2001. *Postcolonialism: An Historical Introduction*. Oxford: Blackwell Publishers.

List of Contributors

Murat Aydemir teaches Comparative Literature and Cultural Analysis at the University of Amsterdam, is research leader at the Amsterdam School of Cultural Analysis (ASCA) on behalf of the KNAW (Royal Dutch Academy of the Arts and Sciences), and project leader of Performative Narratology. He is the author of *Images of Bliss: Ejaculation, Masculinity, and Meaning* (Minnesota University Press, 2006), a book on the representation and conceptualization of male orgasm, ejaculation, and semen in art, literature, theory, and film. He is currently editing two volumes in the Thamyris/Intersecting book series at Rodopi.

Mieke Bal, cultural critic and theorist, holds the position of Royal Dutch Academy of Sciences Professor (KNAW). Her areas of interest include literary theory, semiotics, visual art, cultural studies, postcolonial theory, feminist theory, French, the Hebrew Bible, the seventeenth century and contemporary culture. She is also a video-artist.

Maria Boletsi is a Ph.D. candidate and teaches at Leiden University. She studied Cultural Analysis (MA, 2005) and Comparative Literature (BA, 2003) at the University of Amsterdam, and Greek Philology (BA, 2001) at the Aristotle University of Thessaloniki. Her research deals with the concept of barbarism and the figure of the barbarian in contemporary literature and art.

Bregje van Eekelen has a background in economics and anthropology (Utrecht University). She is a Ph.D. Candidate at the University of California, Santa Cruz. At the Institute of Advanced Feminist Research at UCSC, she co-organized and edited *Shock and Awe: War on Words* (2004), a dictionary on the political trajectories of words. She is writing her dissertation, titled *The Social Life of Ideas*, on the anthropology of knowledge and the travel of ideas. She also works as an editor at the Amsterdam School for Cultural Analysis, University of Amsterdam.

Begüm Özden Firat studied International Relations and Sociology in

Turkey. Currently, she is a PhD candidate at ASCA and working on her dissertation provisionally entitled *Visuality of the Other: Reading the 17th and 18th Century Ottoman Miniature Paintings*. She is a research assistant at the University of Mimar Sinan in Istanbul, Turkey.

Isabel Hoving is working in the fields of intercultural and postcolonial literature, cultural analysis, and gender studies. She is currently affiliated with the University of Leiden, where, in addition to teaching, she is writing a study on the intersection of ecology, globalization and (Caribbean) literature. Her publications include *In Praise of New Travelers* (on Caribbean migrant women's writing, Stanford University Press, 2001), *The Dream Merchant* (awarded youth novel, 2002), *Africa and Its Significant Others* (as editor, 2003), and *Veranderingen van het alledaagse* (as editor, on the question how migrants shaped Dutch everyday culture, 2005). She is also editor of *Thamyris/Intersecting: Place, Sex, and Race*.

Annelies Moors is an anthropologist and holds the ISIM chair at the University of Amsterdam, directing the research programme on Cultural Politics and Islam. She is the author of *Women, Property and Islam: Palestinian Experiences 1920-1990* (Cambridge University Press, 1995), co-editor of *Discourse and Palestine: Power, Text and Context* (Het Spinhuis, 1995), guest-editor of a special issue of *Islamic Law and Society* (2003) about public debates on family law reform, and co-editor of *Religion, Media and the Public Sphere* (Indiana University Press, 2006). She has published widely on visualizing the nation-gender nexus, gold and globalization, Muslims and fashion, and migrant domestic labour in the Middle East.

Patricia Spyer is Professor of Anthropology at Leiden University. She is the author of *The Memory of Trade: Modernity's Entanglements on an Eastern Indonesian Island* (Duke 2000), editor of *Border Fetishisms: Material Objects in Unstable Spaces* (Routledge 1998), and co-editor of the *Handbook of Material Culture* (Sage 2006). She has published on violence, media and photography, historical consciousness, materiality, and religion. Her current research focuses on mediations of violence and postviolence in the Moluccas, Indonesia.

Index of Names and Places

Index of Terms and Concepts